SO YOU WANT TO SING GOSPEL

So You Want to Sing

Guides for Performers and Professionals

A Project of the National Association of Teachers of Singing

So You Want to Sing: Guides for Performers and Professionals is a series of works devoted to providing a complete survey of what it means to sing within a particular genre. Each contribution functions as a touchstone work for not only professional singers, but students and teachers of singing. Titles in the series offer a common set of topics so readers can navigate easily the various genres addressed in each volume. This series is produced under the direction of the National Association of Teachers of Singing, the leading professional organization devoted to the science and art of singing.

So You Want to Sing Music Theater: A Guide for Professionals, by Karen S. Hall, 2013.

So You Want to Sing Rock 'n' Roll: A Guide for Professionals, by Matthew Edwards, 2014.

So You Want to Sing Jazz: A Guide for Professionals, by Jan Shapiro, 2015.

So You Want to Sing Country: A Guide for Performers, by Kelly K. Garner, 2016

So You Want to Sing Gospel: A Guide for Performers, by Trineice Robinson-Martin, 2017

SO YOU WANT TO SING GOSPEL

A Guide for Performers

Trineice Robinson-Martin

Allen Henderson
Executive Editor, NATS

Matthew Hoch
Series Editor

A Project of the National Association of
Teachers of Singing

ROWMAN & LITTLEFIELD
Lanham • Boulder • New York • London

Published by Rowman & Littlefield
A wholly owned subsidiary of The Rowman & Littlefield Publishing Group, Inc.
4501 Forbes Boulevard, Suite 200, Lanham, Maryland 20706
www.rowman.com

Unit A, Whitacre Mews, 26-34 Stannary Street, London SE11 4AB

British Library Cataloguing in Publication Information Available

Library of Congress Cataloging-in-Publication Data

Names: Robinson-Martin, Trineice.
Title: So you want to sing gospel : a guide for performers / Trineice
Robinson-Martin.
Description: Lanham : Rowman & Littlefield, [2017] | Series: So you want
to sing | "A Project of the National Association of Teachers of Singing." |
Includes bibliographical references and index.
Identifiers: LCCN 2016034112 (print) | LCCN 2016034765 (ebook) | ISBN
9781442239203 (pbk. : alk. paper) | ISBN 9781442239210 (electronic)
Subjects: LCSH: Singing—Instruction and study. | Gospel music—Instruction
and study.
Classification: LCC MT820 .R72 2017 (print) | LCC MT820 (ebook) | DDC
783/.09254—dc23
LC record available at https://lccn.loc.gov/2016034112

♾™ The paper used in this publication meets the minimum requirements
of American National Standard for Information Sciences—Permanence of
Paper for Printed Library Materials, ANSI/NISO Z39.48-1992.

Printed in the United States of America

CONTENTS

FIGURES AND TABLES

FIGURES

TABLES

FOREWORD

So You Want to Sing Gospel: A Guide for Performers is the fifth book in the National Association of Teachers of Singing/Rowman & Littlefield So You Want to Sing series and the second book to fall under my editorship. It was truly a pleasure to work with Trineice Robinson-Martin on this project. Trineice brings many years of experience as a performer of gospel and as a singing teacher, and she was the perfect author for this important and invaluable book.

Among American voice pedagogues, Dr. Robinson-Martin stands out as one of the few contemporary commercial music teachers who has performed gospel, jazz, rhythm and blues, rock, country, and pop music professionally while also maintaining a full-time schedule as a singing teacher and clinician. She holds a master's degree in jazz studies from Indiana University and a master's and doctoral degree in music education from Teachers College–Columbia University. She regularly travels nationally and internationally to present her research on gospel music and vocal pedagogy. We are grateful that she has taken time out of her busy schedule to contribute to the So You Want to Sing series.

There are several "common chapters" that are included across multiple titles in the series. These chapters include a chapter on voice science by Scott McCoy, one on vocal health by Wendy LeBorgne, and one on audio technology by Matthew Edwards (author of *So You Want to Sing Rock 'n' Roll*). These chapters help to bind the series together, ensuring consistency of fact when it comes to the most essential matters of voice production.

The collected volumes of the So You Want to Sing series offer a valuable opportunity for performers and teachers of singing to explore new styles and important pedagogies. I am confident that voice specialists, both amateur and professional, will benefit from Dr. Robinson-Martin's important resource on gospel music. It has been a privilege to work with her on this project.

Matthew Hoch

ACKNOWLEDGMENTS

Praise God from whom all blessings flow. I give honor and thanks to God for the unconditional love, mercy, favor, and grace that he bestows upon me every day. I thank him for guiding my footsteps and leading me in directions I wouldn't have otherwise gone, and for making my path cross with people in my life that I otherwise would not have met.

I thank God for a supportive and loving family. To my husband, Lindsay Martin, and my children, Laura-Simone and Lindsay Jr., thank you for your love, support, and patience. I know the long nights of writing, performing, teaching, and working surely put a strain on our family time, so I thank you for continuing to encourage me and for trusting God and his plan for our lives.

To my amazing, unconditionally loving, and supportive parents and siblings, I say thank you. To my mother, Chandra Smith (and Willie); my father, Pastor David Robinson (and Melanie Sue); and my sisters, Chanee Ly and Kimberly Algee, thank you for always being there for me and helping me carry the load even when it means flying across the country to do so. As the African proverb states, "It takes a whole village to raise a child." I am proud to be a product of such upbringing. To my extended family, my maternal grandparents, Murlene Mangle and Jesse Mangle (deceased); paternal grandparents, Bishop John B. and Annie

May Robinson (deceased); and a host of aunts, uncles, and cousins, it was not until I began to travel that I realized the magnitude of the blessing it is to be born to such a close-knit, supportive, loving family. I love you all. Thank you for your prayers and for always being there.

I thank God for supportive and loving friends. I'm grateful that God has blessed me with my adopted family of mentors and friends who treat me as if I were their own blood relative. Starting with the pillars I lost during the process of writing this book, Donald "Jazz Griot" Meade, Dr. David N. Baker, and Saburah Ammattulah, I thank you for your love, dedication, and for believing in me. May you all rest in peace. To Lida Baker, Gloria McCloe, Courtney Leonard, Justin Leonard, Bishop Joseph Ravenell, Ric Minter, Luna Jones, Clint and Marci Youngblood, Cathy Neilley, Dr. Larry Ridley, Ms. Charlie Ianni, Nate Lawrence, and my siblings in the Donald Meade Legacy Foundation, thank you for being my family when I'm away from family. The comfort in knowing I can depend on each of you to be there whenever I need you is what motivates me to keep going when times get hard. My church families at Miraculous Word Christian Center, Oakland, California; Turning Point Methodist Church, Trenton, New Jersey; Samaritan Baptist Church, Trenton, New Jersey; and my pastor, Dr. Dharius Daniels, Kingdom Church, Ewing, New Jersey, thank you for your continued prayers and ministry.

I thank God for my teachers and colleagues. My voice teachers, Jacqueline Hairston, Dr. Katchie Cartwright, Mary Ann Hart, Dr. Jeanne Goffi-Fynn, Robert Edwin, and Jeannette LoVetri, have taught me so much. I appreciated the contribution each of you has made to my development as an artist, teacher, and scholar. I have to give a special thank you to my two pedagogy pillars, Dr. Raymond Wise, my mentor in gospel music pedagogy, and Jeannette LoVetri, my "voice pedagogy mom." To Dr. Wise, thank you for your work and research and for personally helping me understand how to articulate and operate in ministry within the world of academia. To Jeanie, thank you for the countless hours you have spent and continue to spend helping me understand contemporary commercial music voice pedagogy, helping me understand my own voice, helping me develop my approach to teaching gospel and soul music, coaching me on how to teach to voice, helping me with all my published work, and always challenging me to keep getting better as a singer and teacher.

A special thank you to my colleagues Kat Reinhart, Shaun Saunders of GodzChild Productions, and Jacquelyn Pillsbury for giving me advice on organizing my thoughts and proofreading countless revisions. I also thank Chester D. T. Baldwin and Nancy Roncesvalles for offering their expertise and being there to listen and help me talk through concepts I discuss in this book. To my student Nandita Rao, thank you for all you have done to help me through this process; from the glossary to proof-reading to babysitting, I truly appreciate you.

Lastly, I would like to thank the National Association of Teachers of Singing (NATS) for encouraging me to write this book. Thank you to Allen Henderson, president of NATS; Karen Hall and Matthew Hoch, series editors; and Bennett Graff and Natalie Mandziuk of Rowman & Littlefield Publishers for all your service to the teaching community and for your commitment to the completion of this book and all the other books in this series. May your efforts and dedication continue to be beneficial to singing teachers all over the world for years to come.

INTRODUCTION

All research in the field of voice pedagogy aims to determine the most efficient and effective type of vocal technique for the performance of a given style of music. To date, gospel music, because it is primarily taught through oral transmission, has not created a wealth of written resources that document this process. I began my research toward developing a formalized pedagogy for gospel singing about ten years ago. At the time, I was trying to answer some questions I personally had about determining the best techniques for singing African American music styles—particularly jazz, gospel, and rhythm and blues (R&B), as they represented the styles of music I regularly performed. The motivation for this quest stemmed from comments and constructive criticism I received from family, mentors, and other colleagues and band members outside of academia. It was not so much what they said that left me unsettled, rather it was their inability to articulate either what they meant or how to fix the problem.

I was raised in the church and was surrounded by family members active in ministry. In addition to a host of aunts, uncles, and cousins who served as ministers, deacons, missionaries, and worship leaders, my father, Pastor David Robinson, MAT, pastors the church founded by my uncle Bishop Samuel Robinson, DD (Miraculous Word Christian Center, nondenominational), and my grandfather Bishop John the Baptist Robinson pastored and also served as the district bishop for Triumph the Church and Kingdom of God in Christ (COGIC). So my attendance and active participation in church was not only inevitable, it was simply a way of life. I started singing in the family choir at the age of five and began singing solo or with my sisters around the age of eight, but I never once considered the option of singing gospel music professionally. When I did finally start thinking about singing as a profession and began taking voice lessons as a junior in high school, it was with the goal of becoming a professional singer in the style of jazz, not gospel.

I began studying jazz voice intently as a sophomore in college and continued through my graduate studies, and was taught vocal technique predominately by classical singers, all while still singing gospel in church. However, when singing in church, now as a formally trained vocalist, I took a more vocally conservative approach to singing. I wanted my singing to reflect the vocal technique I had been working so hard to achieve. My dad would often lovingly comment after service, "Neice you are so talented, people brag on you all the time. Just imagine what you will sound like when you stop holding back and really push it." I remember thinking to myself, "What does he mean 'push it'! I'm not wrecking my voice. Besides, I'm a jazz singer; I don't need to train myself to do all that." I had become somewhat of an elitist and didn't even realize it. However, after a while I started to recognize what he was talking about but didn't know how to fix it.

The irony was during that time, my jazz mentors would often comment on and acknowledge that they could hear a prominent gospel or blues influence in my jazz interpretation, although in a positive way. My mentor and teacher David Baker would say, "You've got Dinah [Washington] all over you!" or "You got your church hat?" every time we performed "Accentuate the Positive" with the big band. My "musical grandfather," Donald Meade, who watched me develop from the time I started singing jazz seriously, would say, "Boy you've got that gospel thing down!" especially after I sang a ballad. While I did get the occasional criticism from other sources commenting on my use of too much vibrato, since the jazz singers I was most influenced by (Dinah Washington, Sarah Vaughan, and Nancy Wilson) used a lot of vibrato, I didn't think much of it. Then I started questioning, "*Is* my vibrato too much?"

"Why do they keep saying I sound like a gospel singer?" "Is that a bad thing?" "What am I actually doing that makes them say that?" "Should I fix it?" "Should I care?" "Can I fix it if I want to?" Again, no answers.

To help me find the answers I was looking for, I was determined to spend my graduate studies in education understanding how the voice works. At the same time that I began this academic journey, I started singing pop, rock, and R&B in a high-end corporate cover band. It was in that band that my limitations as a trained vocalist were finally exposed, and this time I had to face it head-on. I was getting paid well to perform sixty-five dates per year, and in addition to the stylistic learning curve I endured as I began singing with the band, I also found myself struggling to keep up vocally the longer I was with them. I remember my very first challenge was performing Beyoncé's "Crazy in Love." In the first re-hearsal, besides the fact my throat felt like it was on fire, one of the other singers sitting next to me leaned over and said, "Maybe you shouldn't say the words so properly." I was devastated. Not only was I vocally do-ing something wrong, and didn't know how to fix it, but it turned out I was also subconsciously employing an inappropriate diction by actually enunciating the words as I had been taught. I couldn't understand how I was the only vocalist in the group who had formally and intensively studied music yet was struggling to sing. Eight months into working with the band, while also being a full-time graduate student and a full-time wife and mother of a toddler, I began noticing I was taking longer and longer to recover vocally from the weekend gigs. My voice teacher and graduate advisor at the time recommended I get my vocal folds evalu-ated and that I get voice therapy. I was diagnosed with muscle tension dysphonia (MTD) and an acute polyp. I went through voice therapy and ultimately had surgery to remove the polyp. I began working to retrain my speaking voice, to achieve clarity in my overall sound, and also to find "work-arounds" so I could sing my assigned repertoire with less strain. However, I still didn't know how to fix the problem. I thought to myself, "There has to be a way to sing these notes authentically without damag-ing the voice. With all the people singing these notes on Broadway, eight shows a week, there's got to be a way. With all the gospel and R&B sing-ers that have lasting careers, there's got to be a way."

The following semester I took a special topics course on applied voice pedagogy that featured guest lecturers who specialized in various aspects of voice pedagogy. Jeannette LoVetri of Somatic VoiceWorks™ was the guest lecturer who spoke on a topic I had never heard of: contemporary commercial music (CCM) voice pedagogy. It was that day that I began my journey toward finding the answers to all the questions that had been toiling through my mind all those years. From that day on, I made it my mission to read any and every piece of literature written about the topic so that I could understand and better articulate what *was* going on in my body and what *should have* been going on in my body in order to achieve my desired vocal goals. This research ultimately encompassed my master's research project. In continuing this newfound passion for voice pedagogy research and strategies, I chose to direct my doctoral research toward finding ways to apply this information to the genres of music I sang. I began with gospel music, as it not only represents the first style of music I ever performed, but it also represents the genre in which my questions first began.

This book represents one of the first books I have written to encompass my life experience, teaching experience, performance experience, and my extensive research in the fields of gospel music pedagogy, gospel music history, voice science, classical voice pedagogy, and CCM voice pedagogy in the effort of helping others begin their own journey.

Chapter 1 provides a brief history of gospel music in terms of its cultural function, historical evolution, and influential composers and artists. It's only through a knowledge of history and musical lineage that one can truly appreciate a musical style. Chapters 2 and 3 feature guest authors who provide information defining the various components of vocal anatomy, voice production, and vocal health. In order to develop and protect your instrument (your voice), you must first understand how it functions. Chapter 4 introduces and identifies the components of gospel music voice pedagogy and briefly details those components of vocal training that are related to developing the voice as an instrument. Chapter 5 focuses on stylistic interpretation, briefly identifying the various types of sacred music, introducing style categories that can be used to organize the various styles of gospel music into broader categories, and also identifying the various performance mediums used to perform gospel music. Chapter 6 discusses the development of interpretation from a personal standpoint in terms of self-expression and ministerial function. This chapter also includes suggestions on how performers can establish and organize repertoire. Chapter 7 summarizes some additional notes specific to one's function as a singer, worship leader, choir member/choir director, and voice teacher. The chapter includes a list of resources that, in addition to the resources listed in the works cited section of most chapters, specifically target the development of gospel singing. The final chapter, chapter 8, consists of another guest contribution and focuses on a topic that every singer using amplification must become familiar with: audio technology.

Many of the musical examples cited in this book, as well as other books in this series, are freely available on the Internet. All supplemental materials for this book can be found at www.SoYouWantToSing.org.

No one can learn to sing or learn a style of music from reading a book. This book is intended to provide insights and bring nomenclature to concepts in gospel music voice pedagogy. There are very few books that discuss the pedagogy of gospel singing in this manner, and I hope this book stimulates more resources. Teaching is my ministry. I am humbled that God has blessed me with the gift and skill of being able to present those aspects of singing and performance practices that generations of gospel singers, choir directors, and voice teachers may have already applied through the years but never wrote down.

Though my journey is not over, this is my story, and these are my answers.

ONLINE SUPPLEMENT NOTE

So You Want to Sing Gospel features an online supplement courtesy of the National Association of Teachers of Singing. Visit the link below to discover additional exercises and examples, as well as links to recordings of the songs referenced in this book.

http://www.nats.org/So_You_Want_To_Sing_Book_Series.html

A musical note symbol ♪ in this book will mark every instance of corresponding online supplement material.

❶

WHAT IS GOSPEL MUSIC?

Gospel is not just a musical experience; it is a process of esoteric sharing and affirmation. It is more than the beat; it is more than the movement; it even embodies much more than text, harmonies or instrumental accompaniment.[1]

Gospel music is not just a genre or a type of song or style of music. Like many other genres within the black sacred music tradition, gospel music is the musical and stylistic reflection and representation of a specific aspect of the black religious experience. Its musical style and performance practice evolves with culture yet maintains its roots in work songs, Negro spirituals, hymns, blues, jazz, soul, rhythm and blues (R&B), and hip-hop. Highly improvised, gospel music is the platform to which one's personal expression and experience with Christ can be exhibited through his or her personal interpretation of a song. The following chapter briefly describes the historic function of religious music in black culture, the performance aesthetics associated with gospel music, and the evolution of gospel music through the recognition of historic eras, composers, and artists influential in its development.

BLACK CULTURE AND RELIGIOUS MUSIC EXPRESSION

Much of black life and culture is heard through its music. Black gospel music is deeply rooted in the expression of the contemporary black religious experience. It reflects on the emotional, spiritual, physical, and historical journey of blacks in America.[2] The culture of gospel music is composed of ideologies and belief systems associated with black theology. **Black theology** is defined as the theological explication of the blackness of black people.[3] The lyrics of gospel music typically communicate one's personal knowledge of the meaning of black survival in America, particularly identifying the contribution religion has made to that survival. It is the manner in which black people express and articulate the liberation of the oppressed. This expression can be found in gospel music through the musical and nonmusical components of gospel music performance. At one time, the black church was the only cultural institution enabling black people to express themselves freely; the music in the black church was a direct representation of that free license of expression.[4] For example, the eighteenth- and nineteenth-century Negro spirituals were a collection of lyrical responses to the slave experience in the United States.[5] Marietta Miller provides one example of this in her correlation of the Negro spiritual "Go Down Moses" with the slave experience. Miller explains that the slaves believed God would send Moses down to tell Pharaoh to "let God's people go," and they would apply this to their enslaved status in America as well. Negro spirituals became more than predictable and repetitive melodies; rather, they were songs of power and inspiration.[6] With song lyrics like "Steal away, steal away home, I ain't got long to stay here," slaves declared freedom would come one day, either through emancipation or death.[7] Without question, these songs helped black slaves to persevere in spite of the hardships they endured and to focus on the better days to come.

Just as the spirituals were the voice of the slaves, gospel music is, and continues to be, the voice of the contemporary black church and religious community. The most significant distinction of African American gospel music according to gospel scholar, composer, and director Dr. Raymond Wise, is the presence and implementation of core musical and nonmusical elements from the African American cultural aesthetic.[8]

Core elements such as **pentatonic scales**, flatted thirds and sevenths, 12/8 rhythms, call-and-response, tempos ranging from fast to no strict tempo, instrumental accompaniment, vocal techniques, syncopated rhythms, improvisation, hand clapping, and foot stomping are just a few characteristics associated with black music cultural aesthetics.[9]

The gospel sound specifically was developed in the charismatic church cultures of the Holiness and Pentecostal churches. The cultural norm of expression in these churches is highly energized and charismatic, from preaching to praying to singing to shouting. It is this energy and charismatic nature that provides the foundation for the gospel sound and gospel music performance practices. These characteristics are heavily woven throughout the fabric of both sacred and secular African American music styles due to the constant interaction between the two communities. For example, many church pastors and musicians were born-again blues singers. Many of the church musicians were working blues and jazz musicians who played in the juke joint on Saturday and then played in the church service on Sunday morning.[10] This practice of crossing the sacred and secular lines continues today. Singers like Dinah Washington (jazz), Sarah Vaughan (jazz), Little Richard (rock and roll), Sam Cooke (soul), and Whitney Houston (R&B) are popular secular artists who started in the church and brought their church influences and performance practices into the secular market. This is also true for musicians. Thomas Dorsey, affectionately known as the "Father of Gospel Music," started off as a blues and jazz composer and bandleader. Once he became a believer in Christ, he began writing religious music. Regardless, at the core lives the singers' ability to emotionally communicate at a high spiritual level; an expression of one's personal experience and relationship with Jesus Christ.

BLACK GOSPEL MUSIC PERFORMANCE AESTHETIC

Music plays an important part in the black church, both as rhetoric and as a device for heightening emotions. Glen Hinson writes, "For the saints of the black church, song is an exultant offering of praise, a heartfelt rendering of soul through the vehicles of voice and melody."[11] The black church, at least that which is descended from the Sanctified churches of the rural South, is a setting for many sorts of highly stylized behaviors ranging from preaching to praying to singing.[12] There are musical structures and musical expectations for expression that constitute black gospel music, and they are based on cultural standards.

Samuel Floyd Jr. generalizes these expectations through a music-analysis framework he describes as **call-response**.[13] Not to be confused with the musical term *call-and-response*, although call-and-response is used in the call-response system. Call-response consists of five broad elements that describe the dynamics found in the performance of black folk music when performed within the cultural context of the African American music tradition. These elements consist of:[14]

Signifyin(g). A literary term coined by Henry Louis Gate Jr. and Samuel Floyd. Jr. infers from a musical perspective that **signifyin(g)** consists of improvisatory and performance characteristics found in the performance of black folk music, such as moans, slurs, shouts, and call-and-response.

Audience interactions. There is a general tendency to make performances occasions in which the audience participates in reaction to what the performers do.

Continuous self-criticism in its indigenous cultural context. This is when the performer delves more deeply into him- or herself in order to express his or her own emotional vulnerability through the music as a natural result of the interaction between the performer and the audience.

Competitive exchange. The emphasis on the competition that occurs between the performer and the audience or two performers, in which they encourage each other to do their best and give their all.

Intertwining of song and dance. The performance of black music deals with the complete intertwining of black music and dance.

It is the communal experience—the interchanging dynamics between the instrumentalists and the singer and between the congregation and the singer—when the performance of gospel music is at its best.[15]

Black gospel music aesthetics are represented in the following four primary areas: (1) sound or sound quality; (2) style or technique; (3) delivery style or nonmusical aspects of delivery; and (4) spirit.[16]

Sound or Sound Quality

The *sound* of gospel music is a reflection of core music elements used to create the overall timbres that ultimately define and distinguish gospel music from other styles.[17] For singers, the gospel sound is reflected in terms of the vocal textures, qualities, and nuances used when singing the genre. The gospel sound is almost exclusively associated with a harsh, gravelly, full-chest belt/shout quality to those who are not familiar with the complexities of the gospel style. Coupled with the lack of transparency of a formal vocal-training system for the gospel genre, there stems a major misconception that those who sing in the gospel style will ruin their voices. This is because while it is true that the harsh, gravelly vocal quality found in gospel music is the most imitated vocal quality among singers of both secular and sacred music, there are many other vocal qualities and textures that can be found in the performance of gospel music. Dr. Horace Boyer notes while traditional[18] gospel singers still prefer the "full-throated, strained" sound of James Cleveland, Dorothy Love, and Shirley Caesar, contemporary singers tend to use a "pure" voice because of the lyrical qualities of contemporary gospel music.[19] Acknowledging the variation in vocal qualities, and the reasons for such, Boyer writes: "It was natural for the young singer [of contemporary gospel music] to adopt pure sound, for by the time they began singing, all churches and auditoriums had rather sophisticated sound systems. Additionally, vocal restraint enhances the effect of the harmonic character in contemporary gospel."[20] This is even more apparent today as electronic amplification and recording tendencies continue to expand, in addition to an expanded variety of vocal textures that have become culturally acceptable during gospel music interpretation. Additionally, people who carry this misconception about gospel music ruining the voice fail to acknowledge that any style of music in which the singer lacks the appropriate technique to execute the required sound and volume will result in an injury.

Musical Style or Technique

In gospel performance, one's ability to genuinely and authentically express oneself through song using the appropriate stylistic features dominates the knowledge and exposition of technical musical skills (as thought of in the Western European classical art form).[21] The knowledge and exposition of technical music skills as valued by gospel tradition–bearers are demonstrated by the manner in which the singer articulates his or her interpretation of a song through the use of the following three factors: time, text, and pitch.[22]

Time can be manipulated not only in terms of the juxtaposition and layering of rhythms but also in the continual shift of rhythmic phrases in the melody and through the repetition and expansion of certain sections in the overall form of the song.[23] Text can be manipulated through the addition of personal stories (referred to as "testimony" in the black religious tradition), the addition of text to the original lyrics, and the manner in which important words are stressed within a melodic phrase.[24] Pitch in black gospel music is not valued as absolute as it is in some other musical cultures. Rather, it serves as an element of contrast.[25] Pitch can be manipulated through the use of slurs, bending of notes, growls, changes in color and texture of notes within a single phrase, and any factor of melodic embellishment such as **melismas** and passing tones.

Delivery Style or Nonmusical Elements of Style

In addition to the musical aspects of the black gospel music style, many nonmusical elements are used by gospel performers to enhance the overall communication of the song and musical culture. According to Dr. Mellonee Burnim, the most respected artists in the field not only possess a "good voice" but also have the ability to combine that voice with a culturally prescribed mode of presentation, affirming their immersion in black culture. Performance in black culture symbolizes vitality, a sense of aliveness in which the performer must convey the all-consuming and compelling force of gospel music through every means available. Such nonmusical elements include the movement of hands and feet, bouncing, shouting, body movement, facial expressions, and even the attire a gospel music performer chooses.[26] Combined, all of these elements contribute to the overall sense of celebration traditionally represented in gospel music performance.

Spirit

The spirit (also called *anointing* or *Holy Spirit*) is the ministerial aspect of a gospel music performance and is often referred to as the most important performance aspect by gospel tradition bearers.[27] While not every gospel singer considers himself or herself to be a spiritual leader, two of the many functions of gospel music (arguably the two most important ones) are "praise" and "religious renewal."[28] Gospel tradition bearers view praise as their devotional duty, and often with praise comes ministry, for the Bible says faith comes by hearing (Rom. 10:17).

Gospel music is a direct product of what Rev. R. M. Simmons refers to as "**energized worship**," a multidimensional aspect of the African American religious experience.[29] A retention of the African personality and African aesthetic that African Americans brought into the Christian worship experience, Simmons describes energized worship as "spontaneity, flexibility, expression, movement, rhythmic coordination, fluidity, flow, feelings, energy, language and linguistic styles, spirituality and spiritual perception, affectivity, and cognition (and the inseparable relations between the latter two)."[30] Stemming from the invisible church of the slaves through the black religious response of the Evangelist movements of the Great Awakenings and the urban storefront churches as blacks migrated North, blacks embraced a charismatic style of worship that reflects the spiritual intensity of the black religious celebration. The spiritual intensity represented in energized worship is the "unique understanding of the presence, role and power of the Holy Spirit in the church and in the daily doings," which manifests itself through the music, prayers, sermons, scriptures, and "feelings that evidence the indwelling of [the] Holy Spirit."[31] This is important to know because energized worship cannot be taught, only acquired. When gospel music is learned and performed in a context outside the black religious experience, this component is often missing and as a result affects the authenticity and efficacy of the music.

EVOLUTION OF GOSPEL MUSIC

From the time it was established, gospel music has integrated African American musical aesthetics with other sacred and secular African

American and European musical styles. The practice of combining African rhythm and movement, secular song, and Christian worship to create an experience that is distinctly black American dates back to the 1700s and continues to be illustrated during every historic era throughout the genre's development. There are five distinguishable eras in the evolution of gospel music. They include the congregational era (1900–1920s), the traditional era (1920s–1960s), the contemporary era (1960s–1970s), the ministry era (1980s–1990s), and the crossover era (1990s–present).[32]

The congregational era (1900–1920s) represents a time period when the musical medium focused on the creation and development of congregational music. The development of black religious music that occurred during this era set the stage for the creation of and implementation of gospel music. The traditional era (1920s–1960s) represents the time period during which the gospel music style and performance practices were established. This time period contained the most innovative contributions toward defining what it meant to sing "gospel music." The contemporary era (1960s–1970s) represents the era in which composers of gospel music began to incorporate musical practices of Western European classical musical art tradition, in addition to elements of the contemporary popular music that was developing at the time. The ministry era (1980s–1990s) represents the time period in which gospel music began to move away from using some of the defining musical characteristics of traditional gospel sound and instead put greater compositional focus on the "words" or "text." During this era, there was a stream of composers who sought to clarify and convey the gospel message in a manner that would promote spiritual transformation in addition to an emotional response. The crossover era (1990s–present) represents the "urbanization" of gospel music. During this era, the musical characteristics and performance practices have moved even further away from those established during the traditional gospel era.[33] While maintaining the most basic elements developed in the congregational era, each additional era (and its corresponding dates) represents when specific musical characteristics and performance practices were added and hence further contributed to the creation and development of gospel music.

The Roots: Pre-1900s

The earliest forms of black religious music developed in the United States are commonly categorized as "folk" spirituals.[34] This style of music was vocal music accompanied by "body rhythm," mainly hand clapping and foot stomping, and was typically sung in a call-and-response musical structure. Folk spirituals, named so to be distinguished from "arranged" or "concert" spirituals and made famous by the Fisk Jubilee Singers, were an outgrowth of slavery.[35]

Dating back to the Great Awakening (1740–1800), blacks were converted to Christianity and participated in Christian worship singing. Slaves would attend church and sing the songs with their master, then reinterpret the religious instruction and musical expression of these songs through an African lens and create new songs when they gathered among themselves.[36] It was in these settings, the invisible church, that slaves in the South could freely interpret their religion and freely express themselves in a manner that would not otherwise be permitted. They could sing and dance, change the words, or even create new melodies and performance practices that would create a worship experience more relevant to their needs and concerns.[37]

During the Second Great Awakening in the 1800s, there was another revival movement. Camp meetings were set up in the South in which Protestant denominations, both black and white, would gather in a tent and hold spiritual revival meetings lasting several days to a week.[38] After the main evening services, participants would sing short scraps of affirmations, pledges, and prayers, lengthened with repetition choruses. The songs created during these camp meetings were called *camp meeting spirituals*. These songs consisted of a chorus in irregular meter and rhyme, with paraphrased scriptural references and a refrain that repeated with the word *hallelujah*. Boyer provides examples of the musical form of the camp meeting spiritual as follows:[39]

Leader: Oh, what ship is this we are sailing upon?

Congregation: Oh, glory, hallelujah.

Refrain

All: 'Tis the old ship of Zion. Ha-le-loo.

'Tis the old ship of Zion. Ha-le-loo.

The camp meeting spirituals inspired another type of folk spiritual known as the *shout*, or *ring shout*, or *running spirchil*.[40] The ring shout is called so because of the element of dancing incorporated into its performance.[41] In a ring shout, a group of worshippers would move counterclockwise, singing and dancing in a circle in an energized manner to manifest a religious experience. Burnim describes the performance characteristics of the ring shout as including "(1) a high degree of repetition; (2) the continuation of the songs for indefinite, but sometimes lengthy, periods; (3) variation of tempo in different contexts; (4) robust timbre; and (5) highly embellished melodic lines, with an abundance of 'slides from one note to another and turns and cadences not in articulated notes.'"[42] It was believed that in the ring, sinners would be converted into Christians.

With the establishment of the independent African Methodist Episcopal (AME) Church under the leadership of Richard Allen of Philadelphia in 1787, shouts were further developed in the North.[43] According to Burnim, part of Allen's selective identification with Methodism was the rejection of the standard Methodist hymnal, which he replaced with his own compilation of worship songs that he felt had a greater appeal for blacks. Allen wrote many of the lyrics for his hymn book; however, research suggests some of the music to which the lyrics were sung came from the melodies of popular songs of the day.[44] This practice was not only looked down on by white Methodist ministers but also by some black ministers and black congregants of a higher social-economic status. Burnim cites examples of an account from a white Methodist minister named John Watson in 1819 who strongly objected to the fact that "(1) blacks were known to sing songs of their 'own composing' instead of the established repertoire of the Methodist hymnal; (2) these songs were poetically substandard; and (3) the music was influencing whites to engage in similar practices."[45] These acts were looked upon as heathenish and an abomination to the will of God.

Some black ministers also aligned themselves with the traditional, more refined white Methodist worship tradition. For example, Bishop Daniel Alexander Payne, a nineteenth-century African American minister of the AME Church and a historian, specifically viewed those who practiced the highly charismatic religious expression of the ring shout as "ignorant but well-meaning" and called the songs "cornfield ditties."[46]

This ideology led to a great divide in the style of worship between the denominations within the black church, particularly between the major denominations of Methodist and Baptist. Methodists and Baptists tended to keep their style of worship more closely aligned with the traditional white Methodist and Baptist worship styles, especially those with congregants of a higher economic status.

Another type of religious song popular during the decade before the Emancipation Proclamation was the jubilee spiritual.[47] According to Boyer, the lyrics of the jubilee spiritual employed a slightly more sophisticated kind of poetry and a more Westernized sense of harmony. Boyer writes, "Since these songs were not used for the 'shout,' the rhythm was less intricate and slightly more organized":[48]

Leader: Have you got good religion?

Congregation: Certainly, Lord.

Leader: Have you got good religion?

Congregation: Certainly, Lord.

Leader: Have you got good religion?

Congregation: Certainly, Lord, certainly, certainly, certainly, Lord.

Camp meeting and jubilee spirituals were transformed in the "church song" in 1895 when the first black Holiness church was organized. According to Boyer, the church song was a simple refrain without a contrasting section, usually with four lines of poetry, the second and fourth of which were the same or nearly the same. These songs contained few words and a limited melodic range but lent themselves to considerable rhythmic and textual variety. Boyer provides the following example of a church song:[49]

Leader: I'm a soldier—

Congregation: In the army of the Lord.

Leader: I'm a soldier—

Congregation: In the army.

Leader: I'm a sanctified soldier—

Congregation: In the army of the Lord.

Leader: I'm a sanctified soldier—

Congregation: In the army.

Succeeding lines

For the leader: I'm fighting for my Lord—

I'll live and I'll die—

I'm on my way to glory—

These songs would be sung repetitively, lasting fifteen or twenty minutes, with each variation being more complex than the previous. Holiness churches grew rapidly throughout the South, and these "church songs" ultimately infiltrated black Methodist and Baptist churches and by the turn of the century spread to Northern cities.[50]

Congregational Era/Pre-Gospel Era: 1900s–1920s

In the early 1900s, following the emancipation of the slaves, there was a great movement among Southern blacks to move to Northern cities. The goal for this migration was to find educational and economic freedom. Many blacks migrated from small Southern towns to large Northern cities like Chicago, St. Louis, and New York City to pursue freedom. As a result, there was an increase in storefront churches in the cities and a development of various denominations. The music integrated instruments and musical advancements of the city music, and new songs were written to reflect life in the city and all the troubles accompanying this new lifestyle.[51]

While a cappella spirituals and line-metered hymns were the primary style of congregational music performed in Methodist and Baptist churches, it was in the Holiness and Pentecostal churches where instrumental accompaniment was used and a new form of congregational songs was created. Pentecostal and Holiness singers sang with more passion, seeming abandoned and consequently more improvisational than was sanctioned in the Baptist and Methodist churches, creating a unique style of singing.[52] This practice provided the model and foundation for gospel music. It was in these Pentecostal and Holiness denominations where musical developments such as adding instrumental accompaniment to hymns and congregational spirituals (first with tambourines and washtub bass, then later with piano and other instruments), the development of European hymnody and black hymnody in the traditional black denominations, in addition to development of jazz, blues, and ragtime penetrated the black church.[53] Raymond Wise identifies the fact that many of the black preachers were former blues singers before converting to Christianity, and many blues and jazz musicians worked as part-time church musicians in addition to working in the local juke joint, making inevitable the introduction of blues singing techniques such as flattened notes and pentatonic scales into the musical interpretation of church music.[54]

The transition from spirituals to gospel songs began with composers such as Charles Tindley, Lucie Campbell, and Dr. Isaac Watts. As previously mentioned, gospel music was an avenue where black people could express their perspective. Therefore, while many black churches embraced European hymns and white Evangelistic congregational songs, they "gospelized" them by changing the words and/or music and applying some African American music aesthetics prevalent during that time.[55]

This time period also saw the emergence of the jubilee quartet. The jubilee quartet was a style of singing born in an academic setting when universities began shifting the **performance medium** for Negro spirituals from being sung by mixed choirs of jubilee singers to a male quartet. Historically black colleges and universities such as Fisk University, Hampton University, Tuskegee University (formerly Tuskegee Institute), Hinds Community College at Utica (formerly Utica Junior College), Mississippi Valley State University (formerly Mississippi Vocational College), and Wilberforce University were among the early schools to make this change from jubilee singers to jubilee quartets.[56] Upon graduating from these institutions, many singers created their own groups modeled after these jubilee quartets, making the male quartet a common staple during this time period. One of the university singers who went to teach at a high school in Lowndes County, Alabama, was Vernon W. Barnett, a graduate of Tuskegee Institute (now Tuskegee University). One of his students in quartet singing was R. C. Foster. Foster led a quartet group called the Foster Singers, which featured a repertoire of Negro spirituals, standard Protestant hymns rendered in the jubilee quartet style, and the relatively new gospel hymns of both black and white composers. The Foster Singers were the first black male quartet formed in Bessemer, Alabama, and the first quartet to begin the transition from the university-based and European-informed quartets to what became the gospel quartet.[57]

Icons to Know   Charles Tindley (1851–1933) was a charismatic minister of Tindley Temple Methodist Church in Philadelphia. Tindley migrated to Philadelphia from the South and was greatly influenced by the doctrines of the Holiness movement that sought to reinvigorate religious worship.[58] In 1900, Tindley began composing new songs by setting hymnbook-like verses to the tunes and rhythms of church songs.[59] Most importantly for the development of gospel music, Tindley wrote songs by himself designed to complement his sermons in contrast to the communally written spirituals that were previously a standard practice.[60] Tindley's first set of compositions were published in 1901. He wrote a total of forty-six songs, which include the gospel hymn classics "We'll Understand It Better By and By" (1905), "Stand by Me" (1900), and "The Storm Is Passing Over" (1905).[61] Tindley's composition "I'll Overcome Someday" was freely borrowed from the Emancipation Proclamation spiritual "No More Auction Block for Me" and was later transformed by the freedom marchers of the 1960s into "We Shall Overcome."[62]

Tindley's compositions are largely distinguished from the folk spiritual by the use of instrumental accompaniment (piano and organ) and the prevalence of the verse-chorus external structure.[63] The lineage of the spiritual tradition that remained consistent throughout Tindley's compositions was his incorporation of a call-and-response section into the larger verse-chorus structure. According to Boyer, it is the performance practice rather than the compositional or notated style that yields the distinct character of Tindley's songs.[64] Tindley used pentatonic scales (a specific five-note scale) for many of his melodies and left intentional space within his melodic lines and harmonic structures for the interpolation (insertion) of flatted or blues thirds and sevenths. In addition to leaving space for harmonic improvisation, Tindley also left space within his compositions for the improvisation of text, melody, and rhythm, which "was so characteristic of the black American folk and popular music."[65]

This composition practice was characteristic of pioneering gospel hymn composer Lucie Campbell (1885–1963) and many subsequent composer-arrangers.[66]

Composers and Performers to Know Lucie Campbell, Williams Sherwood, Charles Price Jones, Charles Mason, Garfield T. Haywood, Dixie Hummingbirds, Ravizee Singers, Foster Singers, Birmingham Jubilee Singers, and Ensley Jubilee Singers.

Traditional Era: 1920s–1960s

The traditional era is also known as the "golden era" of gospel music. It was during this era when the gospel style was established as a distinct performance style of music. While the early part of this era was dominated by male quartet singing, by the end of the era female quartets and soloists were the dominant performing force. Thomas A. Dorsey (1899–1993), Mahalia Jackson (1912–1972), and Roberta Martin (1907–1969) were important pioneers of gospel music, all arriving in Chicago after the Great Migration.[67]

The jubilee quartets movement of the 1920s helped develop the gospel style in the first decades of the traditional era. Groups like the Harmonizing Four, Golden Gate Quartet, Silver Leaf Quartet from Virginia, the Fairfield Four from Tennessee, and Dixie Hummingbirds of South Carolina were established during this time period. They began to further expand the traditional quartet sound by incorporating musical components into their performances, such as using complex jazz chords instead of the simple chords found in hymns and spirituals and adding falsetto voice as inherited from African tribal singing. These groups remained a cappella.

Dorsey, regarded by many as the father of gospel music, further developed this practice of introducing African American aesthetics into sacred music in the late 1920s. In the beginning of his career as a composer, Dorsey used quartet singers to sell his music. Born in Villa Rica, Georgia, Dorsey was the son of a Baptist preacher and grew up playing in church. However, before devoting his career to playing gospel music, Dorsey was a prolific composer of both blues and jazz, as well as a bandleader and singer known in the blues world as "Georgia Tom" and "Barrelhouse Tom."[68] Dorsey worked as Gertrude "Ma" Rainey's piano player for many years and also had his own acclaimed recordings and compositions.[69] On his most famous double entendre hokum hit, "It's Tight Like That," he collaborated with guitarist Tampa Red (Hudson Whitaker) in 1928.[70] Dorsey wrote his first gospel song, "If I Don't Get There," after being inspired to greater devotion upon hearing Dr. A. W. Nix sing "I Do, Don't You?" at the 1921 National Baptist Convention of America[71] in Chicago. Dorsey ultimately decided to exclusively dedicate his career to gospel music, perhaps in part due to a series of several personal tragedies, among them the deaths of his wife and newborn son, which inspired him to write the gospel classic "Precious Lord, Take My Hand."[72] Dorsey composed over five hundred gospel songs and many remain popular classics, notably "There Will Be Peace in the Valley," written for Mahalia Jackson and recorded by white country western singer Red Foley, and "Search Me, Lord, I'm Going to Live the Life I Sing About in My Song."[73]

As a direct reflection of his musical background, Dorsey was specifically known for infusing various musical elements and performance practices of blues (i.e., form, textual interpolation, rhythmic variation of text and melody, and the overall expressive quality found in the performance of blues) into white Evangelistic hymns and sacred hymns composed by black composers such as Charles Tindley.[74] Prior to Dorsey, "gospel music relied heavily upon existing compositions for most of its text, harmony, and style. Spirituals were rearranged and the hymns and psalms of [Isaac] Watts, Ira Sankey, Homer Rodeheaver, John Newton, and John Wesley underwent countless transformations. Dorsey set out to capture the specific hopes and frustrations of black Christians with completely original compositions, and succeeded brilliantly."[75]

Dorsey employed male quartets (the most popular performance medium of that time) to tour with him while promoting his songs and publishing company.[76] The black church did not readily accept the new music as it was believed to have too many influences and similarities to secular music of the day. He teamed up with Sallie Martin and later Jackson to develop an audience outside of the black religious and musical establishments.[77]

While the more refined Baptist and Methodist denominations did not like the wild nature of the Pentecostal and Holiness worship style (i.e., the spontaneity in song and dance, fainting, and shouted), the popularity and effectiveness of their music was undeniable.[78] In 1921, the National Baptist Convention, the largest organization of African American Christians in the United States, recognized the music and published the first collection of songs by a black congregation, calling it *Gospel Pearls*, which allowed for singing songs that would capture the essence of Pentecostal and Holiness worship settings without the excess normally added by Pentecostal singers. Excess to the Baptist, as Boyer described, included singing at the extremes of the register with a volume usually reserved for outdoor song, interpolating additional words into the text, hand clapping, and occasional spurts of shouting.[79]

With the Baptists now having access to this music, the growth of two styles of gospel singing began. One style emphasized singing in which the Spirit dictated the amount of embellishment, volume, and improvisation that was applied to a song. The other style, while still attempting to incorporate the dictates of the Spirit, tempered the rendition to the musical taste of the Baptist congregation.[80]

In 1930, the National Baptist Convention officially endorsed gospel music. It was during this time period that the first gospel choirs, female groups, and conventions were established. Gospel soloists and mixed groups became the predominant performance medium over congregational singing. Jubilee quartets, which primarily sang a cappella, now sang with instrumental accompaniments and established specific vocal stylings that transformed the jubilee quartet into the gospel quartet.[81] In 1931, Dorsey and Theodore Frye, another gospel music composer and singer, organized the first large gospel choir at Ebenezer Baptist Church in Chicago.[82] In 1932, Dorsey hired Roberta Martin as the pianist for the choir during his absence. Also in 1932, Dorsey, Martin, Frye, and Magnolia Lewis Butts created an alliance to form the National Convention of Gospel Choirs and Choruses, also known as the Dorsey Convention.[83] The express purpose of this organization was to promote the performance and understanding of gospel music. The Dorsey Convention would be a model for other organizations and training conventions established to teach and promote black gospel music in the decades that followed.

Martin is credited with being the greatest teacher of gospel singers. Her first group was composed of five teenage boys from the Ebenezer Baptist Church choir who joined with Martin and Frye to form the

Martin and Frye Singers. In 1935, Martin replaced two of the men with women, creating the first mixed gospel group, called the Roberta Martin Singers.[84] Boyer writes: "For nearly four decades she [Martin] accepted young singers and pianists as students in her group. Among the famous gospel musicians who started as members of the Roberta Martin Singers are Willie Webb, Delores Barrett, the Gay Sisters (Mildred and Evelyn), Myrtle Scott, Myrtle Jackson, Robert Anderson, Gloria Griffin, Alex Bradford, and the Rev. James Cleveland."[85] Martin's use of piano accompaniment and vocal harmonies made the mixed-group format standard within the gospel musical style.[86]

By 1939, gospel music directly insinuated elements of the blues style into worship music via its rhythms, melodies, and vocal styles. Robert Raymond Allen summarized the new style of music as being "distinctly African American" in its incorporation of "the melismatic moans of the spiritual, the driving music and instrumentation of sanctified music, the syncopated licks and 'bent' notes of jazz and blues, and the ecstatic emotionalism of Southern preaching."[87] While these practices troubled the "waters" between the church and the world, the blending of secular and sacred music became standard practice and established a new style of sacred music that continues to be known as gospel music.

As the decades continued, more Pentecostal churches sprang up across the nation, and "sanctified" singing became the feature. In addition to the ever-popular male quartet, which began touring and recording, the popularity of soloists, mixed-gender choirs, and all-female groups also came into prominence in the 1940s and 1950s. It would be the female singing groups that brought gospel into the mainstream. During this time period, soloists in quartets were the ones who were making innovative additions to the gospel style and became the major influence for the other gospel artists and soul artists that followed.

Icons to Know   Sister Rosetta Tharpe (1915–1973) was a singer and virtuoso steel guitar player who became the first national gospel star and ultimately the first gospel crossover artist, emerging in the 1930s.[88] Born in Cotton Plant, Arkansas, she moved to Chicago at the age of six with her mother, Katie Bell Nubin, a mandolin player and Church of God in Christ (COGIC) evangelist who enlisted her daughter's musical gifts to attract converts. Tharpe was considered a "singing and guitar-playing miracle," giving her first public performance at the age of six at the Fortieth Street Church of God in Christ (later Roberts Temple).[89] She traveled the Southern "gospel highway" with her mother during her childhood and adolescence and by 1938 ultimately moved to New York City in order to pursue her own career as a performer. It was in New York City where she began singing and performing music outside the church, playing clubs like the Café Society Downtown and the Cotton Club on Broadway, where she appeared on a program with Cab Calloway and His Orchestra.[90]

Tharpe was the first gospel singer to sign a recording contract, cutting four sides for Decca Records, including "Rock Me" and "That's All." Less than a few months after recording, Tharpe performed in the 1938 historic "From Spirituals to Swing"[91] concert at Carnegie Hall, displaying her affinity for gospel and jazz. For a gospel singer to sing secular music, especially the blues—"the devil music" during this time period—was considered an abomination to the black church, so her success was met with much dismay on the religious side. This harsh criticism did not deter Tharpe's desire to perform both gospel and secular music. By 1948, she was singing and playing her steel guitar before as many as thirty thousand people in ball parks and stadiums.[92] Boyer attributed her large following to her many recordings, in addition to her ability to "drive audiences into a frenzy with her 'sliding' tones (a moaning technique derived from earlier Dr. Watts hymns, sorrow songs, and chants) and a constant shaking of her head."[93] In analyzing her 1938 recording "Rock Me," Gayle Wald describes Tharpe's vocal style as "precise, sometimes 'talky-y'" elocution, with subtle changes in pitch, volume, and tempo, unfussy melismatic flourishes, and a bouncy but controlled energy.[94] Wald acknowledges the "preacherly touches" apparent in Tharpe's intonation and pronunciation of words as a direct influence of her Pentecostal background. "She had the virtuosic ability to make particular musical choices—in singing, intonation, tone, timbre, pitch, phrasing, elocution, and so on—that could induce an audience to collective joy or sorrow, awe or celebration."[95]

Tharpe's virtuosic guitar playing and flamboyant singing and performing style created such an impact that she influenced many generations of singers and performers in both the religious and secular worlds. Tharpe is recognized for having been an important force in the development of Chicago blues and is considered the "Godmother of Rock and Roll," as she served as an important influence on later generations of singer-guitarists, from Chuck Berry, Little Richard, and Elvis Presley to contemporary artists such as Bonnie Raitt and Eric Clapton.[96]

Mahalia Jackson (1911–1972) was a native of New Orleans who moved to Chicago following the Great Migration. Jackson also embraced both secular and sacred music as a child, although she did so secretly. She was raised Baptist, but there was a Pentecostal church near the house in which she grew up, so she was exposed to that style of religious music at an early age. Listening to secular music was forbidden in her upbringing, but she still found ways to sneak and listen to it anyway. Jackson later admitted that Bessie Smith was her favorite performer. She greatly admired Smith's vocal quality and tried to imitate her sound, a fact she kept hidden from church folk.[97] Jackson was constantly criticized during most of her career for maintaining and perpetuating the style of music now called gospel. As previously mentioned, gospel was looked down upon by African American education elitists as the noneducated style of singing. Many, including her husband, Isaac Hockenhull, who constantly encouraged her to sing classical or semiclassical instead, believed singing gospel was a waste of her talent. Many of the traditional church denominations referred to the style of singing as jazz and thus condemned that style in church. This did not deter Jackson. She felt in her soul that singing gospel was her purpose and that her sound was a culmination of her musical upbringing, one that uniquely resonated with her spirit.[98] Jackson started by singing with an a cappella group, the Johnson Singer's Quartet, as their lead singer. From there, she teamed with Thomas Dorsey, who helped to train her, composed music for her, and also worked as her accompanist from 1937 to 1946.[99] Burnim quotes Jackson as stating:

> I didn't care whether gospel singing wasn't art. It had something for me. It was part of me. I loved it and sang it just the way I heard folks singing it down South during those great Baptist revival meetings on the Mississippi River when I was a child. . . . A lot of times we don't appreciate who we are and what we are. Even education, while it's a wonderful thing, can make a person narrow that way about himself.[100]

Jackson is considered one of the pioneers who established the stylistic features recognized as gospel singing styles. In terms of performance practices, she was the least outwardly physical singer of her time until much later in her career. Instead she took a more pious yet "joyful" approach to singing, using her deep, "dusky" contralto to build a slow, dramatic crescendo in gospel ballads.[101] With her mind on singing the gospel, Jackson died a multimillionaire. She sold the first million-selling gospel record, "Move On Up a Little Higher," in 1947, earned two Grammy awards, had both her own radio show and a TV show, made multiple appearances on variety shows, was a featured soloist at the presidential inauguration of John F. Kennedy, and was the musical preface to Martin Luther King Jr. at the 1963 March on Washington, singing "How I Got Over" and "I've Been 'Buked and I've Been Scorned."[102]

The most famous and innovative of all gospel quartets was the Soul Stirrers, particularly during the years of Rebert H. Harris.[103] Originally from Trinity, Texas, R. H. Harris began singing quartet at the age of ten with a family group at Harris Christian Methodist Church, his father's church. He attended seminary and was exposed to the Western European art music tradition of using the voice in a formal or subscribed manner. Resisting the operatic tone colors required in quartet singing at his school, Harris chose to use a type of mixed registration that would allow him to have the power of his low range and falsetto without maintaining the "opera-singer sound."[104] His sound was one that could alternate between a lyric sweetness and a grainy, passionate intensity.[105] Harris joined the Soul Stirrers in 1937 and was at the forefront of developing many new trends in quartet singing. He inspired the Soul Stirrers to approach their singing with an emotional intensity that until then had been considered too sanctified. He encouraged singers to move around the stage as they sang. He introduced the implementation of "swing lead," where two singers lead one song, one singing the verses and the other rousing the congregations on the choruses. He was also instrumental in distinguishing the gospel quartet from the jubilee quartet in the shift of focus from polished precision to touching some element of soul in the listeners.[106] As a soloist, Harris introduced performance techniques that would eventually become standard practice in gospel singing. They included ad-libbing, the background chanting of key words, and using "delayed time" in the quartet styles to create a form of syncopation that was commonly heard in the jazz styles by horn players.[107] Directly out of Harris came Sam Cooke, the father of soul music, whom Harris personally trained. Cooke eventually took Harris's place as the lead singer of the Soul Stirrers after Harris retired.

Other Artists to Know   Blind Arizona Dranes, Tindley Gospel Singers (Tindley Seven), Golden Gate Singers, the Southernaires, Dixie Hummingbirds, Sallie Martin, Theodore Frye, Magnolia Lewis Butts, Roberta Martin, Eugene Smith, Deloris Barrett, Robert Anderson, Willie Webb, Albertina Walker, Dorothy Love Coates, Julius Cheeks, Blue Jay Singers, Clara Ward and the Ward Singers, Marion Williams, and Ruth "Baby Sis" Davis.

Contemporary Era: 1960s–1970s

With the 1954 *Brown v. Board of Education* Supreme Court decision, the civil rights movement allowed for greater education and social opportunities for blacks and ultimately exposed them to a variety of musical forms. Gospel composers and artists such as Clinton Utterbach, who started his nationally recognized choir in 1961, showed strong influences from Western European classical music. On the side of the Pentecostal and Holiness gospel styles, his choir, often with as many as five hundred singers, became the ideal gospel sound by the end of the 1950s.[108] The mixed group established by Roberta Martin was further refined when it was applied to the gospel choir by Rev. James Cleveland and Mattie Moss Clark. Popularity in style grew nationwide. Gospel choirs were being featured more on television stations, were booked in major auditoriums, and signed contracts with major recording labels. The younger generation of singers during this time period had a greater desire for a modern gospel sound and wanted more access to the popular music market.[109] The trend of taking popular music songs and changing the text to religious content became one of the major gateways to connect with popular music audiences. Cleveland took the lead in revolutionizing the gospel sound through his extravagant arrangements, jazzy piano, soul organ, and semipop vocals that echoed his lead voice.[110] His following and influence was so great that in 1969, Cleveland founded what became the largest organization to be established specially for the purpose of teaching and promoting gospel music, the Gospel Music Workshop of America, annually hosting twenty thousand attendees.[111]

Mattie Moss Clark was the preeminent choral director of the COGIC national convention and served as the director, soloist, and composer for the Southwest Michigan Choir. She was responsible for training, influencing, and highlighting numerous gospel talents. Clark's daughter, Elbernita "Twinkie" Clark, became a star keyboardist at COGIC conventions and, after attending Howard University, rejoined her sisters to create a series of albums that made them the most significant and celebrated female gospel-singing group of their time.[112] Their harmonies and rhythmic syncopations were complex. They used **vowel distortion**, repetition of words and syllables, and spoke in tongues (i.e., a signifyin(g) capturing of the spirit through a fluent kind of utterance filled with Hebraic-sounding syllables) in their performances.

The 1960s and 1970s came to represent an era of gospel music in which new vocal harmonies, chordal progressions, and musical influences from around the world were incorporated into the gospel sound. In the late 1960s, gospel music composers, arrangers, and soloists like Andraé Crouch and later Edwin and Walter Hawkins, the Clark Sisters, and the Winans would include new harmonies and chordal progressions from the emerging contemporary popular music styles of the time. The pivotal gospel song that overtook the popular music industry in a way never before accomplished by a gospel group was the Edwin Hawkins Singers' 1969 release of "Oh Happy Day."

Gospel music also spread to Broadway during this time. While religious dramas, complete with costumes, lights, scenery, and music, had been part of African American church activities since the first quarter of the nineteenth century, it was in the late 1950s when gospel song-plays came to Broadway.[113] After creating the musical titled *Tambourines to Glory, a Musical Melodrama*, which was staged in summer stock in Westport, Connecticut, in 1957, the prolific author and poet Langston Hughes created *Black Nativity*, a gospel song-play that celebrated the birth of Christ through a tapestry of African American religious and musical expressions.

Icons to Know   Reverend James Cleveland (1931–1991) was born and raised in Chicago and affectionately became known as "the Crown Prince of Gospel." He attended Pilgrim Baptist Church with his grandmother as a child and sang in the choir as a boy soprano. The choir director and minister of music at the time was none other than Thomas

Dorsey, and the accompanist was Roberta Martin. Upon hearing his voice, Dorsey wrote a song for Cleveland that jump-started his career as a professional musician at a very young age.[114] Greatly influence by Dorsey and Martin, by the time he was a teenager Cleveland was traveling with the Roberta Martin Singers as a composer and arranger. He scarred his vocal folds as a teenager while singing with a local gospel group, leaving him with his distinctive husky, gravelly vocal quality, which ultimately became his hallmark.[115] As a result of the change in his voice, Cleveland turned his focus toward playing the piano, composing, and arranging until the hard, gravelly sound became popular in the 1970s, when he was again popular as a soloist. Albertina Walker later hired him as a composer, arranger, pianist, and occasional singer/narrator and gave him the opportunity to make his first recording. Though he no longer maintained the pretty voice of his childhood, he was particularly skilled in song delivery and in compelling his audience to a collective joy or sorrow. While working with organist Billy Preston and the Angelic Choir of Nutley, New Jersey, Rev. Cleveland recorded an album that made gospel history, selling over eight hundred thousand albums, with the eighteenth-century madrigal "Peace Be Still" as the title section.[116] Although many of his peers in the 1960s, 1970s, and 1980s migrated toward the "crossover" contemporary sound that began during the "Jesus movement" in the 1960s, Cleveland remained true to the traditional black gospel music tradition and the black church. Consistently and intently speaking to the black experience through his music and preaching, Cleveland never stepped away from the black church in search of greater success. With the creation of the Gospel Music Workshop of America and the perpetuation of all the organization represented—in terms of workshops, classes, bringing together church choirs from all over the country—Cleveland gave dignity to the music that comprised the very roots of the black church and its music.[117] Over his career, Cleveland won five Grammys and numerous awards and was the first gospel singer to receive a star on the Hollywood Walk of Fame.[118]

Andraé Crouch (1942–2015) was a pivotal figure in the contemporary gospel music era, helping to bring contemporary Christian music to the church and bridging the gap between black and white Christian music. Born and raised in San Francisco, California, Crouch was raised in the church where his father, Bishop Benjamin Crouch, was the pastor of

Christ Memorial Church of God in Christ. In the early 1960s, Crouch formed a group called the COGIC Singers, which featured Billy Preston on keyboards, and later formed the Disciples in 1965 while attending college. Though he began singing early in church and was composing as a teenager (he composed "The Blood Will Never Lose Its Power" at the age of fifteen), it wasn't until he signed with Light Records, a white religious label, that his group made their first recording in 1968. His biggest hits, "Through It All" and "I Don't Know Why Jesus Loves Me," combined traditional messages with heavily pop- and rock-inspired melodies.[119] It was through his connection and success with Light Records that he was able to bring in other black artists such as Walter and Tramaine Hawkins, Jessy Dixon, and the Winans to the label. Crouch has collaborated with a myriad of other gospel and secular music artists, including Take 6, Stevie Wonder, Michael Jackson, and Paul Simon. His compositions are a staple in churches and hymnbooks all around the world, with his most popular being "Soon and Very Soon," "Through It All," "The Blood Will Never Lose Its Power," "Bless His Holy Name," "Jesus Is the Answer," and "My Tribute." Crouch has earned numerous awards and honors, including seven Grammy awards, induction into the Gospel Music Hall of Fame in 1998, and a star on the Hollywood Walk of Fame.[120]

Other Artists to Know   Mattie Moss Clark, Alex Bradford, Albertina Walker and the Caravans, Inez Andrews, Dorothy Norwood, Pastor Shirley Caesar, Bessie Griffin, Marion Williams, Gertrude Ward, Joe Ligon and the Mighty Clouds of Joy, Staple Singers, Walter and Tramaine Hawkins, the O'Neal Twins, the Boyer Brothers, Cleophus Robinson and Josephine James, and the Winans.

Ministry Era: 1980s–1990s

Just as "Oh Happy Day" blended musical elements of gospel, jazz, and R&B in the 1960s, gospel composers and performers of the ministry era began experimenting with the popular music styles of the 1980s and 1990s.[121] Moving away from highlighting traditional gospel musical elements, gospel composers and performers began to incorporate musical and performance components from rap, R&B, and pop music and performance practices. The musical characteristics, once clearly separating

African American sacred and secular sound, became so diluted that the words or text of a song became *the* identifying factor for gospel music.[122] Starting in the 1960s and 1970s, this era solidified two distinct streams of contemporary artists: traditional and inspirational. Each maintained two different approaches to ministry, two different approaches to music, and sometimes even two different audiences. Those contemporary artists who maintained a traditional gospel approach proposed to clarify and convey the gospel message in a way that would lead gospel music listeners to both an emotional response and spiritual transformation.[123] These artists had their roots in the church choir and, musically, in blues and older R&B.[124] These inspirational artists sought to reach listeners that were non-Christian and to be able to speak into their lives and tell them about Christ by combining Bible messages with the contemporary R&B, Motown influences, jazz, and disco sound heard on the radio.[125] The contemporary sound appealed to young audiences whose ties to the church were not as strong, while those artists who maintained the traditional sound appealed to older audiences and those who grew up with strong ties to the church.[126] Overall, gospel singing moved toward a smoother vocal sound by the end of the 1980s. Black gospel artists recognized that this sound was key to permeating the white gospel market, and it ultimately became the impetus for traditionally white gospel labels to embrace the music and promote it through the Christian bookstores and other Christian media.

One of the most powerful musical trends in the 1990s was praise and worship music—music to be sung in church and sung to God by believers with believers. Both black and white churches began replacing traditional hymns with newly composed, contemporary praise and worship songs.[127] Judith Christie McAllister, "the first lady of praise and worship," is recognized as being one of the forerunners of the praise and worship movement in the black church.[128]

Other Artists to Know Andraé Crouch, Judith Christie, the Winans, Commissioned, Walter Hawkins, Vanessa Bell Armstrong, Clark Sisters, Darryl Coley, Take 6, Thomas Whitfield, Kim Burrell, Richard Smallwood, Donald Lawrence, Kurt Carr, Rickie Dillard, Carlton Pearson, Ron Kenoly, Larnelle Harris, Wintley Phipps, and Rance Allen.

Crossover Era: 1990s–Present

The crossover era of gospel music represents the "urbanization" of the gospel. Starting in the 1990s, gospel composers and performers continued the trend of infusing secular musical components with biblical messages with the targeted market of the urban youth in mind.[129] These compositions not only appealed to urban communities, they were also appealing to mainstream markets, which now began playing gospel music recordings on mainstream radio stations. This era also signifies a time period in which religious music as a whole becomes a prominent money-making industry in the sales of music, videos, books, and other merchandise. Music categories were developed in the 1990s that distinguish black religious music as *gospel music* and white religious music as *Christian music*, using the term *contemporary Christian music* to denote contemporary white religious music.[130] While both white and black religious music grew exponentially in sales through the 1990s, black gospel music showed the most gain during this time period, particularly with the 1997 release of Kirk Franklin's album *God's Property from Kirk Franklin's Nu Nation*. A trailblazer in the gospel music industry, Kirk Franklin's album sold 115,000 units within the first week of its release and, spurred by the hit single "Stomp" and a video on MTV, landed at number 3 on Billboard's Top Album charts. The "Tour of Life" tour that accompanied the promotion of the album was a major tour, with start-up costs of $250,000, yet was extremely successful, selling out in major cities.[131] Gospel music as an industry ministry continues to grow in sales and in popularity nationally and internationally.

Other Artists to Know   Yolanda Adams, Tramaine Hawkins, Donnie McClurkin, Donald Lawrence, BeBe and CeCe Winans, Hezekiah Walker, John P. Kee, Fred Hammond, Mary Mary, Smokie Norful, Luther Barnes, Thompson Community Choir, Dottie Peoples, Chester D. T. Baldwin, Israel Houghton, J. Moss, and Marvin Sapp.

NOTES

1. Mellonee Burnim, "Functional Dimensions of Gospel Music Performance," *Western Journal of Black Studies* 12, no. 2 (1988): 112.

2. Burnim, "Functional Dimensions."

3. James H. Cone, "Black Consciousness and the Black Church: A Historical-Theological Interpretation," *ANNALS of the American Academy of Political and Social Science* 387, no. 1 (1970): 49–55.

4. Mellonee Burnim, "Culture Bearer and Tradition Bearer: An Ethnomusicologist's Research on Gospel Music," *Ethnomusicology* 29, no. 3 (1985): 432–47.

5. Ibid.; Marietta Miller, "Qualitative Study of the American Black Spiritual and Gospel Music" (master's thesis, Morgan State University, 2003).

6. Mellonee Burnim, "The Black Gospel Music Tradition: A Complex of Ideology, Aesthetic, and Behavior," in *More than Dancing: Essays on Afro-American Music and Musicians*, ed. Irene V. Jackson (Westport, CT: Greenwood, 1985), 147–67.

7. Horace Clarence Boyer, "Black Gospel Music," in *Oxford Music Online*, vol. 2, ed. L. Macy (Oxford: Oxford University Press, 2008).

8. Raymond Wise, "Defining African American Gospel Music by Tracing Its Historical and Musical Development from 1900 to 2000" (PhD diss., Ohio State University, 2002).

9. Ibid.

10. Ibid.

11. Glenn Douglas Hinson, "When the Words Roll and the Fire Flows: Spirit, Style and Experience in African-American Gospel Performance" (PhD diss., University of Pennsylvania, 1989), 82.

12. Robert Raymond Allen, "Singing in the Spirit: An Ethnography of Gospel Performance in New York City's African-American Church Community" (PhD diss., University of Pennsylvania, 1987); Burt Feintuch, "A Noncommercial Black Gospel Group in Context: We Live the Life We Sing About," *Black Music Research Journal* 1 (1980): 37–50.

13. Samuel A. Floyd Jr., "Ring Shout! Literary Studies, Historical Studies, and Black Music Inquiry," *Black Music Research Journal* 11, no. 2 (1991): 265–87.

14. Ibid., 285.

15. Horace Clarence Boyer, "Gospel Music," *Music Educators Journal* 64, no. 9 (1978): 34–43.

16. Burnim, "Culture Bearer and Tradition Bearer"; Wise, "Defining African American Gospel."

17. Wise, "Defining African American Gospel Music."

18. "Traditional" is a generic term used to describe the stylistic aspects of gospel music performers or music written before 1960. "Contemporary" is the generic term used to describe the stylistic aspects of gospel music performers or music written after 1960.

19. Horace Clarence Boyer, "A Comparative Analysis of Traditional and Contemporary Gospel Music," in *More than Dancing: Essays on Afro-American Music and Musicians*, ed. Irene V. Jackson (Westport, CT: Greenwood, 1985), 127–45.

20. Ibid., 139–40.

21. Horace Clarence Boyer, "Contemporary Gospel Music," *Black Perspective in Music* 7, no. 1 (1979): 5–58; Lloyd Benjamin Mallory Jr., "The Choral Singing of the Negro Spiritual versus the Singing of Contemporary Gospel without Harming the Vocal Apparatus: A Choral Concept" (DMA diss., University of California, Los Angeles, 2006; ProQuest Order No. 3240942); Pearl Williams-Jones, "Afro-American Gospel Music: A Crystallization of the Black Aesthetic," *Ethnomusicology* 19, no. 3 (1975): 373–85.

22. Burnim, "Black Gospel Music Tradition."

23. Ibid.; Miller, "Qualitative Study of the American Black Spiritual and Gospel Music."

24. Boyer, "Contemporary Gospel Music"; Burnim, "Black Gospel Music Tradition"; Wise, "Defining African American Gospel Music."

25. Burnim, "Black Gospel Music Tradition."

26. Boyer, "Comparative Analysis of Traditional and Contemporary Gospel Music"; Burnim, "Black Gospel Music Tradition"; Wise, "Defining African American Gospel Music."

27. Allen, "Singing in the Spirit"; Feintuch, "Noncommercial Black Gospel Group in Context"; Hinson, "When the Words Roll"; Wise, "Defining African American Gospel Music"; Williams-Jones, "Afro-American Gospel Music."

28. Burnim, "Functional Dimensions of Gospel Music Performance"; Hinson, "When the Words Roll."

29. R. M. Simmons, *Good Religion: Expressions of Energy in Traditional African-American Worship* (Columbus, OH: Layman Christian Leadership, 1998), 1.

30. Ibid., 1.

31. Ibid., 47.

32. Mellonee Burnim, "Religious Music," in *African American Music: An Introduction*, ed. Mellonee Burnim and Portia K. Maultsby (New York: Taylor and Francis, 2006).

33. Wise, "Defining African American Gospel Music."

34. Burnim, "Religious Music."

35. Ibid.

36. Ibid.

37. Ibid.

38. Boyer, "Gospel Music."

39. Ibid., 36.

40. Ibid.

41. Burnim, "Religious Music."

42. Ibid., 56.

43. Ibid.

44. Ibid.; Eileen Southern, *The Music of Black Americans: A History* (New York: W. W. Norton, 1997).

45. Burnim, "Religious Music," 53.

46. Ibid., 58.

47. Boyer, "Gospel Music."

48. Ibid., 36.

49. Ibid.

50. Boyer, "Black Gospel Music."

51. Joyce Marie Jackson, "The Performing Black Sacred Quartet: An Expression of Cultural Values and Aesthetics" (PhD diss., Indiana University, 1988); Wise, "Defining African American Gospel Music"; Trineice Murlene Robinson-Martin, "Developing a Pedagogy for Gospel Singing: Understanding the Cultural Aesthetics and Performance Components of a Vocal Performance in Gospel Music" (PhD diss., Teachers College, Columbia University, 2010).

52. Horace Clarence Boyer, *How Sweet the Sound: The Golden Age of Gospel*, 1st ed. (Washington, DC: Elliott and Clark, 1995).

53. Wise, "Defining African American Gospel Music by Tracing Its Historical and Musical Development from 1900 to 2000"; Bernice Johnson Reagon, *We'll Understand It Better by and by: Pioneering African American Gospel Composers* (Washington, DC: Smithsonian Institution Press, 1992).

54. Wise, "Defining African American Gospel Music."

55. Boyer, *How Sweet the Sound*; Burnim, "Functional Dimensions of Gospel Music Performance"; Wise, "Defining African American Gospel Music."

56. Horace Clarence Boyer, *The Golden Age of Gospel* (Urbana: University of Illinois Press, 2000).

57. Ibid.

58. Burnim, "Religious Music."

59. Boyer, "Gospel Music."

60. Burnim, "Religious Music."

61. Boyer, "Gospel Music"; Burnim, "Religious Music."

62. Boyer, "Gospel Music."

63. Burnim, "Religious Music."

64. Horace Clarence Boyer, "Charles Albert Tindley: Progenitor of African-American Gospel Music," in *We'll Understand It Better By and By: Pioneering*

African American Gospel Composers, ed. Bernice Johnson Reagon (Washington, DC: Smithsonian Institution Press, 1992), 53–78.

65. Ibid. See also, "Defining African American Gospel Music"; Burnim, "Religious Music"; Robinson-Martin, "Developing a Pedagogy for Gospel Singing," 137.

66. Burnim, "Religious Music."

67. Ibid.

68. Mellonee Burnim, "The Gospel Music Industry," in *African American Music: An Introduction*, ed. Mellonee Burnim and Portia K. Maultsby (New York: Taylor and Francis, 2006).

69. Boyer, "Gospel Music."

70. Burnim, "Gospel Music Industry."

71. The National Baptist Convention of America was organized by a group of black Baptists in 1866; the music department within the convention was established by 1900 (Boyer, "Gospel Music").

72. Burnim, "Gospel Music Industry."

73. Boyer, "Gospel Music."

74. Wise, "Defining African American Gospel Music"; Burnim, "Religious Music."

75. Boyer, "Gospel Music," 38.

76. Ibid.

77. Burnim, "Religious Music"; Anthony Heilbut, *The Gospel Sound: Good News and Bad Times*, 25th anniversary ed. (New York: Limelight Editions, 1997).

78. Boyer, *Golden Age of Gospel*.

79. Ibid., 42.

80. Ibid.

81. Wise, "Defining African American Gospel Music."

82. Boyer, "Gospel Music."

83. Burnim, "Religious Music"; Wise, "Defining African American Gospel Music."

84. Boyer, "Gospel Music"; Wise, "Defining African American Gospel Music."

85. Boyer, "Contemporary Gospel Music," 18.

86. Wise, "Defining African American Gospel Music."

87. Allen, "Singing in the Spirit," 13.

88. Gayle Wald, *Shout, Sister, Shout! The Untold Story of Rock-and-Roll Trailblazer Sister Rosetta Tharpe* (Boston: Beacon Press, 2007).

89. Gayle Wald, "From Spirituals to Swing: Sister Rosetta Tharpe and Gospel Crossover," *American Quarterly* 55, no. 3 (2003): 388.

90. Ibid.

91. "From Spirituals to Swing" was a cultural event with a social mission: to transform attitudes about race by displaying exemplars of black musical achievement to an urban white audience. The roster of musicians included blues shouters Jimmy Rushing and Joe Turner, the North Carolina–based quartet Mitchell's Christian Singers, boogie-woogie pianist Albert Ammons, jazz soloist Sidney Bechet, and star-studded swing bands led by Count Basie and Benny Goodman (Wald, "From Spirituals to Swing," 387).

92. Boyer, "Gospel Music."

93. Ibid., 38.

94. Wald, "From Spirituals to Swing," 397.

95. Ibid., 398.

96. Ibid.

97. Mellonee Burnim, "Women in African American Music: Gospel," in *African American Music: An Introduction*, ed. Mellonee Burnim and Portia K. Maultsby (New York: Taylor and Francis, 2006).

98. Ibid.

99. Boyer, "Gospel Music."

100. Burnim, "Women in African American Music," 501–2.

101. Boyer, "Gospel Music."

102. Burnim, "Women in African American Music."

103. Boyer, *Golden Age of Gospel*.

104. Ibid., 96.

105. Heilbut, *Gospel Sound*.

106. Boyer, *Golden Age of Gospel*.

107. Heilbut, *Gospel Sound*.

108. Boyer, *Golden Age of Gospel*.

109. Ibid.

110. Heilbut, *Gospel Sound*.

111. Burnim, "Religious Music."

112. Heilbut, *Gospel Sound*.

113. Boyer, *Golden Age of Gospel*.

114. "Biography of Rev. James Cleveland," JCChorus.org, accessed May 20, 2016, http://jcchorus.com/Biography.htm.

115. "Reverend James Cleveland—Gospel Music Workshop of America, Inc.," GMW National website, accessed May 20, 2016, www.gmwanational.net/about-gmwa/reverend-james-cleveland/; "Biography of Rev. James Cleveland."

116. Heilbut, *Gospel Sound*; "Reverend James Cleveland"

117. Don Cusic, *The Sound of Light: A History of Gospel and Christian Music* (Milwaukee, WI: Hal Leonard Corporation, 2002).

118. "Biography of Rev. James Cleveland"; "James Cleveland," *Wikipedia*, accessed March 31, 2016, https://en.wikipedia.org/w/index.php?title=James _Cleveland&oldid=712823783.

119. Heilbut, *Gospel Sound*.

120. "Andraé Crouch," *Wikipedia*, accessed May 14, 2016, https://en.wiki pedia.org/w/index.php?title=Andra%C3%A9_Crouch&oldid=720253132.

121. Wise, "Defining African American Gospel Music."

122. Ibid.

123. Ibid.

124. Cusic, *Sound of Light*.

125. Wise, "Defining African American Gospel Music"; Cusic, *Sound of Light*.

126. Cusic, *Sound of Light*.

127. Ibid.

128. "Dr. Judith McAllister," Never Ending Worship, accessed May 21, 2016, www.neverendingworship.com/Dr._Judith_McAllister/.

129. Wise, "Defining African American Gospel Music."

130. Cusic, *Sound of Light*.

131. Ibid.

WORKS CITED

Allen, Robert Raymond. "Singing in the Spirit: An Ethnography of Gospel Performance in New York City's African-American Church Community." PhD diss., University of Pennsylvania, 1987.

"Andraé Crouch." *Wikipedia*. Accessed May 14, 2016. https://en.wikipedia .org/w/index.php?title=Andra%C3%A9_Crouch&oldid=720253132.

"Biography of Rev. James Cleveland." JCChorus.com. Accessed May 20, 2016. http://jcchorus.com/Biography.htm.

Boyer, Horace Clarence. "A Comparative Analysis of Traditional and Contemporary Gospel Music." In *More than Dancing: Essays on Afro-American Music and Musicians*, edited by Irene V. Jackson, 127–45. Westport, CT: Greenwood, 1985.

———. "Black Gospel Music." In *Oxford Music Online*, vol. 2, edited by L. Macy. Oxford: Oxford University Press, 2008.

———. "Charles Albert Tindley: Progenitor of African-American Gospel Music." In *We'll Understand It Better By and By: Pioneering African American Gospel Composers*, edited by Bernice Johnson Reagon, 53–78. Washington, DC: Smithsonian Institution Press, 1992.

———. "Contemporary Gospel Music." *Black Perspective in Music* 7, no. 1 (1979): 5–58.

———. *The Golden Age of Gospel*. Urbana: University of Illinois Press, 2000.

———. "Gospel Music." *Music Educators Journal* 64, no. 9 (1978): 34–43.

———. *How Sweet the Sound: The Golden Age of Gospel*. 1st ed. Washington, DC: Elliott and Clark, 1995.

Burnim, Mellonee. "The Black Gospel Music Tradition: A Complex of Ideology, Aesthetic, and Behavior." In *More than Dancing: Essays on Afro-American Music and Musicians*, edited by Irene V. Jackson, 147–67. Westport, CT: Greenwood, 1985.

———. "Culture Bearer and Tradition Bearer: An Ethnomusicologist's Research on Gospel Music." *Ethnomusicology* 29, no. 3 (1985): 432–47.

———. "The Gospel Music Industry." In *African American Music: An Introduction*, edited by Mellonee Burnim and Portia K. Maultsby. New York: Taylor and Francis, 2006.

———. "Functional Dimensions of Gospel Music Performance." *Western Journal of Black Studies* 12, no. 2 (1988): 112–21.

———. "Religious Music." In *African American Music: An Introduction*, edited by Mellonee Burnim and Portia K. Maultsby. New York: Taylor and Francis, 2006.

———. "Women in African American Music: Gospel." In *African American Music: An Introduction*, edited by Mellonee Burnim and Portia K. Maultsby. New York: Taylor and Francis, 2006.

Cone, James H. "Black Consciousness and the Black Church: A Historical-Theological Interpretation." *ANNALS of the American Academy of Political and Social Science* 387, no. 1 (1970): 49–55.

Cusic, Don. *The Sound of Light: A History of Gospel and Christian Music*. Milwaukee, WI: Hal Leonard, 2002.

"Dr. Judith McAllister." Never Ending Worship. Accessed May 21, 2016. www .neverendingworship.com/Dr._Judith_McAllister/.

Feintuch, Burt. "A Noncommercial Black Gospel Group in Context: We Live the Life We Sing About." *Black Music Research Journal* 1 (1980): 37–50.

Floyd, Samuel A., Jr. "Ring Shout! Literary Studies, Historical Studies, and Black Music Inquiry." *Black Music Research Journal* 11, no. 2 (1991): 265–87.

Heilbut, Anthony. *The Gospel Sound: Good News and Bad Times*. 25th anniversary ed. New York: Limelight Editions, 1997.

Hinson, Glenn Douglas. "When the Words Roll and the Fire Flows: Spirit, Style and Experience in African-American Gospel Performance." PhD diss., University of Pennsylvania, 1989.

Jackson, Joyce Marie. "The Performing Black Sacred Quartet: An Expression of Cultural Values and Aesthetics." PhD diss., Indiana University, 1988.

"James Cleveland." *Wikipedia*. Accessed March 31, 2016. https://en.wikipedia .org/w/index.php?title=James_Cleveland&oldid=712823783.

Mallory, Lloyd Benjamin, Jr. "The Choral Singing of the Negro Spiritual versus the Singing of Contemporary Gospel without Harming the Vocal Apparatus: A Choral Concept." DMA diss., University of California, Los Angeles, 2006. ProQuest Order No. 3240942.

Miller, Marietta. "Qualitative Study of the American Black Spiritual and Gospel Music." Master's thesis, Morgan State University, 2003.

Reagon, Bernice Johnson, ed. *We'll Understand It Better By and By: Pioneering African American Gospel Composers*. Washington, DC: Smithsonian Institution Press, 1992.

"Reverend James Cleveland—Gospel Music Workshop of America, Inc." GMWA National website. Accessed May 20, 2016. www.gmwanational.net/ about-gmwa/reverend-james-cleveland/.

Robinson-Martin, Trineice Murlene. "Developing a Pedagogy for Gospel Singing: Understanding the Cultural Aesthetics and Performance Components of a Vocal Performance in Gospel Music." PhD diss., Teachers College, Columbia University, 2010.

Simmons, R. M. *Good Religion: Expressions of Energy in Traditional African-American Worship*. Columbus, OH: Layman Christian Leadership, 1998.

Southern, Eileen. *The Music of Black Americans: A History*. New York: W. W. Norton, 1997.

Wald, Gayle. "From Spirituals to Swing: Sister Rosetta Tharpe and Gospel Crossover." *American Quarterly* 55, no. 3 (2003): 387–416.

———. *Shout, Sister, Shout! The Untold Story of Rock-and-Roll Trailblazer Sister Rosetta Tharpe*. Boston: Beacon Press, 2007.

Williams-Jones, Pearl. "Afro-American Gospel Music: A Crystallization of the Black Aesthetic." *Ethnomusicology* 19, no. 3 (1975): 373–85.

Wise, Raymond. "Defining African American Gospel Music by Tracing Its Historical and Musical Development from 1900 to 2000." PhD diss., Ohio State University, 2002.

2

SINGING GOSPEL AND VOICE SCIENCE

Scott McCoy

This chapter presents a concise overview of how the voice functions as a biomechanical, acoustic instrument. We will be dealing with elements of anatomy, physiology, acoustics, and resonance. But don't panic: the things you need to know are easily accessible, even if it has been many years since you last set foot in a science or math class!

All musical instruments, including the human voice, have at least four things in common, consisting of a *power source*, *sound source* (vibrator), *resonator*, and a system for *articulation*. In most cases, the person who plays the instrument provides power by pressing a key, plucking a string, or blowing into a horn. This power is used to set the sound source in motion, which creates vibrations in the air that we perceive as sound. Musical vibrators come in many forms, including strings, reeds, and human lips. The sound produced by the vibrator, however, needs a lot of help before it becomes beautiful music—we might think of it as raw material, like a lump of clay that a potter turns into a vase. Musical instruments use resonance to enhance and strengthen the sound of the vibrator, transforming it into sounds we identify as a piano, trumpet, or guitar. Finally, instruments must have a means of articulation to create the nuanced sounds of music. Let's see how these four elements are used to create the sounds of singing.

PULMONARY SYSTEM: THE POWER SOURCE
OF YOUR VOICE

The human voice has a lot in common with a trumpet: both use flaps of tissue as a sound source, both use hollow tubes as resonators, and both rely on the respiratory (pulmonary) system for power. If you stop to think about it, you quickly realize why breathing is so important for singing. First and foremost, it keeps us alive through the exchange of blood gasses—oxygen in, carbon dioxide out. But it also serves as the storage depot for the air we use to produce sound. Most singers rarely encounter situations in which these two functions are in conflict, but if you are required to sustain an extremely long phrase, you could find yourself in need of fresh oxygen before your lungs are totally empty.

Misconceptions about breathing for singing are rampant. Fortunately, most are easily dispelled. We must start with a brief foray into the world of physics in the guise of *Boyle's law*. Some of you no doubt remember this principle: the pressure of a gas within a container changes inversely with changes of volume. If the quantity of a gas is constant and its container is made smaller, pressure rises. But if we make the container get bigger, pressure goes down. Boyle's law explains everything that happens when we breathe, especially when we combine it with another physical law: *nature abhors a vacuum*. If one location has reduced pressure, air flows from an area of higher pressure to equalize the two and vice versa. So if we can create a zone of reduced air pressure by expanding our lungs, air automatically flows in to restore balance. When air pressure in the lungs is increased, it has no choice but to flow outward.

As we all know, the air we breathe goes in and out of our lungs. Each lung contains millions and millions of tiny air sacs called *alveoli*, where gasses are exchanged. The alveoli also function like ultraminiature versions of the bladder for a bag pipe, storing the air that will be used to set the vocal folds into vibration. To get the air in and out of them, all we need to do is make the lungs larger for inhalation and smaller for exhalation. Always remember this relationship between cause and effect during breathing: we inhale because we make ourselves large; we exhale because we make ourselves smaller. Unfortunately, the lungs are organs, not muscles, and have no ability on their own to accomplish this feat. For this reason, your bodies came from the factory with special muscles designed to enlarge and compress your entire thorax (rib cage), while simultaneously moving your lungs. We can classify these muscles in two main categories: any muscle that has the ability to increase the volume capacity of the thorax serves an *inspiratory* function; any muscle that has the ability to decrease the volume capacity of the thorax serves an *expiratory* function.

Your largest muscle of inspiration is called the *diaphragm* (figure 2.1). This dome-shaped muscle originates from the bottom of your sternum (breastbone) and completely fills the area from that point around your ribs to your spine. It's the second-largest muscle in your body, but you probably have no conscious awareness of it or ability to directly control

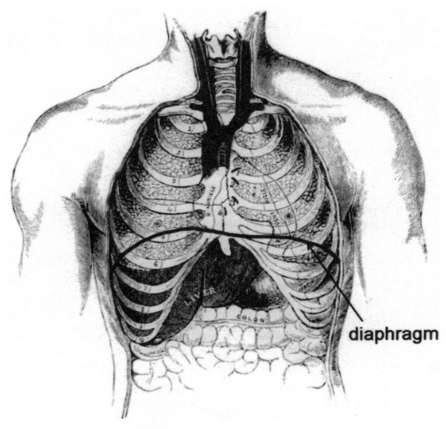

diaphragm

Figure 2.1. Location of Diaphragm.
Dr. Scott McCoy

it. When we take a deep breath, the diaphragm contracts and the central portion flattens out and drops downward a couple inches into your abdomen, pressing against all of your internal organs. If you release tension from your abdominal muscles as you inhale, you will feel a gentle bulge in your upper or lower belly, or perhaps in your back, resulting from the displacement of your innards by the diaphragm. This is a good thing and can be used to let you know you have taken a good inhalation.

The diaphragm is important, but we must remember that it cannot function in isolation. After you inhale, it relaxes and gently returns to its resting position through an action called *elastic recoil*. This movement, however, is entirely passive and makes no significant contribution to generating the pressure required to sustain phonation. Therefore, it makes no sense at all to try to "sing from your diaphragm"—unless you intend to sing while you inhale, not exhale!

Eleven pairs of muscles assist the diaphragm in its inhalatory efforts, which are called the *external* **intercostal muscles** (figure 2.2). These muscles start from ribs one through eleven and connect at a slight angle downward to ribs two through twelve. When they contract, the entire thorax moves up and out, somewhat like moving a bucket handle. With the diaphragm and intercostals working together, you are able to increase the capacity of your lungs by about three to six liters, depending on your gender and overall physical stature; thus, we have quite a lot of air available to power our voices.

Eleven additional pairs of muscles are located directly under the external intercostals, which, not surprisingly, are called the *internal intercostals* (figure 2.2). These muscles start from ribs two through twelve and connect upward to ribs one through eleven. When they contract, they induce the opposite action of their external partners: the thorax is made smaller, inducing exhalation. Four additional pairs of expiratory muscles are located in the abdomen, beginning with the *rectus* (figure 2.2). The two rectus abdominis muscles run from your pubic bone to your sternum and are divided into four separate portions, called *bellies* of the muscle (lots of muscles have multiple bellies; it is coincidental that the bellies of the rectus are found in the location we colloquially refer to as our belly). Definition of these bellies results in the so-called ripped abdomen or six-pack of body builders and others who are especially fit.

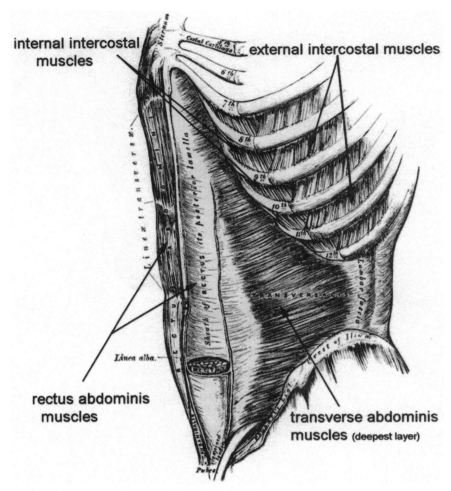

Figure 2.2. Intercostal and Abdominal Muscles.
Dr. Scott McCoy

The largest muscles of the abdomen are called the *external obliques* (figure 2.3), which run at a downward angle from the sides of the rectus, covering the lower portion of the thorax, and extend all the way to the spine. The *internal obliques* lie immediately below, oriented at an angle that crisscrosses the external muscles. They are slightly smaller, beginning at the bottom of the thorax rather than extending over it. The deepest muscle layer is the *transverse abdominis* (figure 2.3), which is

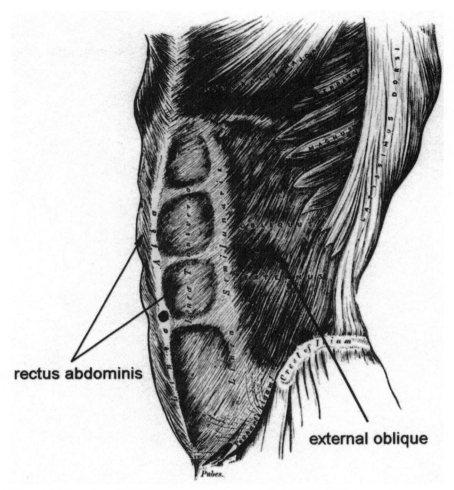

rectus abdominis

external oblique

Figure 2.3. External Oblique and *Rectus Abdominis* Muscles.
Dr. Scott McCoy

oriented with fibers that run horizontally. These four muscle pairs completely encase the abdominal region, holding your organs and digestive
system in place while simultaneously helping you breathe.

Your expiratory muscles are quite large and can produce a great deal of
pulmonary or air pressure. In fact, they easily can overpower the **larynx**.
Healthy adults generally can generate more than twice the pressure that
is required to produce even the loudest sounds; therefore, singers must
develop a system for moderating and controlling airflow and breath pres-

sure. This practice goes by many names, including *breath support*, *breath control*, and *breath management*, all of which rely on the principle of *muscular antagonism*. Muscles are said to have an antagonistic relationship when they work in opposing directions, usually pulling on a common point of attachment, for the sake of increasing stability or motor control. You can see a clear example of muscular antagonism in the relationship between your biceps (flexors) and triceps (extensors) when you hold out your arm. In breathing for singing, we activate inspiratory muscles (e.g., diaphragm and external intercostals) during exhalation to help control respiratory pressure and the rate at which air is expelled from the lungs.

One of the things you will notice when watching a variety of singers is that they tend to breathe in many different ways. You might think that voice teachers and scientists, who have been teaching and studying singing for hundreds, if not thousands of years, would have come to an agreement on the best possible breathing technique. But for many reasons, this is not the case. For one, different musical and vocal styles place varying demands on breathing. For another, humans have a huge variety of body types, sizes, and morphologies. A breathing strategy that is successful for a tall, slender woman might be completely ineffective in a short, robust man. Our bodies actually contain a large number of muscles beyond those we've already discussed that are capable of assisting with respiration. For an example, consider your *latissimi dorsi* muscles. These large muscles of the arm enable us to do pull ups (or pull downs, depending on which exercise you perform) at the fitness center. But because they wrap around a large portion of the thorax, they also can exert an expiratory force. We have at least two dozen such muscles that have secondary respiratory functions, some for exhalation and some for inhalation. When we consider all these possibilities, it is no surprise at all that there are many ways to breathe that can produce beautiful singing. Just remember to practice some muscular antagonism—maintaining a degree of inhalation posture during exhalation—and you should do well.

LARYNX: THE VIBRATOR OF YOUR VOICE

The larynx, sometimes known as the *voice box* or *Adam's apple*, is a complex physiologic structure made of cartilage, muscle, and tissue.

Biologically, it serves as a sphincter valve, closing off the airway to prevent foreign objects from entering the lungs. When firmly closed, it also is used to increase abdominal pressure to assist with lifting heavy objects, childbirth, and defecation. But if we gently close this valve while we exhale, tissue in the larynx begins to vibrate and produce the sounds that become speech and singing.

The human larynx is a remarkably small instrument, typically ranging from the size of a pecan to a walnut for women and men, respectively. Sound is produced at a location called the *glottis*, which is formed by two flaps of tissue called the *vocal folds* (a.k.a. vocal cords). In women, the glottis is about the size of a dime; in men, it can approach the diameter of a quarter. The two folds are always attached together at their front point, but open in the shape of the letter V during normal breathing, an action called *abduction*. To phonate, we must close the V while we exhale, an action called *adduction* (just like the machines you use at the fitness center to exercise your thigh and chest muscles).

Phonation only is possible because of the unique multilayer structure of the vocal folds (figure 2.4). The core of each fold is formed by muscle, which is surrounded by a layer of gelatinous material called the *lamina propria*. The *vocal ligament* also runs through the lamina propria, which helps to prevent injury by limiting how far the folds can be stretched for high pitches. A thin, hairless epithelial layer that is constantly kept moist with mucus secreted by the throat, larynx, and trachea surrounds all of this. During phonation, the outer layer of the fold glides independently over the inner layer in a wavelike motion, without which phonation is impossible.

We can use a simple demonstration to better understand the independence of the inner and outer portions of the folds. Explore the palm of your hand with your other index finger. Note that the skin is attached quite firmly to the flesh beneath it. If you poke at your palm, that flesh acts as padding, protecting the underlying bone. Now explore the back of your hand. You will observe that the skin is attached quite loosely— you easily can move it around with your finger. And if you poke at the back of your hand, it is likely to hurt; there is very little padding between the skin and your bones. Your vocal folds combine the best attributes of both sides of your hand. They provide sufficient padding to help reduce impact stress while permitting the outer layer to slip like the skin on

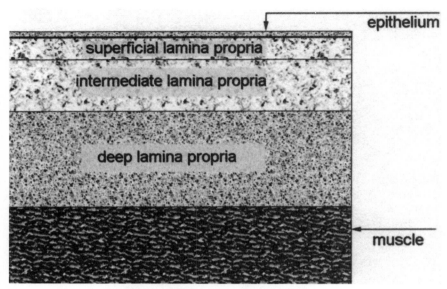

Figure 2.4.   Layered Structure of the Vocal Fold.
Dr. Scott McCoy

the back of your hand, enabling phonation to occur. When you are sick with laryngitis and lose your voice (a condition called *aphonia*), inflammation in the vocal folds couples the layers of the folds tightly together. The outer layer no longer can move independently over the inner and phonation becomes difficult or impossible.

The vocal folds are located within the five cartilaginous structures of the larynx (figure 2.5). The largest is called the *thyroid cartilage*, which is shaped like a small shield. The thyroid connects to the *cricoid* cartilage below it, which is shaped like a signet ring—broad in the back and narrow in the front. Two cartilages that are shaped like squashed pyramids sit atop the cricoid, called the *arytenoids*. Each vocal fold runs from the thyroid cartilage in front to one of the arytenoids at the back. Finally, the *epiglottis* is located at the top of the larynx, flipping backward each time we swallow to prevent food and liquid from entering our lungs. Muscles connect between the various cartilages to open and close the glottis and to lengthen and shorten the vocal folds for ascending and descending pitch, respectively. Because they sometimes are used to identify vocal function, it is a good idea to know the names of the

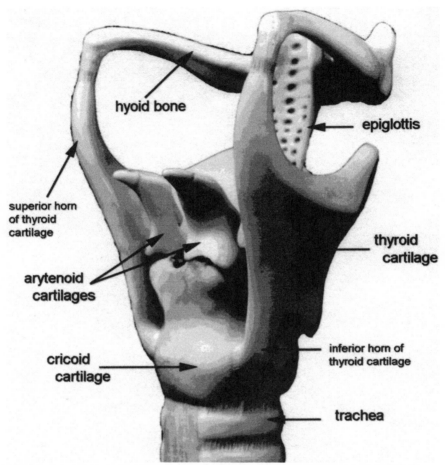

Figure 2.5.   Cartilages of the Larynx, Viewed at an Angle from the Back.
Dr. Scott McCoy

muscles that control the length of the folds. We've already mentioned that a muscle forms the core of each fold. Because it runs between the thyroid cartilage and an arytenoid, it is named the ***thyroarytenoid muscle*** (formerly known as the *vocalis* muscle). When the thyroarytenoid or TA muscle contracts, the fold is shortened and pitch goes down. The folds are elongated through the action of the ***cricothyroid or CT muscles***, which run from the thyroid to cricoid cartilage.

Vocal color (timbre) is created by the combined effects of the sound produced by the vocal folds and the resonance provided by the vocal tract. While these elements can never be completely separated, it is useful to consider the two primary modes of vocal fold vibration and their resulting sound qualities. The main differences are related to the relative thickness of the folds and their cross-sectional shape (figure 2.6). The first option depends on short, thick folds that come together with nearly square-shaped edges. Vibration in this configuration is given a variety of names, including *mode 1*, *thyroarytenoid* (TA) *dominant*, *chest mode*, or *modal voice*. The alternate configuration uses longer, thinner folds that only make contact at their upper margins. Common names include *mode 2*, *cricothyroid* (CT) *dominant*, *falsetto mode*, or *loft voice*. Singers vary the vibrational mode of the folds according to the quality of sound they wish to produce.

Before we move on to a discussion of resonance, we must consider the quality of the sound that is produced by the larynx. At the level of the glottis, we create a sound not unlike the annoying buzz of a duck call. That buzz, however, contains all the raw material we need to create speech and singing. Vocal or glottal sound is considered to be *complex*, meaning it consists of many simultaneously sounding frequencies (pitches). The lowest frequency within any tone is called the *fundamental*, which corresponds to its named pitch in the musical scale. Orchestras tune to a pitch called A-440, which means it has a frequency of 440 vibrations per second or 440 *Hertz* (abbreviated Hz). Additional frequencies are included above the fundamental, which are called *overtones*. Overtones in the glottal sound are quieter than the fundamental. In voices, the overtones usually are whole-number multiples of the fundamental, creating a pattern called the *harmonic series* (e.g., 100 Hz,

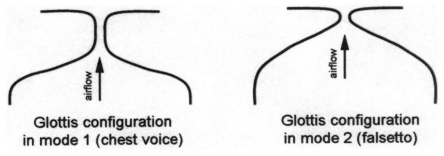

Glottis configuration in mode 1 (chest voice)

Glottis configuration in mode 2 (falsetto)

Figure 2.6. Primary Modes of Vocal Fold Vibration.
Dr. Scott McCoy

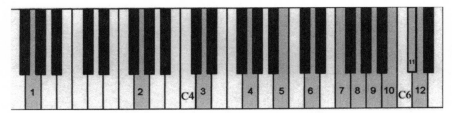

Figure 2.7.   Natural Harmonic Series, Beginning at G2.
Dr. Scott McCoy

200 Hz, 300 Hz, 400 Hz, 500 Hz, etc., or G2, G3, C4, G4, B4; note that pitches are named by the international system, in which the lowest C of the piano keyboard is C1. Middle C therefore becomes C4, the fourth C of the keyboard; see figure 2.7).

Singers who choose to make coarse or rough sounds, as might be appropriate for rock or blues, often add overtones that are *inharmonic* or not part of the standard numerical sequence. Inharmonic overtones also are common in singers with damaged or pathological voices.

Under most circumstances, we are completely unaware of the presence of overtones—they simply contribute to the overall timbre of a voice. In some vocal styles, however, harmonics become a dominant feature. This is especially true in *throat singing* or *overtone singing*, as is found in places like Tuva. Throat singers tune their vocal tracts so precisely that single harmonics are highlighted within the harmonic spectrum as a separate, whistle-like tone. These singers sustain a low-pitched drone and then create a melody by moving from tone to tone within the natural harmonic series. You can learn to do this too. Sustain a comfortable pitch in your range and slowly morph between the vowels /ee/ and /oo/. If you listen carefully, you will hear individual harmonics pop out of your sound.

The mode of vocal fold vibration has a strong impact on the overtones that are produced. In mode 1, high-frequency harmonics are relatively strong; in mode 2, they are much weaker. As a result, mode 1 tends to yield a much brighter, brassier sound.

VOCAL TRACT: YOUR SOURCE OF RESONANCE

Resonance typically is defined as the amplification and enhancement (or enrichment) of musical sound through *supplemental vibration*. What does this really mean? In layman's terms, we could say that resonance makes instruments louder and more beautiful by reinforcing the original vibrations of the sound source. This enhancement occurs in two primary ways that are known as *forced* and *free resonance* (there is nothing pejorative in these terms: free resonance is not superior to forced resonance). Any object that is physically connected to a vibrator can serve as a forced resonator. For a piano, the resonator is the soundboard (on the underside of a grand or on the back of an upright); the vibrations of the strings are transmitted directly to the soundboard through a structure known as the bridge, which also is found on violins and guitars. Forced resonance also plays a role in voice production. Place your hand on your chest and say *ah* at a low pitch. You almost certainly felt the vibrations of forced resonance. In singing, this might best be considered your *private* resonance; you can feel it, and it might impact your self-perception of sound, but nobody else can hear it. To understand why this is true, imagine what a violin would sound like if it were encased in a thick layer of foam rubber. The vibrations of the string would be damped out, muting the instrument. Your skin, muscles, and other tissues do the same thing to the vibrations of your vocal folds.

By contrast, free resonance occurs when sound travels through a hollow space, such as the inside of a trumpet, an organ pipe, or your vocal tract, which consists of the pharynx (throat), oral cavity (mouth), and nasal cavity. As sound travels through these regions, a complex pattern of echoes is created; every time sound encounters a change in the shape of the vocal tract, some of its energy is reflected backward, much like an echo in a canyon. If these echoes arrive back at the glottis at the precise moment a new pulse of sound is created, the two elements synchronize, resulting in a significant increase in intensity. All of this happens very quickly—remember that sound is traveling through your vocal tract at over seven hundred miles per hour.

Whenever this synchronization of the vocal tract and sound source occurs, we say that the system is *in resonance*. The phenomenon occurs at specific frequencies (pitches), which can be varied by changing the position of the tongue, lips, jaw, palate, and larynx. These resonant frequencies or areas in which strong amplification occurs are called *formants*. Formants provide the specific amplification that changes the raw, buzzing sound produced by your vocal folds into speech and singing. The vocal tract is capable of producing many formants, which are labeled sequentially by ascending pitch. The first two, F1 and F2, are used to create vowels; higher formants contribute to the overall timbre and individual characteristics of a voice. In some singers, especially those who train to sing in opera, formants three through five are clustered together to form a super formant, eponymously called the *singer's formant*, which creates a ringing sound and enables a voice to be heard in a large theater without electronic amplification.

Formants are vitally important in singing, but they can be a bit intimidating to understand. An analogy that works really well for me is to think of formants like the wind. You cannot see the wind, but you know it is present when you see leaves rustling in a tree or feel a breeze on your face. Formants work in the same manner. They are completely invisible and directly inaudible. But just as we see the rustling leaf, we can hear and perhaps even feel the action of formants through how they change our sound. Try a little experiment. Sing an ascending scale beginning at B-flat3, sustaining the vowel /ee/. As you approach the D-natural or E-flat of the scale, you likely will feel (and hear) that your sound becomes a bit stronger and easier to produce. This occurs because the scale tone and formant are on the same pitch, providing additional amplification. If you change to an /oo/ vowel, you will feel the same thing at about the same place in the scale. If you sing to an /oh/ or /eh/ and continue up the scale, you'll feel a bloom in the sound somewhere around C5 (an octave above middle C). An /ah/ is likely to come into its best focus at about G5.

To remember the approximate pitches of the first formants for the main vowels, /ee/-/eh/-/ah/-/oh/-/oo/, just think of a C-major triad in first inversion, open position, starting at E4: /ee/ = E4, /eh/ = C5, /ah/ = G5,

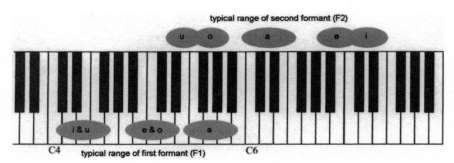

Figure 2.8. Typical Range of First and Second Formants for Primary Vowels. *Dr. Scott McCoy*

/oh/ = C5, and /oo/ = E4 (figure 2.8). If your music theory isn't strong, you could use the mnemonic "**e**very **c**hild **g**ets **c**andy **e**agerly." These pitches might vary by as much as a minor third higher and lower but no farther: once a formant changes by more than that interval, the vowel that is produced *must* change.

Formants have absolutely no preference for what they amplify—they are indiscriminate lovers, just as happy to bond with the first harmonic as the fifth. When men or women sing low pitches, there almost always will be at least one harmonic that comes close enough to a formant to produce a clear vowel sound. The same is not true for women with high voices, especially sopranos, who routinely must sing pitches that have a fundamental frequency *higher* than the first formant of many vowels. Imagine what happens if she must sing the phrase "and I'll leave you forever" with the word "leave" set on a very high, climactic note. The audience won't be able to tell if she is singing *leave* or *love* forever; the two will sound identical. This happens because the formant that is required to identify the vowel /ee/ is too far below the pitch being sung. Even if she tries to sing *leave*, the sound that comes out of her mouth will be heard as some variation of /ah/.

Fortunately, this kind of mismatch between formants and musical pitches rarely causes problems for anyone but opera singers, choir sopranos, and perhaps ingénues in classic music theater shows. Almost everyone else generally sings low enough in their respective voice ranges to produce easily identifiable vowels.

Second formants also can be important but more so for opera singers than anyone else. They are much higher in pitch, tracking the pattern /oo/ = E5, /oh/ = G5, /ah/ = D6, /eh/ = B6, /ee/ = D7 (you can use the mnemonic "**e**very **g**ood **d**ad **b**uys **d**iapers" to remember these pitches; figure 2.8). Because they can extend so high, into the top octave of the piano keyboard for /ee/, they interact primarily with higher tones in the natural harmonic series. Unless you are striving to produce the loudest unamplified sound possible, you probably never need to worry about the second formant; it will steadfastly do its job of helping to produce vowel sounds without any conscious thought or manipulation on your part.

If you are interested in discovering more about resonance and how it impacts your voice, you might want to install a spectrum analyzer on your computer. Free (or inexpensive) programs are readily available for download over the Internet that will work with either a PC or Mac. You don't need any specialized hardware—if you can use Skype or FaceTime, you already have everything you need. Once you've installed something, simply start playing with it. Experiment with your voice to see exactly how the analysis signal changes when you change the way your voice sounds. You'll be able to see how harmonics change in intensity as they interact with your formants. If you sing with vibrato, you'll see how consistently you produce your variations in pitch and amplitude. You'll even be able to see if your tone is excessively nasal for the kind of singing you want to do. Other programs are available that will help you improve your intonation (how well you sing in tune) or enhance your basic musicianship skills. Technology truly has advanced sufficiently to help us sing more beautifully.

MOUTH, LIPS, AND TONGUE: YOUR ARTICULATORS

The articulatory life of a singer is not easy, especially when compared to the demands placed on other musicians. Like a pianist or brass player, we must be able to produce the entire spectrum of musical articulation, including dynamic levels from hushed pianissimos to thunderous fortes, short notes, long notes, accents, crescendos, diminuendos, and so on. We produce most of these articulations the same way instrumentalists do, which is by varying our power supply. But singers have another layer of articulation that makes everything much more complicated; we must produce these musical gestures while simultaneously singing words.

As we learned in our brief examination of formants, altering the resonance characteristics of the vocal tract creates the vowel sounds of language. We do this by changing the position of our tongue, jaw, lips, and sometimes palate. Slowly say the vowel pattern /ee/-/eh/-/ah/-/oh/-/oo/. Can you feel how your tongue moves in your mouth? For /ee/, it is high in the front and low in the back, but it takes the opposite position for /oo/. Now slowly say the word *Tuesday*, noting all the places your tongue comes into contact with your teeth and palate, and how it changes shape as you produce the vowels and diphthongs. There is a lot going on in there—no wonder it takes so long for babies to learn to speak!

Our articulatory anatomy is extraordinarily complex, in large part because our bodies use the same passageway for food, water, air, and sound. As a result, our tongue, larynx, throat, jaw, and palate are all interconnected with common physical and neurologic points of attachment. Our anatomical Union Station in this regard is a small structure called the *hyoid bone*. The hyoid is one of only three bones in your entire body that do not connect to other bones via a joint (the other two are your *patellae* or kneecaps). This little bone is suspended below your jaw, freely floating up and down every time your swallow. It is a busy place, serving as the upper suspension point for the larynx, the connection for the root of the tongue, and the primary location of the muscles that open your mouth by dropping your jaw.

Good singing—in any genre—requires a high degree of independence in all these articulatory structures. Unfortunately, nature conspires against us to make this difficult to accomplish. From the time we were born, our bodies have relied on a reflex reaction to elevate the palate and raise the larynx each time we swallow. This action becomes habitual: palate goes up, larynx also lifts. But depending on the style of music we are singing, we might need to keep the larynx down while the palate goes up (opera and classical) or palate down with the larynx up (country and bluegrass). As we all know, habits can be very hard to change, which is one of the reasons that it can take a lot of study and practice to become an excellent singer. Understanding your body's natural reflexive habits can make some of this work a bit easier.

There is one more significant pitfall to the close proximity of all these articulators: tension in one area is easily passed along to another. If your jaw muscles are too tight while you sing, that hyperactivity will likely be transferred to the larynx and tongue—remember, they all are interconnected through the hyoid bone. It can be tricky to determine the primary offender in this kind of chain reaction of tension. A tight tongue could just as easily be making your jaw stiff, or an elevated, rigid larynx could make both tongue and jaw suffer.

Neurology complicates matters even further. You have sixteen muscles in your tongue, fourteen in your larynx, twenty-two in your throat and palate, and another sixteen that control your jaw. Many of these are very small and lie directly adjacent to each other, and you often are required to contract one quite strongly while its next-door neighbor must remain totally relaxed. Our brains need to develop laser-like control, sending signals at the right moment with the right intensity to the precise spot where they are needed. When we first start singing, these brain signals come more like a blast from a shotgun, spreading the neurologic impulse over a broad area to multiple muscles, not all of which are the intended target. Again, with practice and training we learn to refine our control, enabling us to use only those muscles that will help while disengaging those that would get in the way of our best singing.

CONCLUSION

This brief chapter has only scratched the surface of the huge field of voice science. To learn more, you might visit the websites of the National Association of Teachers of Singing, the Voice Foundation, or the National Center for Voice and Speech. You can easily locate the appropriate addresses through any Internet search engine. Remember: knowledge is power. Occasionally, people are afraid that if they know more about the science of how they sing, they will become so analytical that all spontaneity is lost or they will become paralyzed by too much information and thought. In my forty-plus years as a singer and teacher, I've never encountered somebody who actually suffered this fate. To the contrary, the more we know, the easier—and more joyful—singing becomes.

RESOURCES

National Association of Teachers of Singing: nats.org
The National Center for Voice and Speech: ncvs.org
The Voice Foundation: voicefoundation.org

3

VOCAL HEALTH AND THE GOSPEL VOCAL ATHLETE

Wendy DeLeo LeBorgne

GENERAL PHYSICAL WELL-BEING

All singers, regardless of genre, should consider themselves to be "vocal athletes." The physical, emotional, and performance demands required for optimal output require that the artist consider training and maintaining their instrument as an athlete trains for an event. With increased vocal and performance demands, it is unlikely that a vocal athlete will have an entire performing career completely injury free. This may not be the fault of the singer, as many injuries occur due to circumstances beyond the singer's control, such as singing through an illness or being on a new medication seemingly unrelated to the voice.

Vocal injury has often been considered taboo to talk about in the performing world as it has been considered to be the result of faulty technique or poor vocal habits. In actuality, the majority of vocal injuries presenting in the elite performing population tend to be overuse and/ or acute injury. From a clinical perspective over the last twenty years, younger, less experienced singers with fewer years of training (who tend to be quite talented) generally are the ones who present with issues related to technique or phonotrauma (nodules, edema, contact ulcers), while more mature singers with professional performing careers tend to present with acute injuries (hemorrhage) or overuse and misuse injuries (muscle tension dysphonia, edema, gastroesophageal reflux disease) or injuries following an illness. There are no current studies documenting use and training in correlation to laryngeal pathologies. However, there are studies that document that somewhere between 35 to 100 percent of professional vocal athletes have abnormal vocal fold findings upon stroboscopic evaluation. Many times these "abnormalities" are in singers who have no vocal complaints or symptoms of vocal problems. From a performance perspective, uniqueness in vocal quality often gets hired, and perhaps a slight aberration in the way a given larynx functions may become quite marketable. Regardless of what the vocal folds may look like, the most integral part of performance is that the singer must maintain agility, flexibility, stamina, power, and inherent beauty (genre appropriate) for their current level of performance, taking into account physical, vocal, and emotional demands.

Unlike sports medicine and the exercise physiology literature where much is known about the types and nature of given sports injuries, there is no common parallel for the vocal athlete model. However, because the vocal athlete uses the body systems of alignment, respiration, phonation, and resonance with some similarities to physical athletes, a parallel protocol for vocal wellness may be implemented/considered for vocal athletes in order to maximize injury prevention knowledge for both the singer and teacher. This chapter aims to provide information on vocal wellness and injury prevention for the vocal athlete.

CONSIDERATIONS FOR WHOLE BODY WELLNESS

Nutrition

You have no doubt heard the saying "you are what you eat." Eating is a social and psychological event. For many people, food associations and eating have an emotional basis resulting in either overeating or being malnourished. Eating disorders in performers and body image issues may have major implications and consequences for the performer on both ends of the spectrum (obesity and anorexia). Singers should be encouraged to reprogram the brain and body to consider food as fuel. You want to use high-octane gas in your engine, as pouring water in your car's gas tank won't get you very far. Eating a poor diet or a diet that lacks appropriate nutritional value will have negative physical and vocal effects on the singer. The effects of poor dietary choices for the vocal athlete may result in physical and vocal consequences, ranging from fatigue to life-threatening disease over the course of a lifetime. Encouraging and engaging in healthy eating habits from a young age will potentially prevent long-term negative effects from poor nutritional choices. It is beyond the scope of this chapter to provide a complete overview of all the dietary guidelines for pediatrics, adolescents, adults, and the mature adult; however, a listing of additional references to help guide your food and beverage choices for making good nutritional choices can be found online at websites such as Dietary Guidelines for Americans, Nutrition.gov Guidelines for Tweens and Teens, and Fruits and Veggies Matter. See the online companion webpage on the National Association of Teachers of Singing (NATS) website for links to these and other resources.

Hydration

"Sing wet, pee pale." This phrase was echoed in the studio of Van Lawrence regarding how his students would know if they were hydrated well enough. Generally, this rule of pale urine during your waking hours is a good indicator that you are well hydrated. Medications, vitamins, and certain foods may alter urine color despite adequate hydration. Due to the varying levels of physical and vocal activity of many performers, in order to maintain adequate oral hydration, the use of a hydration calculator based on activity level may be a better choice. These hydration calculators are easily accessible online and take into account the amount and level of activity the performer engages in on a daily basis. In a recent study of the vocal habits of musical theater performers, one of the findings indicated a significantly underhydrated group of performers.[1]

Laryngeal and pharyngeal dryness as well as "thick, sticky, mucus" are often complaints of singers. Combating these concerns and maintaining an adequate viscosity of mucus for performance has resulted in some research. As a reminder of laryngeal and swallowing anatomy, nothing that is swallowed (or gargled) goes over or touches the vocal folds directly (or one would choke). Therefore, nothing that a singer eats or drinks ever touches the vocal folds, and in order to adequately hydrate the mucus membranes of the vocal folds, one must consume enough fluids for the body to produce a thin mucus. Therefore, any "vocal" effects from swallowed products are limited to potential pharyngeal and oral changes, not changes to the vocal folds themselves.

The effects of systemic hydration are well documented in the literature. There is evidence to suggest that adequate hydration will provide some protection of the laryngeal mucosal membranes when they are placed under increased collision forces as well as reducing the amount of effort (phonation threshold pressure) to produce voice. This is important for the singer because it means that with adequate hydration and consistency of mucus, the effort to produce voice is less and the vocal folds are better protected from injury. Imagine the friction and heat produced when two dry hands rub together and then what happens if you put lotion on your hands. The mechanisms in the larynx to provide appropriate mucus production are not fully understood, but there is enough evidence at this time to support oral hydration as a vital component of every singer's vocal-health regime to maintain appropriate mucosal viscosity.

Although very rare, overhydration (hyperhidrosis) can result in dehydration and even illness or death. An overindulgence of fluids essentially makes the kidneys work "overtime" and flushes too much water out of the body. This excessive fluid loss in a rapid manner can be detrimental to the body.

In addition to drinking water and systemically monitoring hydration, there are many nonregulated products on the market for performers that lay claim to improving the laryngeal environment (e.g., Entertainer's Secret, Throat Coat Tea, Greathers Pastilles, Slippery Elm, etc.). Although there may be little detriment in using these products, quantitative research documenting change in laryngeal mucosa is sparse. One study suggests that the use of Throat Coat when compared to a placebo treatment for pharyngitis did show a significant difference in decreasing the perception of sore throat. Another study compared the use of Entertainer's Secret to two other nebulized agents and its effect on phonation threshold pressure (PTP). There was no positive benefit in decreasing PTP with Entertainer's Secret.

Personal steam inhalers and/or room humidification to supplement oral hydration and aid in combating laryngeal dryness are used by many singers. There are several considerations for singers who choose to use external means of adding moisture to the air they breathe. Personal steam inhalers are portable and can often be used backstage or in the hotel room for the traveling performer. Typically, water is placed in the steamer and the face is placed over the steam for inhalation. Because the mucus membranes of the larynx are composed of a saltwater solution, one study looked at the use of nebulized saline in comparison to plain water and its potential effects on effort or ease to sound production in classically trained sopranos.[2] Data suggested that perceived effort to produce voice was less in the saline group than the plain water group. This indicated that the singers who used the saltwater solution reported less effort to sing after breathing in the salt water than singers who used plain water. It was hypothesized by the researchers that because the body's mucus is not plain water (rather it is a salt water—think about your tears), when you use plain water for steam inhalation, it may actually draw the salt from your own saliva, resulting in a dehydrating effect.

In addition to personal steamers, other options for air humidification come in varying sizes of humidifiers, from room size to whole-house humidifiers. When choosing between a warm air or cool mist humidifier, considerations include both personal preference and needs. One of the primary reasons warm mist humidifiers are not recommended for young children is due to the risk of burns from the heating element. Both the warm mist and cool air humidifiers act similarly in adding moisture to the environmental air. External air humidification may be beneficial and provide a level of comfort for many singers. Regular cleaning of the humidifier is vital in order to prevent bacteria and mold buildup. Also, depending on the hardness of the water, it is important to avoid mineral buildup on the device and distilled water may be recommended for some humidifiers.

For traveling performers who often stay in hotels, fly on airplanes, or are generally exposed to other dry-air environments, there are products on the market designed to help minimize drying effects. One such device is called a Humidfly, which is a facemask designed with a filter to recycle the moisture from a person's own breath and replenish moisture on each breath cycle.

For dry nasal passages or to clear sinuses, singers sometimes use Neti Pots. Many singers use this homeopathic flushing of the nasal passages regularly. When used properly, research supports the use of a Neti Pot as a part of allergy relief and chronic rhinosinusitis control, sometimes in combination with medical management.[3] Conversely, long-term use of nasal irrigation (without taking intermittent breaks from daily use) may result in washing out the "good" mucus of the nasal passages, which naturally help to rid the nose of infections. A study presented at the 2009 American College of Allergy, Asthma, and Immunology (ACAAI) Annual Scientific Meeting reported that when a group of individuals who were using twice-daily nasal irrigation for one year discontinued using it, they had an increase in acute rhinosinusitis.[4]

Tea, Honey, and Gargle to Keep the Throat Healthy

Regarding the use of general teas (which many singers combine with honey or lemon), there is likely no harm in the use of decaffeinated tea (caffeine may cause systemic dryness). The warmth of the tea may provide a soothing sensation to the pharynx, and the act of swallowing can be relaxing for the muscles of the throat. Honey has shown to be promising as an effective cough suppressant in the pediatric population.[5] The dose of honey given to the children in the study was two teaspoons. Gargling with salt or apple cider vinegar and water are also popular home remedies for many singers, with the uses ranging from soothing the throat to curing reflux. Gargling plain water has been shown to be efficacious in reducing the risk of contracting upper respiratory infections. This author suggests that when gargling, the singer only "bubble" the water with air and avoid engaging the vocal folds in sound production. Salt water as a gargle has long been touted as a sore throat remedy and can be traced back to 2700 BCE in China for treating gum disease. The science behind a saltwater rinse for everything from oral hygiene to a sore throat is that salt (sodium chloride) may act as a natural analgesic (pain killer) and may also kill bacteria. Similar to the effects that not enough salt in the water may have on drawing the salt out of the tissue in the steam inhalation, if you oversaturate the water solution with excess salt and gargle it, it may act to draw water out of the oral mucosa, thus reducing inflammation.

Another popular home remedy reported by singers is the use of apple cider vinegar to help with everything from acid reflux to sore throats. Dating back to 3300 BCE, apple cider vinegar was reported as a medicinal remedy, and it became popular in the 1970s as a weight-loss diet cocktail. Popular media reports that apple cider vinegar can improve conditions from acne and arthritis to nosebleeds and varicose veins. Specific efficacy data regarding the beneficial nature of apple cider vinegar for the purpose of sore throat, pharyngeal inflammation, and/or reflux have not been reported in the literature at this time. Of the peer-reviewed studies found in the literature, one discussed possible esophageal erosion and inconsistency of actual product in tablet form.[6] Therefore, at this time, strong evidence supporting the use of apple cider vinegar is not published.

Medications and the Voice

Medications (over the counter, prescription, and herbal) may have resultant drying effects on the body and often the laryngeal mucosa. General classes of drugs with potential drying effects include antidepressants, antihypertensives, diuretics, attention deficit disorder and attention deficit/hyperactivity disorder medications, some oral acne medications, hormones, allergy drugs, and vitamin C in high doses. The National Center for Voice and Speech (NCVS) provides a listing of some common medications with potential voice side effects, including laryngeal dryness. This listing does not take into account all medications, so singers should always ask their pharmacist of the potential side effects of a given medication. Due to the significant number of drugs on the market, it is safe to say that most pharmacists will not be acutely aware of "vocal side effects," but if dryness is listed as a potential side effect of the drug, you may assume that all body systems could be affected. Under no circumstances should you stop taking a prescribed medication without consulting your physician first. As every person has a different body chemistry and reaction to medication, just because a medication lists dryness as a potential side effect, it does not necessarily mean you will experience that side effect. Conversely, if you begin a new medication and notice physical or vocal changes that are unexpected, you should consult with your physician. Ultimately, the goal of medical management for any condition is to achieve the most benefits with the least side effects. Please see the companion page on the NATS website for a list of possible resources for the singer regarding prescription drugs and herbs.

In contrast to medications that tend to dry, there are medications formulated to increase saliva production or alter the viscosity of mucus. Medically, these drugs are often used to treat patients who have had a loss of saliva production due to surgery or radiation. Mucolytic agents are used to thin secretions as needed. As a singer, if you feel that you need to use a mucolytic agent on a consistent basis, it may be worth considering getting to the root of the laryngeal dryness problem and seeking a professional option by an otolaryngologist.

Reflux and the Voice

Gastroesophageal reflux disease (GERD) and/or laryngopharyngeal reflux (LPR) can have a devastating effect on the singer if not recognized and treated appropriately. Although GERD and LPR are related, they are considered slightly different diseases. GERD (Latin root meaning "flowing back") is the reflux of digestive enzymes, acids, and other stomach contents into the esophagus (food pipe). If this backflow is propelled through the upper esophagus and into the throat (larynx and pharynx), it is referred to as LPR. It is not uncommon to have both GERD and LPR, but they can occur independently.

More frequently, people with GERD have decreased esophageal clearing. Esophagitis or inflammation of the esophagus is also associated with GERD. People with GERD often feel heartburn. LPR symptoms are often "silent" and do not include heartburn. Specific symptoms of LPR may include some or all of the following: lump in the throat sensation, feeling of constant need to clear the throat/post nasal drip, longer vocal warm-up time, quicker vocal fatigue, loss of high-frequency range, worse voice in the morning, sore throat, bitter/raw/brackish taste in the mouth. If you experience these symptoms on a regular basis, it is advised that you consider a medical consultation for your symptoms. Prolonged, untreated GERD or LPR can lead to permanent changes in both the esophagus and/or larynx. Untreated LPR also provides a laryngeal environment that is conducive for vocal fold lesions as it inhibits normal healing mechanisms.

Treatment of LPR and GERD generally include both dietary and lifestyle modifications in addition to medical management. Some of the dietary recommendations include elimination of caffeinated and carbonated beverages, smoking cessation, no alcohol use, and limiting tomatoes, acidic foods and drinks, and raw onions or peppers, to name a few. Also, avoidance of high-fat foods is recommended. From a lifestyle perspective, changes include not eating within three hours of laying down, eating small meals frequently (instead of large meals), elevating the head of your bed, avoiding tight clothing around the belly, and avoiding bend over or exercising too soon after you eat.

Reflux medications fall in three general categories: antacids, H_2 blockers, and proton pump inhibitors (PPI). There are now combination drugs that include both an H_2 blocker and PPI. Every medication has both associated risks and benefits, and singers should be aware of the possible benefits and side effects of the medications they take. In general terms, antacids (e.g., Tums, Mylanta, Gaviscon) neutralize stomach acid. H_2 (histamine) blockers such as Axid (nizatidine), Tagamet (cimetidine), Pepcid (famotidine), and Zantac (ranitidine) work to decrease acid production in the stomach by preventing histamine from triggering the H_2 receptors to produce more acid. Then there are the PPIs: Nexium (esomeprazole), Prevacid (lansoprazole), Protonix (pantoprazole), AcipHex (rabeprazole), Prilosec (omeprazole), Dexilant (dexlansoprazole). PPIs act as a last line of defense to decrease acid production by blocking the last step in gastric juice secretion. Some of the most recent drugs to combat GERD/LPR are combination drugs (e.g., Zegrid [sodium bicarbonate plus omeprazole]), which provide a short-acting response (sodium bicarbonate) and a long release (omeprazole). Because some singers prefer a holistic approach to reflux management, strict dietary and lifestyle compliance is recommended, and consultation with both your primary care physician and naturopath are warranted in that situation. Efficacy data on nonregulated herbs, vitamins, and supplements are limited, but some data do exist.

Physical Exercise

Vocal athletes, like other physical athletes, should consider how and what they do to maintain both cardiovascular fitness and muscular strength. In today's performance culture, it is rare for a performer to stand still and sing unless in a recital or choral setting. The range of physical activity can vary from light movement to high-intensity choreography with acrobatics. As performers are being required to increase their on-stage physical activity level from the operatic stage to the popstar arena, overall physical fitness is imperative in order to avoid compromise in the vocal system. Breathlessness will result in compensation by the larynx, which will now attempt to regulate the air. Compensatory vocal behaviors over time may result in a change in vocal performance. The health benefits of both cardiovascular training and strength training are well documented in the literature for physical athletes but relatively rare for vocal performers.

Mental Wellness

Vocal performers must maintain a mental focus during performance and a mental toughness during auditioning and training. Rarely during vocal performance training programs is this important aspect of performance addressed, and it is often left to the individual performer to develop his or her own strategy or coping mechanism. Yet many performers are on antianxiety or antidepressant drugs (which may be the direct result of performance-related issues). If the sports world is again used as a parallel for mental toughness, there are no elite-level athletes (and few junior-level athletes) who don't make use of the services of a performance/sports psychologist in order to maximize focus and performance. It is the recommendation of this author that performers consider the potential benefits of a performance psychologist to help maximize vocal performance. Several references that may be of interest to the singer include Joanna Cazden's *Visualization for Singers* and Shirlee Emmons and Alma Thomas's *Power Performance for Singers: Transcending the Barriers*.

Unlike instrumentalists, whose performance is dependent on the accurate playing of an external musical instrument, the singer's instrument is uniquely intact and subject to the emotional confines of the brain and body in which it is housed. Musical performance anxiety (MPA) can be career threatening for all musicians, but perhaps the vocal athlete is more severely impacted. The majority of literature on MPA is dedicated to instrumentalists, but the basis of definition, performance effects, and treatment options can be considered for vocal athletes. Fear is a natural reaction to a stressful situation, and there is a fine line between emotional excitation and perceived threat (real or imagined). The job of a performer is to convey to an audience through vocal production, physical gestures, and facial expression a most heightened state of emotion. Otherwise, why would audience members pay top dollar to sit for two or three hours for a mundane experience? Not only is there the emotional conveyance of the performance but also the internal turmoil often experienced by the singer her- or himself in preparation for elite performance. It is well documented in the literature that even the most elite performers have experienced debilitating performance anxiety. MPA is defined on a continuum with anxiety levels ranging from low to high and has been reported to comprise four distinct components: affect, cognition, behavior, and physiology. Affect comprises feelings (e.g., doom, panic, anxiety); compromised cognition will result in altered levels of concentration; while the behavior component results in postural shifts, quivering, and trembling, and finally, physiologically the body's autonomic nervous system (ANS) will activate resulting in the "fight or flight" response. In recent years, researchers have been able to define two distinct neurological pathways for MPA. The first pathway happens quickly and without conscious input (ANS), resulting in the same fear stimulus as if a person were put into an emergent, life-threatening situation. In those situations, the brain releases adrenaline, resulting in physical changes of increased heart rate, increased respiration, shaking, pale skin, dilated pupils, slowed digestion, bladder relaxation, dry mouth, and dry eyes, all of which severely affect vocal performance. The second pathway that has been identified results in a conscious identification of the fear/threat and a much slower physiologic response. With the second neuromotor response, the performer has a chance to recognize the fear, process how to deal with the fear, and respond accordingly.

Treatment modalities to address MPA include psychobehavioral therapy (including biofeedback) and drug therapies. Elite physical-performance athletes have been shown to benefit from visualization techniques and psychological readiness training, yet within the performing arts community, stage fright may be considered a weakness or character flaw precluding readiness for professional performance. On the contrary, vocal athletes, like physical athletes should mentally prepare themselves for optimal competition (auditions) and performance. Learning to convey emotion without eliciting an internal emotional response by the vocal athlete may take the skill of an experienced psychologist to help change ingrained neural pathways. Ultimately, control and understanding of MPA will enhance performance and prepare the vocal athlete for the most intense performance demands without vocal compromise.

VOCAL WELLNESS: INJURY PREVENTION

In order to prevent vocal injury and understand vocal wellness in the singer, general knowledge of common causes of voice disorders is imperative. One common cause of voice disorders is vocally abusive behaviors or misuse of the voice, including phonotraumatic behaviors such as yelling, screaming, loud talking, talking over noise, throat clearing, coughing, harsh sneezing, and boisterous laughing. Chronic or less than optimal vocal properties such as poor breathing techniques, inappropriate phonatory habits during conversational speech (glottal fry, hard glottal attacks), inapt pitch, loudness, rate of speech, and/or hyperfunctional laryngeal-area muscle tone may also negatively impact vocal function. Medically related etiologies, which also have the potential to impact vocal function, range from untreated chronic allergies and sinusitis to endocrine dysfunction and hormonal imbalance. Direct trauma, such as a blow to the neck or the risk of vocal fold damage during intubation, can impact optimal performance in vocal athletes depending on the nature and extent of the trauma. Finally, external irritants ranging from cigarette smoke to reflux directly impact the laryngeal mucosa and ultimately can lead to laryngeal pathology. Vocal hygiene education and compliance may be one of the primary essential components for maintaining the voice throughout a career. This section will provide the singer with information on the prevention of vocal injury. However, just like a professional sports athlete, it is unlikely that a professional vocal athlete will go through an entire career without some compromise in vocal function. This may be from a common upper respiratory infection that creates vocal fold swelling for a short time, or it may be from a "vocal accident" that is career threatening. Regardless, the knowledge of how to take care of your voice is essential for any vocal athlete.

Train Like an Athlete for Vocal Longevity

Performers seek instant gratification in performance, sometimes at the cost of gradual vocal building for a lifetime of healthy singing. Historically, voice pedagogues required their students to perform vocalises exclusively for up to two years before beginning any song literature. Singers gradually built their voice by ingraining appropriate muscle memory and neuromotor patterns through the development of aesthetically pleasing tones, onsets, breath management, and support. There was an intensive master-apprentice relationship and rigorous vocal guidelines to maintain a place within a given studio. Time off was taken if a vocal injury ensued, or careers potentially were ended and students were asked to leave a given singing studio if their voice was unable to withstand the rigors of training. Training vocal athletes today has evolved and appears driven to create a "product" quickly, perhaps at the expense of the longevity of the singer. Pop stars emerging well before puberty are doing international concert tours, yet many young artist programs in the classical arena do not consider singers for their programs until they are in their mid- to late twenties.

Each vocal genre presents with different standards and vocal demands. Therefore, the amount and degree of vocal training is varied. Some would argue that performing extensively without adequate vocal training and development is ill advised, yet singers today are thrust onto the stage at very young ages. Dancers, instrumentalists, and physical athletes all spend many hours per day developing muscle strength, memory, and proper technique for their craft. The more advanced the artist or athlete, generally, the more specific the training protocol becomes. Consideration of training vocal athletes in this same fashion is recommended. One would generally not begin a young, inexperienced singer without previous vocal training on a Wagner aria. Similarly, in nonclassical vocal music, there are easy, moderate, and difficult pieces to consider pending the level of vocal development and training.

Basic pedagogical training of alignment, breathing, voice production, and resonance are essential building blocks for the development of good voice production. Muscle memory and the development of appropriate muscle patterns happens slowly over time with appropriate repetitive practice. Doing too much, too soon for any athlete (physical or vocal) will result in an increased risk for injury. When the singer is being asked to do "vocal gymnastics," they must be sure to have a solid basis of strength and stamina in the appropriate muscle groups in order to perform consistently with minimal risk of injury.

Vocal Fitness Program

One generally does not get out of bed first thing in the morning and try to do a split. Yet many singers go directly into a practice session or audition without proper warm-up. Think of your larynx like your knee, made up of cartilages, ligaments, and muscles. Vocal health is dependent on appropriate warm-ups (to get things moving), drills for technique, and then cooldowns (at the end of your day). Consider vocal warm-ups a "gentle stretch." Depending on the needs of the singer, warm-ups should include physical stretching; postural alignment self-checks; breathing exercises to promote rib cage, abdominal, and back expansion; vocal stretches (glides up to stretch the vocal folds and glides down to contract the vocal folds); articulatory stretches (yawning, facial stretches); and mental warm-ups (to provide focus for the task at hand). Vocalises, in the opinion of this author, are designed as exercises to go beyond warm-ups and prepare the body and voice for the technical and vocal challenges of the music they sing. They are varied and address the technical level and genre of the singer in order to maximize performance and vocal growth. Cooldowns are a part of most athletes' workouts. However, singers often do not use cooldowns (physical, mental, and vocal) at the end of a performance. A recent study looked specifically at the benefits of vocal cooldowns in singers and found that singers who used a vocal cooldown had decreased effort to produce voice the next day.[7]

Systemic hydration as a means to keep the vocal folds adequately lubricated for the amount of impact and friction that they will undergo has been previously discussed in this chapter. Compliance with adequate oral hydration recommendations is important, as is subsequently the minimization of agents that could potentially dry the membranes (e.g., caffeine, medications, dry air). The body produces approximately two quarts of mucus per day. If not adequately hydrated, the mucus tends to be thick and sticky. Poor hydration is similar to not putting enough oil in a car engine. Frankly, if the gears do not work as well, there is increased friction and heat, and the engine is not efficient.

Speak Well, Sing Well

Optimize the speaking voice using ideal frequency range, breath, intensity, rate, and resonance. Singers generally are vocally enthusiastic individuals who talk a lot and often talk loudly. During typical conversation, the average fundamental speaking frequency (times per second the vocal folds are impacting) for men varies from 100 to 150 Hz and from 180 to 230 Hz for women. Because of the delicate structure of the vocal folds and the importance of the layered microstructure vibrating efficiently and effectively to produce voice, vocal behaviors or outside factors that compromise the integrity of the vibration patterns of the vocal folds may be considered phonotrauma.

Phonotraumatic behaviors can include yelling, screaming, loud talking, harsh sneezing, and harsh laughing. Elimination of phonotraumatic behaviors is essential for good vocal health. The louder one speaks, the further apart the vocal folds move from midline, the harder they impact, and the longer they stay closed. A tangible example would be to take your hands, move them only six inches apart, and clap as hard and as loudly as you can for ten seconds. Now, move your hands two feet apart and clap as hard, loudly, and quickly as possible for ten seconds. The further apart your hands are, the more air you move, the louder the clap. The skin on the hands becomes red and ultimately swollen (if you do it long enough and hard enough). This is what happens to the vocal folds with repeated impact at increased vocal intensities. The vocal folds are approximately 17 mm in length and vibrate at 220 times per second on A3, 440 on A4, 880 on A5, and over 1,000 times per second when singing a high C. That is a lot of impact for little muscles. Consider this fact when singing loudly or in a high tessitura for prolonged periods of time. It becomes easy to see why women are more prone to laryngeal impact injuries than men due to the frequency range of the voice alone.

In addition to the amount of cycles per second the vocal folds are impacting, singers need to be aware of their vocal intensity (volume). Check the volume of the speaking and singing voice and for conversational speech, and consider using a distance of three to five feet as a gage for how loud you need to be in general conversation (about an arm's-length distance). Cell phones and speaking on a Bluetooth device in a car generally result in louder than conversational vocal intensity, and singers are advised to minimize unnecessary use of these devices.

Singers should be encouraged to take "vocal naps" during their day. A vocal nap is a short period of time (five minutes to an hour) of complete silence. Although the vocal folds are rarely completely still (because they move when you swallow and breathe), a vocal nap minimizes impact and vibration for a short window of time. A physical nap can also be refreshing for the singer mentally and physically.

Avoid Environmental Irritants: Alcohol, Smoking, Drugs

Arming singers with information on the actual effects of environmental irritants so that they can make informed choices on engaging in exposure to these potential toxins is essential. The glamour that continues to be associated with smoking, drinking, and drugs can be tempered with the deaths of popular stars such as Amy Winehouse and Cory Monteith, both of whom engaged in life-ending choices. There is extensive documentation about the long-term effects of toxic and carcinogenic substances, but here are a few key facts to consider when choosing whether to partake.

Alcohol, although it does not go over the vocal folds directly, does have a systemic drying effect. Due to the acidity in alcohol, it may increase the likelihood of reflux, resulting in hoarseness and other laryngeal pathologies. Consuming alcohol generally decreases one's inhibitions, and therefore while under the influence of alcohol, you are more likely to sing and do things that you would not typically do.

Beyond the carcinogens in nicotine and tobacco, the heat at which a cigarette burns is well above the boiling temperature of water (water boils at 212° F; cigarettes burn at over 1400°F). No one would consider pouring a pot of boiling water on their hand, and yet the burning temperature for a cigarette results in significant heat over the oral mucosa and vocal folds. The heat alone can create a deterioration in the lining resulting in polypoid degeneration. Obviously, cigarette smoking has been well documented as a cause of laryngeal cancer.

Marijuana and other street drugs are not only addictive but can cause permanent mucosal lining changes depending on the drug used and the method of delivery. If you or one of your singer colleagues is experiencing a drug or alcohol problem, seek or provide your colleague with information and support on getting appropriate counseling and help.

SMART PRACTICE STRATEGIES FOR SKILL DEVELOPMENT AND VOICE CONSERVATION

Daily practice and drills for skill acquisition is an important part of any singer's training. However, overpracticing or inefficient practicing may be detrimental to the voice. Consider the practice sessions of athletes: they may practice four to eight hours per day broken into one- to two-hour training sessions with a period of rest and recovery in between sessions. Although we cannot parallel the sports model without adequate evidence in the vocal athlete, the premise of short, intense, focused practice sessions is logical for the singer. Similar to physical exercise, it is suggested that practice sessions do not have to be all "singing." Rather, structuring sessions so that one-third of the session is spent on warm-up; one-third on vocalise, text work, rhythms, character development, etc.; and one-third on repertoire will allow the singer to function in a more efficient vocal manner. Building the amount of time per practice session, increasing duration by five minutes per week up to sixty to ninety minutes may be effective (e.g., week 1—twenty minutes, three times per day; week 2—twenty-five minutes, three times per day, etc.).

Vary the "vocal workout" during your week. For example, if you do the same physical exercise in the same way day after day with the same intensity and pattern, you will likely experience repetitive strain–type injuries. However, cross-training or varying the type and level of exercise aids in injury prevention. So when planning your practice sessions for a given week (or rehearsal process for a given role), consider varying your vocal intensity, tessitura, and exercises in order to maximize your training sessions, building stamina, muscle memory, and skill acquisition. For example, one day you may spend more time on learning rhythms and translation, and the next day you may spend thirty minutes performing coloratura exercises to prepare for a specific role. Take one day a week off from vocal training and give your voice a break. This does not mean complete vocal rest (although some singers find this beneficial) but rather a day without singing and with limited talking.

Practice Your Mental Focus

Mental wellness and stress management are equally as important as vocal training for vocal athletes. Addressing any mental health issues is paramount to developing the vocal artist. This may include anything from daily mental exercises/meditation/focus to overcoming performance anxiety to more serious mental health issues/illness. Every person can benefit from improved focus and mental acuity.

SPECIFIC VOCAL WELLNESS CONCERNS FOR THE GOSPEL SINGER

General vocal wellness guidelines for all singers hold true for the gospel singer. However, due to the high vocal demands and lack of "formal voice training and pedagogy" for the gospel singer, much of the information on vocal wellness is implied from information on similar singing styles. An article written in 2001 titled "When Hoarseness Is the Goal" discusses the challenges with potential hoarseness in a high-demand Christian music setting. Specifically, the mind-set is that if one is not hoarse following a worship service, there is a question about whether they have adequately fulfilled worship. The opposite side of this argument may be, how can you adequately worship if your voice is hoarse? Below are several considerations for singers performing in a gospel style, both in and out of worship settings.

Vocal Wellness Tips for Gospel Worship (Choral)

For the worship vocalist (which may include choral music and solo singing), some of the most common vocal injuries tend to be related to inadequate stamina and/or training for a given piece of music. Specifically, many choristers go to rehearsal once a week for several hours and then sing for several hours for services. However, they do not exercise their voice the rest of the week. A physical analogy can be made to this type of singing. If you only go to the gym and exercise two hours two days a week, you are more likely to fatigue and get injured then if you spread out your training and condition for a "longer" (two-hour) workout. Therefore, if you are in a choir, try to sing for twenty to forty-five minutes daily (when you do not have choir practice) in order to keep your voice conditioned and "in shape" for those long rehearsals.

Another likely time when choral vocalists experience vocal injury is during the holiday seasons (e.g., Christmas, Kwanzaa, Easter) and during times of workshops or worship weekends because there is often a major uptick in the duration and intensity of voice use. Cantatas, musicals, and long-duration singing activities are typically a part of the holiday season, regardless of religious denomination. Outside of actual rehearsals and performances, there is generally increased family activity during these parts of the year, leading to lack of normal sleeping and eating habits. It is important for vocalists to take care of themselves physically and vocally as the intensity of the season increases. Vocal conservation during long rehearsals, taking "vocal naps" when possible, and avoiding overindulgence of food and beverages become imperative during heavy voice-use seasons in the church.

Solo Gospel Singers

Similar to contemporary pop singers, you are required to put on high physical-intensity shows. Therefore, both physical and vocal fitness should be foremost in the mind of anyone desiring to perform gospel music today. Gospel singers should be physically and vocally in shape in order to meet the necessary performance demands.

Performance of gospel music requires that the singer has a flexible, agile, dynamic instrument with appropriate stamina. The singer must have a good command of his or her instrument as well as exceptional underlying intention to what she or he is singing as it is about relaying a message and connecting with the audience. The voices that convey the gospel song must reflect the mood and intent of the composer, requiring dynamic control, vocal control/power, and an emotional connection to the text.

Similar to other commercial music vocalists, gospel singers use microphones and personal amplification. If used correctly, amplification can be used to maximize vocal health by allowing the singer to produce voice in an efficient manner, while the sound engineer is effectively able to mix, amplify, and add effects to the voice. Understanding both the utility and limits of a given microphone and sound system is essential for the singer both for live and studio performances. Using an appropriate microphone not only can enhance the singer's performance but can reduce vocal load. Emotional extremes (intimacy and exultation) can be enhanced by appropriate microphone choice, placement, and acoustical mixing, thus saving the singer's voice.

Not everything a singer does is "vocally healthy," sometimes because the emotional expression may be so intense it results in vocal collision forces that are extreme. Even if the singer does not have formal vocal training, the concept of "vocal cross-training" (which can mean singing in both high and low registers with varying intensities and resonance options) before and after practice sessions and services is likely a vital component to minimizing vocal injury.

Ultimately, the singer must learn to provide the most output with the least "cost" to the system. Taking care of the physical instrument through daily physical exercise, adequate nutrition and hydration, and maintaining focused attention on performance will provide a necessary basis for vocal health during performance. Small doses of high-intensity singing (or speaking) will limit impact stress on the vocal folds. Finally, attention to the mind, body, and voice will provide the singer with an awareness when something is wrong. This awareness and knowledge of when to rest or seek help will promote vocal well-being for the singer throughout his or her lifetime.

NOTES

1. W. LeBorgne, E. Donahue, S. Brehm, and B. Weinrich, "Prevalence of Vocal Pathology in Incoming Freshman Musical Theatre Majors: A 10-Year Retrospective Study," Fall Voice Conference, October 4–6, 2012, New York City, NY.

2. K. Tanner, N. Roy, R. Merrill, F. Muntz, D. Houtz, C. Sauder, M. Elstad, and J. Wright-Costa, "Nebulized Isotonic Saline versus Water Following a Laryngeal Desiccation Challenge in Classically Trained Sopranos," *Journal of Speech, Language, and Hearing Research* 53, no. 6 (2010): 1555–66.

3. C. Brown and S. Graham, "Nasal Irrigations: Good or Bad?" *Current Opinion in Otolaryngology, Head and Neck Surgery* 12, no. 1 (2004): 9–13.

4. T. Nsouli, "Long-Term Use of Nasal Saline Irrigation: Harmful or Helpful?" American College of Allergy, Asthma & Immunology (ACAAI) 2009 Annual Scientific Meeting, Abstract 32, presented November 8, 2009.

5. M. Shadkam, H. Mozaffari-Khosravi, and M. Mozayan, "A Comparison of the Effect of Honey, Dextromethorphan, and Diphenhydramine on Nightly

Cough and Sleep Quality in Children and Their Parents," *Journal of Alternative and Complementary Medicine* 16, no. 7 (2010):787–93.

6. L. Hill, L. Woodruff, J. Foote, and M. Barreto-Alcoba, "Esophageal Injury by Apple Cider Vinegar Tablets and Subsequent Evaluation of Products," *Journal of the American Dietetic Association* 105, no. 7 (2005): 1141–44.

7. R. O. Gottliebson, "The Efficacy of Cool-Down Exercises in the Practice Regimen of Elite Singers" (PhD diss., University of Cincinnati, 2011).

WORKS CITED

Brown, C., and S. Graham. "Nasal Irrigations: Good or Bad?" *Current Opinion in Otolaryngology, Head and Neck Surgery* 12, no. 1 (2004): 9–13.

Gottliebson, R. O. "The Efficacy of Cool-Down Exercises in the Practice Regimen of Elite Singers." PhD diss., University of Cincinnati, 2011.

Hill, L., L. Woodruff, J. Foote, and M. Barreto-Alcoba. "Esophageal Injury by Apple Cider Vinegar Tablets and Subsequent Evaluation of Products." *Journal of the American Dietetic Association* 105, no. 7 (2005): 1141–44.

LeBorgne, W., E. Donahue, S. Brehm, and B. Weinrich. "Prevalence of Vocal Pathology in Incoming Freshman Musical Theatre Majors: A 10-Year Retrospective Study." Fall Voice Conference, October 4–6, 2012, New York City, NY.

Nsouli, T. "Long-Term Use of Nasal Saline Irrigation: Harmful or Helpful?" American College of Allergy, Asthma & Immunology (ACAAI) 2009 Annual Scientific Meeting, Abstract 32, presented November 8, 2009.

Shadkam, M., H. Mozaffari-Khosravi, and M. Mozayan. "A Comparison of the Effect of Honey, Dextromethorphan, and Diphenhydramine on Nightly Cough and Sleep Quality in Children and Their Parents." *Journal of Alternative and Complementary Medicine* 16, no. 7 (2010):787–93.

Tanner, K., N. Roy, R. Merrill, F. Muntz, D. Houtz, C. Sauder, M. Elstad, and J. Wright-Costa. "Nebulized Isotonic Saline versus Water Following a Laryngeal Desiccation Challenge in Classically Trained Sopranos." *Journal of Speech, Language, and Hearing Research* 53, no. 6 (2010): 1555–66.

4

GOSPEL MUSIC VOICE PEDAGOGY

The primary and traditional way to learn gospel music is by singing in the church. Through imitation, participation, and constant exposure to gospel music and culture, singers learn the musical vocabulary, interpretation, and aesthetic execution associated with gospel music. The voice studio serves as a secondary yet necessary platform for musical and technical development. Gospel voice pedagogy consists of teaching strategies and ideologies derived from voice science, contemporary commercial music voice pedagogy, historical research, ethnomusicology topics related to the performance of gospel music, and professional experience that aims to address ways to sing gospel music styles in a culturally viable yet healthy and vocally efficient manner.

Gospel music voice pedagogy consists of four major components for musical development: anatomical awareness, vocal fitness training, style conditioning, and style coaching.[1] This structure can be applied to vocal training of any style of music.

Anatomical awareness entails learning about the anatomy of the body as it relates to the production of sound: becoming kinesthetically, visually, and aurally aware of what specific muscles feel like when contracted and relaxed. Dr. Scott McCoy addressed some of the primary physiological aspects of producing sound in chapter 2. Other aspects will be presented in this chapter.

Vocal fitness training consists of developmental exercises that are designed to specifically strengthen and condition the vocal instrument for singing and speaking. Without the consideration of specific style-based parameters, vocal fitness training addresses the various aspects of developing the voice for the sake of developing the instrument itself. This includes but is not limited to posture, breathing, balanced registration, and freeing the **articulators**. The importance of vocal fitness in the vocal studio is synonymous to the importance of a sports athlete going to the gym to maintain overall physical fitness. Any physical exercise, including singing, requires the body to be conditioned appropriately in order to function with the necessary strength, endurance, stamina, and flexibility. Through research, scientists and fitness experts recognize that certain exercises, when executed in a specific manner, effectively strengthen muscles. Voice scientists and pedagogues have determined the same and refer to such as functional voice training. The acclaimed voice pedagogue Jeannette LoVetri eloquently describes functional voice training as a methodology aiming to develop, condition, and strengthen the vocal instrument as an instrument within itself, separate from sound and stylistic effects specifically associated with a particular style of music.[2] Since this type of training is not specific to style of music, many of the exercises and pedagogic concepts are similar for all voice types and to voice training for other styles of music.

Style conditioning consists of exercises specifically designed to train the body, voice, and mind to execute the various components of style and performance practices represented in a given genre. Again, to use the sports analogy, style-conditioning exercises for singers are equivalent to dribbling and passing drills for basketball players. While these exercises in themselves do not constitute a basketball game or classify one as a professional basketball player, executed correctly, these exercises are recognized as necessary and fundamental skills for playing the game. In gospel singing, style conditioning includes but is not limited to the development of ear training, execution of vocal effects, **vocal agility**, specific development of registration, and development of improvisation tools. Examples of style-conditioning exercises will be provided later in this chapter.

Style coaching is the final component of vocal and musical development. This aspect of development focuses on performance, specifically assisting singers in the development of personalized strategies for executing the most vocally, spiritually, emotionally effective musical performance of a song. Through style coaching, voice teachers can help nurture singers' abilities to implement vocal strategies in the context of style and repertoire, channel emotional interpretation of the music and align its execution with corresponding musical articulation, and help manage the overall vocal production of performance and output. Though introduced in this chapter as part of a complete pedagogic system, aspects of style coaching will be discussed in detail in the next chapter.

COMPONENTS OF ANATOMICAL AWARENESS AND VOCAL FITNESS TRAINING

Before aspects of stylization can be implemented in a vocally efficient manner, the foundation for a strong, stable, and free voice must be acquired.

Posture

Proper alignment of the skeletal structure is the foundation of the body's ability to work in harmony. When the body is properly aligned, the muscles can operate in a balanced manner conducive to producing free vocal sounds. When the body is misaligned, the muscles have to work harder to compensate for the misalignment. When this happens, the body has the tendency to tense or stiffen, become tender or sore, and fatigue. Regardless of style, in order to sing efficiently singers cannot afford to become stiff in the neck or the torso.

The proper positioning of the skeletal structure in the torso greatly impacts the body's ability to take in air and support and stabilize the sound. If the torso is misaligned by slouching or by bending over at the level of the rib cage and/or caving the shoulders inward, it impacts how we breathe. With the spine comfortably and appropriately aligned, the rib cage is lifted to an appropriate position. With the rib cage lifted, the shoulders slightly pulled back as in figure 4.1, and the abdominal muscles relaxed, the expansion potential of the lungs is maximized. The more the rib cage can expand and the more room the diaphragm has to descend when it contracts, the more air the lungs can take in.

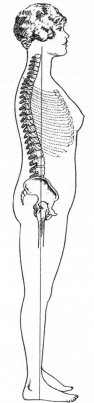

Figure 4.1.   Efficient Body Alignment.
By Unknown—a catalogue, page 18, copyrighted free use, https://commons.wikimedia
   .org/w/index.php?curid=2904917

   If the rib cage is collapsed or overly lifted, the shoulders are curved inward as in figure 4.2, and the stomach muscles are not relaxed. Consequently, the potential for expansion is greatly diminished. In this compromised position, the singer will have difficulty breathing deeply, as well as sustaining and controlling the rate of the airflow when singing.

   Efficient alignment of the head, neck, and shoulders allows for muscular freedom in the neck. Since the neck muscles suspend the larynx, maximizing freedom in this area will help maximize laryngeal function. This is particularly true in relationship to pitch and registration. The larynx, where the vocal folds are housed, is suspended between the head and clavicle, surrounded by neck muscles. In order for the larynx to adjust its position freely, the neck muscles need to be relaxed. If the neck muscles are overactive by trying to hold the weight of the head

Figure 4.2.   Inefficient Body Alignment.
*Public domain/[fatigue posture]. By Unknown—a catalogue, page 18, copyrighted free use.
Retrieved from https://commons.wikimedia.org/w/index.php?curid=2904987*

in an imbalanced manner, the muscles will be tense, and the laryngeal muscles will have to work harder to make necessary adjustments in order to achieve the desired pitches and tone color. Furthermore, if the head position is too far down or too far pushed back, a similar strain on the muscles of the neck and larynx will occur.

It is important to note that part of gospel music performance includes animated gestures or body positioning to aid the cultural aesthetic of expression. Some of these positions will throw the body out of alignment (i.e., leaning back, bending forward, and holding the head back). While these misaligned positions can affect the overall efficiency of the instrument at that moment, this genuine expressive behavior is perfectly viable and vocally acceptable as long as the position does not become the default alignment. Being aware of body posture when practicing and producing sound allows singers to occasionally sing outside of this realm while performing.

Developing the Power Source: Breathing

Breath is fuel and energy and provides the power necessary to produce sound. It helps determine the stability of the tone and how long we can hold that particular tone. Breath helps determine how loud or soft singers will be and helps determine the intensity of vocal output.

An ideal breathing strategy for singers is one that relaxes the vocal mechanism and rejuvenates the body during inhalation, allowing for the most efficient control over the rate and pressure of airflow during exhalation. There are a variety of breathing techniques and breath management theories to address this strategy. However, there is not a one-size-fits-all strategy that works for everyone, every time. By understanding the principles about breathing for singing, singers are more likely to find a breath management strategy that is most effective for their body type. This aspect of voice training, like posture, can be applied to any style of music.

A complete breath cycle can be broken into three phases.[3] Phase 1 is the inhalation/rejuvenation phase. Phase 2 is the transition phase and slightly overlaps phases 1 and 3. Phase 3 is the exhalation phase. When breathing for singing, each phase has a function and a goal that, when executed efficiently, can create the ideal breathing strategy.

Phase 1: Inhaling/Recovery   Whether it is the breath at the beginning of a musical phrase or quick breaths within a phrase, as previously explained, posture and tension in the body can greatly affect how much air is taken in during inhaling. The goal while inhaling is to replenish the body's air supply and to take in enough air to sing a musical phrase or passage. In order to accomplish this, the lungs must be able to expand in an efficient manner. In order for the lungs to have the space and freedom to expand to their fullest potential, certain structural and muscular components have to be in position and relaxed. This includes

- *Comfortably lifting the rib cage without overly arching the back and without lifting the shoulders.* Lifting the rib cage allows the necessary space for the lungs and bottom ribs to expand outward.

Over-raising the rib cage by excessively arching the back typically tightens the abdomen and limits the downward expansion of the lungs. Conversely, when the rib cage is collapsed and the body is hunched over, the bottom ribs are pressed into the abdomen and proper expansion is limited.

- *Completely relaxing the abdominal muscles during inhalation.* With the rib cage comfortably lifted, relaxing the abdominal muscles will allow full contraction of the diaphragm and full downward expansion of the lungs. If the abdominal muscles contract as the diaphragm tries to descend, then pressure and resistance will be created and expansion of the lungs will be greatly restricted to the upper portion of the rib cage.

- *Relaxing the muscles along the vocal tract (i.e., the tongue, jaw, and throat muscles) during inhalation.* Ideally, these muscles should be relaxed in the vowel position of the vowel sound used for the first word sung after the breath. When these muscles are not relaxed, the airflow is restricted and the sound will include unnecessary tension that will be more difficult to remove once the sound begins. Inhaling by using the anticipated vowel-sound position helps keep that vowel sound free once the tone is initiated.

- *Inhaling adequate air for the intended phrase length and volume.* Sometimes breathing in too much air can be as problematic as not breathing in enough air. If the intended phrase is short or soft in volume and the singer inhales too much air, there will be too much pressure in the lungs and the airflow will be difficult to control. If the intended phrase is long or loud in volume and the singer does not inhale enough air, the singer will not be able to maintain appropriate support to execute the phrase.

In singing, the purpose of focusing on efficient inhalation is not simply to maximize lung capacity with air. Often when maximizing lung capacity, it makes the airflow harder to control and causes unnecessary tension in the chest and throat. While the primary function of inhalation *is* to replenish the body's air supply, singers can make this process more efficient by allowing the body to reset and release any muscular tension that may have been introduced in the sound-making process. This makes the process of exhaling easier to control.

Phase 2: Transition Period—Preparing for Exhalation, Coordinating the Onset   There is a moment, or slight pause, in the breathing process that occurs at a point between the completion of inhalation and the beginning of exhalation. In the context of singing, this pause can be very quick or exaggerated depending on the timing or tempo (speed) of the song being performed. It is this moment that defines the transition period. During the transition period, the singer prepares the body for controlled exhalation. The manner in which the body prepares for exhalation not only affects how quickly the air will expel from the body, it is also directly connected to the characteristics of the start or onset of a sung tone. The most efficient manner to control exhalation starts with efficient preparation. As the torso expands during inhalation, the singer has to engage the necessary muscles in order to maintain the expanded position without adding unnecessary pressure or **constriction** in the body. This includes

- *Slightly contracting rib and abdominal muscles.* This keeps the torso in the expanded position that was created during the inhalation phase. This effort creates a resistance with the diaphragm's ability to easily return to its relaxed position, slowing down the exhalation rate.
- *Making sure the breath is not held in the body.* This can occur through the stiffening or contracting of muscles in the throat or clavicle area. Novice singers tend to hold their breath as they prepare for the entrance of a phrase or before making a sound. Maintaining freedom in the throat during this moment can be the difference between a relaxed tone and a restricted tone.
- *Freely positioning the articulators to produce the first consonant at the beginning of the phrase.* Depending on a singer's dialect, there is a tendency to overproduce certain vowels and consonant sounds. During the transition phase, the singer should focus on ensuring these first sounds are produced freely.

Phase 3: Controlling Exhalation/Breath Management   Singers control exhalation by managing the breath flow. Specifically, singers manage the rate in which air passes through the vocal folds (which affects how quickly they run out of air) and also the pressure of the air under the vocal folds (called *subglottic pressure*, which affects how loud singers sound). Efficient breath management allows singers to provide a stable supply of air from which the vocal cords will vibrate, supply an unwavering sound, and give relief from any obstructive tension in the throat. With proper posture and a relaxed inhalation in place, the intercostal and abdominal muscles will work together to manage how quickly breath leaves the body.

Efficient breath management includes

- *Using the support muscles.* (Rib and abdominal muscles shown in figure 4.3.) These muscles supply resistance against the return of the diaphragm to the resting position. The support muscles help control the rate of airflow and the pressure under the vocal folds. If these muscles are not working in this manner, air will quickly escape the body and the singer will run out of breath.
- *Maintaining the expansion in the ribs even as exhalation continues.* Keeping the rib cage expanded throughout the exhalation phase is a learned muscular behavior. Having a stable rib cage will help stabilize the sound and will help provide the much-needed support when belting and dancing.
- *Matching the contraction level with the intended volume.* Various volume levels require different amounts of muscular contraction. During this phase, singers need to match the muscular support with the intended sound; not starting with too much support for a soft sound, and not starting with sufficient support for a loud sound.
- *Gradually increasing the contraction level as the breath supply diminishes.* Singers have to use enough muscular resistance to keep the body expanded but also need to increase the muscular resistance as the breath supply decreases to counter their bodies' collapse.
- *Maintaining a consistent and stable flow of the breath energy throughout the sung phrase.* This allows the sound to remain steady, consistent, and unwavering.
- *Keeping excessive tension out of the throat, particularly as the breath supply diminishes.* With less tension in the throat, there is less constriction and the vowel sound and timbre will remain consistent throughout the sung phrase or note.

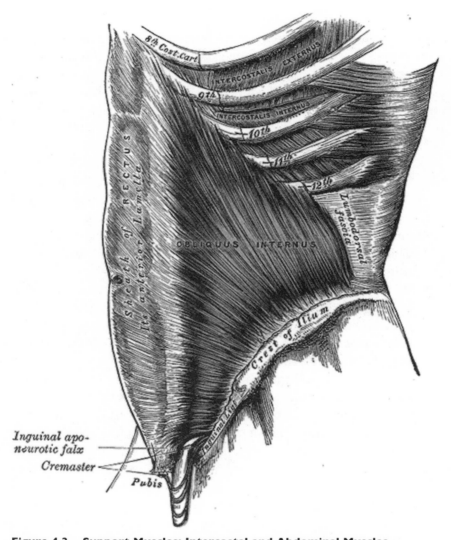

Figure 4.3. Support Muscles: Intercostal and Abdominal Muscles.
By Henry Vandyke Carter—Henry Gray, Anatomy of the Human Body *(1918), Bartleby.com: Gray's Anatomy, plate 395, public domain, https://commons.wikimedia.org/w/index.php?curid=531410*

When the functional purpose of each of these phases are met, efficient breath management results. Singers experience each of the phases differently, so they must pay special attention to how their bodies feel. For gospel singing specifically, the stamina needed to sustain energized worship (i.e., song, dance, lifting of hands, and clapping) requires the ability to stabilize the rib cage and isolate the rhythm of breath pattern from the rhythm of movement, particularly for up-tempo songs.

Onsets—Starting the Tone: Coordinating the Power Source and Vibrator

When developing the voice, it is necessary to understand the proper way to start the tone during training. The start of a tone is called the *onset* of the tone. There are three main types of onsets: **hard onset**, **breathy onset**, and **balanced onset**. In gospel music, there is an additional onset called a *"gravel" onset*.

A hard onset occurs when the vocal folds are firmly pressed together and air pressure builds up underneath the vocal folds, creating a harsh, pressurized sound when the tone starts. This produces a hard or popping, abrupt start to the tone but is commonly heard in spoken English when a vowel starts a word or phrase. For example, when speaking the phrase "I am, that I am" one can hear a pop or hard sound preceding the vowels *a* and *i*.

A breathy onset occurs when an audible breathy sound starts before the vocal folds close/vibrate to make the sound. The sound that results from a breathy onset is an /h/ sound just before the intended consonant or vowel sound.

A balanced onset occurs when the start of the breath and the start of the tone are coordinated. The tone starts smoothly, and there are no abrupt or breathy sounds added to the intended sound.

A gravel onset occurs when the tone starts as a vocal fry (i.e., a toneless popping sound) and then slides into a pitched tone. This type of onset is generally used when a singer is adding a squall or growl texture to the tone. (This type of vocal coloring will be discussed in chapter 5.)

While each of these onsets can be used as tools of expression in gospel singing, the balanced onset is the healthiest way to start a tone. The other three types of onsets—breathy, hard, and gravel—should only be used as a stylistic choice.

How the tone starts typically affects how a tone is sustained. If a tone starts breathy, there is a greater chance that the sustained tone that follows will be breathy and unsupported. Ultimately, this will create fatigue for the singer, particularly when trying to sustain long phrases or sing at loud volumes. If the tone starts with a hard sound, there is a greater chance of the sustained tone that follows being overpressurized. An overpressurized sound will not only be fatiguing for the singer but will also cause other vocal problems, including lack of flexibility and eventually intonation issues. If the tone starts with a gravel onset, there is a greater chance that the sustained tone that follows will be either unstable or overpressurized A balanced onset is the only onset of the four that encourages a stable and balanced tone to follow and should thus be the singer's default onset.

Take a moment to start a tone, and try all four types of onset.

- Hard onset—start a tone with a loud pressurized /ae/ vowel sound as in the word "a(t)."
- Breathy onset—start a tone with an /h/ sound preceding an unpressurized /ae/ vowel sound, as if saying the word "ha(t)" without pronouncing the "t."
- Balanced onset—start a tone on an /ae/ vowel as in "a(t)," smoothly, with no hard or breathy onset.
- Gravel onset—start a sound with a growling sound and slide into the vowel sound /ae/ as in "a(t)."

When training the voice, it is important to use a healthy default sound. When the tone is clear, it means the vocal folds are completely closed when vibrating. It is only when using a clear, balanced tone that the voice can truly be strengthened and developed.

Vocal Folds and Vocal Registration

All of the sounds and pitches created in the voice are a result of coordinated airflow through and vibration of the vocal folds. Pitch and sound quality are determined by the thickness and length of the vocal folds while vibrating. The two primary sets of muscles that control the thickness and length of the vocal folds are the thyroarytenoid (TA) muscle and the cricothyroid (CT) muscle. When the TA muscle is contracted, the vocal folds shorten and thicken. The sound that results is a heavy, weighted, edgy sound and is commonly referred to as *chest voice* or *modal voice* for simplicity. If you were to make the "woof" sound of a big dog barking or say "Ho, Ho, Ho" with your best Santa Claus impersonation, the sound you produce emanates from the chest/TA register function. When the CT muscle is contracted, the vocal folds are lengthened and thinned. The sound that results is a light, smooth sound and is commonly referred to as a *falsetto* when referring to the male voice or *head register* or *loft voice* when referencing the female voice. If you were to make a sound like a hooting owl or began howling like a ghost, you would more than likely be using this register function.

Each register quality, whether chest/TA dominant or head/CT dominant register function, has its own vocal quality and natural limits in pitch range. The term **vocal registration** or **vocal register** is what voice scientists call a particular series of tones (or ranges) that is produced in the same manner (or with the same muscular coordination) and has the same basic vocal quality. This is why for every vocal quality a singer makes, he or she will only be able to go so high or so low before reaching a noticeable limitation. When a singer tries to sing past these limitations, noticeable "breaks" or "cracks" will appear throughout a singer's range. This is particularly evident in what voice teachers and voices scientists refer to as the **passaggio**. The passaggio (passage areas) are specific transition areas of the voice (around E♭, E, F and B♭, B, and C above middle C) where "breaks" in the voice are most obvious for both men and women. One of the goals in vocal training is to teach singers how to navigate through, and transition from, one registration to the next so that the voice can seamlessly create one blended voice quality throughout the overall range of the singer.

Most beginning singers will have one vocal register that is more dominant than the other, simply because one register is used more than the other. Some singers have access to only heavy or loud sounds within their accessible pitch range, and some only have access to light or soft sounds, as both types of singers may consider the alternative sound "unnatural" or "fake" or even a "different personality."[4] These singers will have to be reintroduced to their voice as being one voice that can create different qualities that can and should be equally developed to maximize vocal efficiency.

Isolating and Strengthening Vocal Registers

The foundation of one's vocal range, dynamic range, and vocal stamina rests heavily in the development of vocal registration. It is important that both registers are fully developed to maintain a healthy voice and to maximize the capabilities of your instrument. Pitch ranges are considered developed in a particular registration when you can easily sing loud or soft and on any vowel sound without the throat squeezing or without the back of the tongue pulling or depressing down. When both register functions are developed in isolation and then blended, the results are

- an extended vocal range,
- better accuracy in hitting pitches/intonation,
- greater flexibility in the voice,
- a variety in tonal color and vocal quality from which to choose,
- a variety of dynamic levels from which to choose,
- less vocal fatigue,
- greater vocal stamina.

When developing the voice, there are four aspects of development to consider: (1) the identification of each individual register; (2) the strengthening of each register; (3) the extension of each register; and (4) the combining of vocal registers.[5] This can be acquired through a four-phase development strategy in which exercises are used to target specific objectives.

Phase 1: Identifying Registers   First you have to understand what both your chest register and your falsetto (head voice) sound like in your voice. For chest register, starting with a spoken quality on a relatively low pitch (men can start around C3 or D3 and women around G3 or A3) can help initiate this voice production. Falsetto/head imitations of a soft or light, comfortable high-pitched sound can help initiate this voice production. Below are a few examples of exercises that develop these concepts.

Phase 1, Exercise 1: Identifying Chest Register   Try simply speaking in a relatively loud, low-pitched voice, as if reprimanding someone in an assertive tone. Say "Hey! You!" then sustain with an exaggerated speaking voice.

Figure 4.4. Phase 1, Exercise 1: Identifying Chest Voice

Phase 1, Exercise 2: Identifying Falsetto/Head Voice For falsetto/head voice, start on a relatively high but easily obtainable pitch. Start with some simple owl sounds and then say "You too?" imitating a "damsel in distress" sound.

Figure 4.5. Phase 1, Exercise 2: Identifying Falsetto

Phase 2: Strengthening Registers The simplest yet most efficient way to strengthen vocal registers is to sustain pitches on a specific vowel at a consistent dynamic level. The goal when doing exercises in this stage is to focus on maintaining a clear and stable vocal sound. This maintains the initiated vocal sound throughout the exercise without changing the vowel sound or the vocal texture. Note: As previously noted, stable vocal sound is reflected through maintaining a consistent airflow. A clear and focused vocal tone is reflected in complete closure of the vocal folds and released tension in the throat when singing. Vocal exercises are less effective when one's tone is breathy and noisy. Below are a few examples of exercises that develop this concept.

Phase 2, Exercise 1, Part 1: Strengthening Chest Register For chest voice, sustain the vowel sound /ah/ as in "father," as the natural characteristic of the vowel sound employs more of a chest register function. Once the /ah/ vowel sound can be sustained with ease, change the

Figure 4.6. Phase 2, Exercise 1, Part 1: Strengthening Chest Register

vowel sound to /ee/ as in "be." The /ee/ vowel sound is a strengthening vowel sound in which its natural vocal tract positioning employs a firmer closure of the vocal folds.[6] Repeat the exercise, changing the note one semitone higher (i.e., change pitch up one half step).

Phase 2, Exercise 1, Part 2: Develop Control in Chest Register To develop control, start at a moderate volume and sustain the note used for part 1 of this exercise. This time, while sustaining the note for eight counts, gradually get louder by pushing on the belly muscles and not squeezing the throat, and then gradually get softer by partially releasing the contraction of the belly muscles. Note: There will be a subconscious urge to press the vocal folds together more firmly as the air pressure underneath the vocal folds increases. Therefore, as you push on the belly muscles to increase breath pressure, you have to simultaneously release the pressure that will build at the vocal fold level.

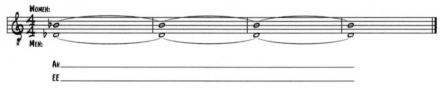

Figure 4.7.   Phase 2, Exercise I, Part 2: Developing Control in Chest Register

Phase 2, Exercise 2, Part 1: Strengthening Falsetto/Head Register For falsetto voice, sustain the vowel sound /oo/ as in "who," as the natural characteristic of the vowel sound employs more of a head register function. Once the /oo/ vowel sound can be sustained with ease, change the vowel sound to /ee/ as in "be," as done in exercise 1. Repeat the exercise, changing the note one semitone higher or lower (i.e., change pitch up or down one half step) depending on your goal.

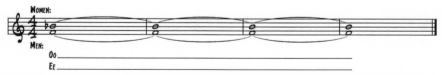

Figure 4.8.   Phase 2, Exercise 2, Part I: Strengthening Falsetto/ Head Register

Phase 2, Exercise 2, Part 2: Develop Control in Falsetto Register   To develop control, start at a moderate volume and sustain the note used for part 1. This time, while sustaining the note for eight counts, gradually get louder by pushing on the belly muscles and not squeezing the throat, and then gradually get softer by partially releasing the contraction of the belly muscles. Note: Again, there will be a subconscious urge to press the vocal folds together more firmly as the air pressure underneath the vocal folds increases. Therefore, as you push on the belly muscles to increase breath pressure, you have to simultaneously release the pressure that will build at the vocal fold level.

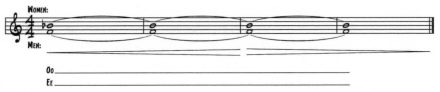

Figure 4.9.   Phase 2, Exercise 2, Part 2: Developing Control in Falsetto/ Head Register

Phase 3: Extending Range   In the extension phase, the goal is to be able to sing through intervals of an octave or more, comfortably and in each register, at moderate to low volumes for chest voice and moderate volumes for falsetto/head voice, using a variety of vowel sounds. Start by singing exercise patterns that remain within a small vocal range of an interval of a sixth. Gradually increase the vocal range by a semitone (or half step) only when the established range can be successfully executed without tension in the throat, without changing the vowel sound from note to note, and without a change in the dynamic level from note to note. Continue this pattern of increasing the range and strengthening the range until a minimum of one octave can be comfortably executed in each registration. Below are a few examples of exercises that develop this concept.

Phase 3, Exercise 1: Vocal Exercise with Range of a Major Third   Use exercises with intervals of a major third to vocalize within a vocal range of a perfect fifth. Transpose up one semitone with each repetition until the highest note reaches a fifth above the original starting pitch. For example, the exercise below starts on C4 and the highest note is E4. Transpose this exercise up by one semitone for each repetition for three repetitions (i.e., to C♯4, then D4, then D♯4) and then back down for three repetitions (i.e., to D4, then C♯4, back to the original C4).

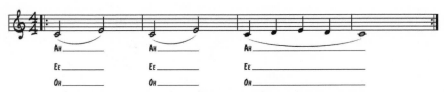

Figure 4.10. Phase 3, Exercise 1: Vocal Exercise with Range of a Major Third

Phase 3, Exercise 2: Vocal Exercise with Range of a Major Sixth   Use exercises with intervals of a perfect fifth to vocalize within vocal range of a perfect fifth or higher to vocalize in within a pitch range of a major sixth or higher. The exercise below combines both stepwise motions and leaps with large intervals for variation.

Figure 4.11. Phase 3, Exercise 2: Vocal Exercise with Range of a Major Sixth

Phase 4: Combining Registers   Combining registers together and being able to switch back and forth between registers in a distinct manner. The goal of this phase is to encourage flexibility when switching between vocal registrations so that the voice doesn't get "stuck" in one register as the pitch ascends or descends and also to maintain the same vowel sound while doing so. Below are a few examples of exercises that develop this concept.

Phase 4, Exercise 1: Blending Registers while Maintaining a Chest-Dominant Sound   Consistency in vowel sound, texture, and volume are the keys to executing this exercise in an efficient manner.

Starting at a moderately loud level in your chest, gradually decrease in volume as the pitch ascends an octave, remaining in chest as long as possible before flipping into a soft falsetto tone. On the descending portion of the exercise, gradually blend back into chest and increase the volume.

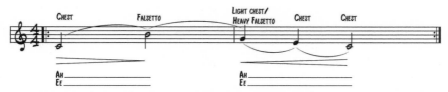

Figure 4.12.   Phase 4, Exercise 1: Blending Register with a Chest-Dominant Sound

Phase 4, Exercise 2: Flexibility between Registers   The following exercise is geared toward flipping between large leaps and flipping quickly within a melodic phrase.

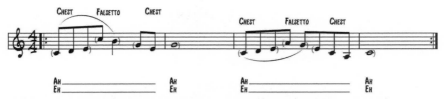

Figure 4.13.   Phase 4, Exercise 2: Flexibility in Switching Registers

Maximizing the Resonator: Effects of the Vocal Tract

The **resonating chamber** is the area of the instrument that allows its sound to carry or project. The shape and the texture of the resonating chamber greatly determine the characteristics of the sound created. In the voice, the chamber from which vocal sounds resonate is called the *pharynx or vocal tract*. The vocal tract consists of all the open space in the head and neck above the vocal folds, including the oral cavity (mouth), nasal cavity (nose), and pharynx (throat). (See figure 4.14.)

We can change the shape of our vocal tract to create different resonance patterns or textures in the voice with even the subtlest movement. Some of the ways we can change the shape of our pharynx are by changing the position of the pharyngeal wall (the walls of the throat), the position of the tongue, the position of the soft palate, the position of the jaw, and the height position of the larynx. Every combination of positioning creates what is commonly referred to as a ***pharyngeal shape***. Each shape has specific acoustic properties and characteristics that result in a distinct sound. The primary component for shaping the sound is the creation of vowel shapes with the positioning of the tongue and jaw. Secondary components of the vocal tract shape include the position of the soft palate, the position of the larynx, and whether or not the con-

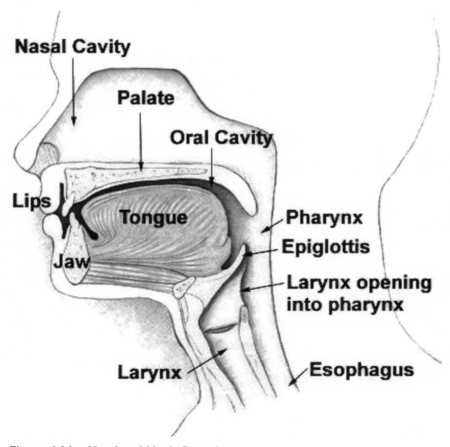

Figure 4.14.   Head and Neck Overview.
*U.S. Cancer Institute/[Head and Neck Overview from U.S. National Cancer Institute website SEER training module.]
     Retrieved from https://commons.wikimedia.org/wiki/File:Illu01_head_neck.jpg*

strictor muscles are engaged or relaxed. These secondary components add specific textures to the sound quality.

In gospel singing, the vocal texture or sound quality created is often used as one of the tools for interpretation in the expression of emotion. Learning to control these components of resonance allows singers to control their sounds at will. In order to do so, we must first learn to identify them, understand their natural function and tendencies, and recognize how their adjustments contribute to the quality of the sound produced.

Vowels: Tongue and Jaw Positions There are specific pharyngeal shapes that are naturally created with the production of a vowel sound. Vowel sounds can be categorized as those sounds produced with specific adjustments to the tongue (e.g., [ɑ] for "father," [æ] for "at," [ɛ] for "bet," etc.), adjustments to the lips (i.e., [oʊ], [u]), or adjustments to both the lips and jaw (i.e., [ɔɪ] for "joy" or [aʊ] for "out"). (See figure 4.15.) Because the production of vowels is a direct result of the position of the tongue, jaw, and lips, the International Phonetic Alphabet (IPA) chart of vowel sounds is categorized by how open or closed the mouth is (i.e., open, mid, close), where the sound is produced in the mouth (i.e., front, central, or back), and if the lips are rounded or not. There is also an exact science behind which pitch ranges are most resonant for each vowel sound, but acoustic measures of these vowel shapes will not be detailed in this book. What is important to know is that vocal textures used in gospel singing are typically described as having bright, robust, speech-like qualities that are sometimes brassy, edgy, or twangy in texture. Voice scientists[7] have determined that front vowel sounds help create and accentuate the "bright" characteristics of the belt voice qualities, like those found in musical genres such as gospel music. This is opposed to back vowels, which result in a "dark" sound, more commonly used in classical or jazz music. As a result, the vocal tract shape most predominantly used by gospel singers tends to be modifications toward front and central vowel shapes.

The Soft Palate The soft part of the top, back of the mouth from which the uvula hangs is called the ***soft palate***. The soft palate can be a tricky part of the mouth to manipulate for some people, but even its most subtle movements can create a noticeable difference in the texture and/or quality of sound. In a relaxed position, one can see the uvula

VOWELS

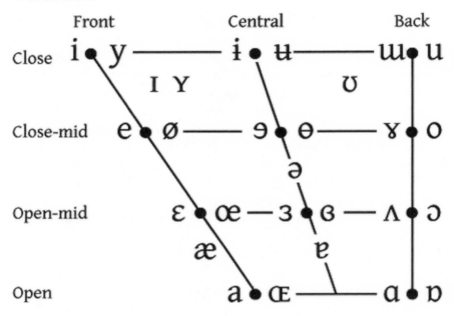

Figure 4.15. International Phonetic Alphabet Vowel Chart.
*Public domain/N. Grendelkhan (redrawn IPA vowel chart; 2004). Retrieved from https://commons.wikimedia.org/
wiki/File:Ipa-chart-vowels.png*

hanging down like normal (see figure 4.16). If you sing or make sound
with the uvula in this neutral position, the resulting sound will be nasal,
as air and sound enter the nasal passage.

The soft palate can be contracted and the uvula can be lifted up to
close off the nasal cavity and eliminate the nasal sound. This sometimes
happens naturally while yawning. However, if you have large or over-
sized tonsils, there is a greater chance of maintaining a bright or even
nasally sound even when attempting to lift the soft palate, as sometimes
the tonsils are inhibiting the soft palate from lifting, or they are simply
blocking the resonating space that would otherwise be available.

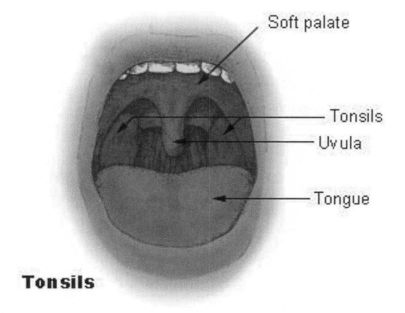

Figure 4.16. Tonsils and Uvula.
US Cancer Institute/[Diagram of the palatine tonsils from U.S. National Cancer Institute website. SEET training module] Retrieved from https://en.wikipedia.org/wiki/File:Tonsils_diagram.jpg

Whether or not a singer should be able to control nasality by way of lifting the soft palate is a subjective matter. Unlike in classical music, a nasal sound is an accepted sound in gospel singing. It is not necessarily a required gospel sound; however, many singers, particularly those with high voices, commonly employ nasal sounds.

The soft palate can even slightly widen using the top-back jaw muscles (the muscles above the back teeth and gums and back cheek muscles). This contraction can be felt by opening your mouth wide, tilting your head all the way back, and smiling with the sensation of spreading your top molars apart. It feels more like a "smirk" with the mouth open or smiling with your mouth open while keeping the bottom jaw and bottom lip relaxed. The trick, however, is to be able to contract the top jaw without overly tensing the bottom jaw (as if sarcastically saying, "Ha, ha, ha, very funny"). Isolating the contraction of the top and bottom jaw and being able to focus on only the top jaw allows the singer to maintain brightness in his or her sound without the usually added pressure in the bottom jaw. This adjustment can add a brighter, edgier texture to a fuller, robust sound.

The Throat   The final part of the vocal tract to be addressed is the throat or **pharyngeal wall**. The muscles in the throat can contract and close tightly (like when we swallow or gargle) by engaging a group of muscles called *constrictor muscles*. The primary function of the constrictor muscles is to swallow. There are three sets of constrictor muscles along the vocal tract.

The upper set of constrictor muscles are called *superior muscles*, and are located at the top of the vocal tract, behind the nose and throat. Under the superior muscles are the *middle constrictor muscles*. This set of muscles is connected to the hyoid bone (Note: The base of the tongue connects to the front of the hyoid bone.) and connects around the vocal tract about the level of the bottom jaw. The function of these upper two sets of constrictors is to narrow the back of the throat and assist in pushing food to the esophagus. The lowest set of constrictor muscles, the *inferior constrictors*, constricts the pharynx and lifts the larynx. The inferior constrictors are attached to both sides of the thyroid cartilage (the cartilage that primarily houses the vocal folds), wraps around the base of the vocal tract, which includes connection to the cricoid cartilage (a cartilage to which a portion of the vocal folds are also attached), and attaches at the top of the esophagus.

The Sound of the Constrictors and Relation to Voice Production

In terms of sound production, these muscles can be engaged consciously or subconsciously when speaking or singing. For example, constrictor muscles are almost always contracted when yelling or screaming. Untrained singers readily engage the constrictor muscles when singing to create a bright, edgy, high-pressured, and/or growl sound in the voice because contracting the constrictor muscles is an easy way to press the vocal folds together and close the back of the throat. The contraction of the constrictor muscle is also partially to blame when a singer's sound is perceived as having a "squeezed" sound or when they sound like they are "singing from their throat." It is possible that their sound is being produced and stabilized primarily by engaging the constrictor muscles,

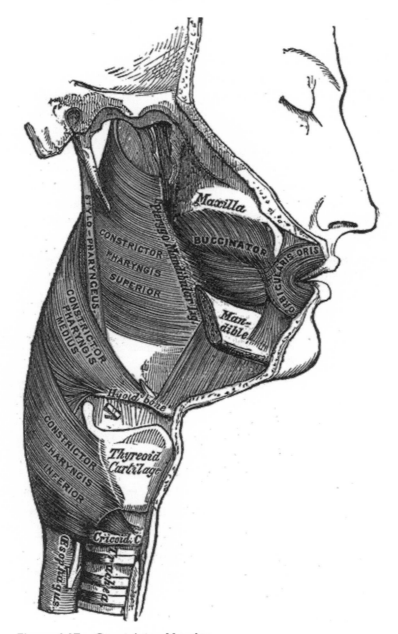

Figure 4.17. Constrictor Muscles.
Public domain/H. V. Carter (Illustrator). Muscles in the pharynx and cheeks. In H. Gray, Anatomy of the Human Body (1918). Retrieved from https://commons.wikimedia.org/wiki/ File:Gray1030.png#/media/File:Gray1030.png

and this is typically the default for singers with underdeveloped vocal registers and/or those who do not know how to support their tone with breath. While this may be the easiest way to create a loud, edgy sound, it is also the quickest way to encounter vocal trouble. With prolonged use, contracting the constrictor muscles will make the voice tired/fatigued, the throat sore, and for some, result in hoarseness and/or temporary to permanent loss of high notes.

The constrictor muscles are often subconsciously or consciously engaged when the body is under emotional and physical stress (good or bad), and the muscles around the larynx contract as a natural response to the protective fight or flight process.[8] In addition to being extremely happy, sad, or mad, vocally tired and/or damaged, when singing high notes in one's chest voice, the body actually responds to this type of vocal production as stress. Therefore, to properly train in a chest-dominant sound means to learn techniques to override this natural response.

Signs of singing or speaking with prolonged use of the constrictors include

- you are vocally tired or hoarse after only a couple hours of singing or speaking,
- your speaking or singing voice consistently sounds edgy or growly,
- your throat hurts after singing or speaking at a social event or religious gathering,
- you feel like you're choking when singing or speaking,
- you feel like there is a tickle in your throat when singing (making you want to clear it),
- you are stuck in one vocal registration (as if there were a ceiling you cannot get through) and cannot flip to a higher registration/sound.

How to Maximize the Vocal Quality Advantages of Singing with Your Constrictors while Minimizing the Vocal Fatigue Disadvantages

While there are many reasons why singers should keep their constrictors relaxed when singing, there are times when a singer will desire the vocal effects that result from using constrictor muscles. The brassy, edgy, growly sounds found in the gospel sound are, from a cultural perspective, an endeared and expected acoustical aspect of musical expression in gospel singing. This is also true for many other African American music styles. It is impossible to produce these sounds without any involvement with the constrictors. Thus it would be highly unrealistic to state one can achieve all stylistically appropriate vocal qualities found in gospel singing without the use of constrictor muscles. However, the key to longevity and stamina in the voice is not only to understand and identify which muscles to contract and which to release but also to understand the difference between **contraction** versus **constriction**, and vocal effect versus vocal sound.

Contraction refers to the tightening and shortening of a muscle. It is necessary for muscles to contract in order to produce and/or sustain vocal sounds. However, constriction occurs when the muscle is stuck in the contracted position and is not easily pliable. When singing, singers want certain areas of the vocal mechanism to contract yet still remain flexible enough to easily adjust to the next vocal function/objective. When constriction occurs, limitation in stamina also occurs, which eventually results in fatigue and sometimes ultimately in damage.

The first objective when purposely adding an increased amount of contraction to any muscle along the vocal tract is learning how to contract the target muscle while keeping the surrounding muscles relaxed. In terms of the constrictor muscles, if you want to use the constrictor muscles but you do not want to allow those muscles to become constricted, you must first learn to isolate[9]/identify each area in the throat that houses the three sets of constrictor muscles: upper, middle, and lower. Please note this requires an advance level of awareness on the part of the singer; however, it is ultimately necessary for vocal health and maintenance.

Working with the Articulators: Awareness of the Articulators

We established that vocal qualities are directly related to the singer's vocal tract shape, vocal registration, and breath pressure. As we continue to further explore the vocal tract, now we will focus on the aspect of vocal tract shaping that can subconsciously cause the most problems: the articulators.

The **articulators** are the parts of the mouth used to create vowel and consonant sounds during speech. The articulators consist of the lips, tongue, teeth, and the soft palate. Most singers, regardless of the style of music they sing, have some difficulty with their articulators. This is generally due to the difficult task of trying to maintain a certain vocal quality and vocal tract position while singing words and using a variety of different mouth positions all at the same time. Since the goal is to maintain a specific vocal quality or vowel shape throughout our singing, singers have to consistently adjust their vocal tracts to ensure the words are both easily executed and understood by listeners. Knowing which articulator to adjust and how to adjust it is a learned behavior combining kinesthetic awareness with aural perception. In other words, the singer must define for him- or herself how to sing words that are intelligible while maintaining a sound that is appropriate for the style of music he or she is singing, all while keeping the whole "voice machine" flexible and free of tension and strain.

The following sections describe each of the articulators and will discuss some physical, aural, and visual cues that allow singers to gain more awareness of their articulators and their roles in the production of singing.

The Tongue   The tongue changes shape and position regularly as we speak and eat. The tongue moves in, out, up, down, and all around our mouth as it performs its various functions. As mentioned earlier in the chapter, every vowel produced is a direct result of the change in the shape of our tongue and with every movement thereafter, will follow with a variation of that vowel sound. For example, if you simply sustain an "ahh" sound and then start moving your tongue around your mouth while sustaining the "ahh," you will notice that different sounds are created. If you listen carefully, you may notice that once you start moving your tongue, the vowel may sound more muffled than when your tongue was in its starting position, particularly as you pull your tongue to the back of your mouth. You may also notice that the vowel sound can sound more "brassy" than it sounded when you made the initial sound, particularly when you stick your tongue out and down. Depending on the shape of your tongue, the vowel can sound more nasally, particularly if you raise the back of the tongue, or the vowel sounds can be a combination of all the sounds described. Take a second to try this for yourself.

The Importance of Taming the Tongue   "Taming the tongue" is
a biblical principle found throughout scripture (Prov. 10:19, 12:18, 15:1,
18:21, 21:23; Eph. 4:29; James 1:26, 3:2–10; Ps. 34:13; 1 Pet. 34:13;
etc.). These Bible verses teach Christians about the power of their
words, stating that we need to control the words that come out of our
mouth as they can bring life or death to any situation. The Bible also says
it is not enough to simply decide not to say bad things, for the result is
only surface. To tame the tongue, Christians must go to the source from
which the language was derived, and that source is the heart (James
3:13–18; Luke 6:45).

Just as with the spiritual taming of the tongue, so it goes for physically
taming the tongue; one has to go to the source of its problem to seek
the solution. Regardless of what style of music a person sings, tongue
tension has a major influence on the accuracy and effectiveness of vocal production. There are many root sources that can cause a singer's
tongue to be tense. For example, some singers tense the tongue to stabilize a sound as a physical response to a lack of proper support. Some
singers squeeze the base of the tongue to make a louder sound or to
sing a higher pitch/note as a physical response to an undeveloped chest
or head register. Some singers may also tense their tongue as a result
of imitating or even approximating an intended vowel sound or vocal
quality. Regardless of the root source, I believe the primary reason for
the continuation of this tension is the singer's inability to kinesthetically
feel/track the specific behaviors of the tongue. In other words, if the
singer cannot internally track and control the physical sensations of the
tongue, then the singer will not be able to self-monitor and ultimately
self-correct the counterproductive behaviors that result.

This concept is particularly true for gospel singing and other genres
whose vowel sounds are a reflection of vernacular speech and specific
dialects. Unlike the classical singing style in which the vocal sound
is based on the production and approximation of pure, scientifically
proven, and measured vowel sounds that established specific measures
of what constitutes *a* correct sound, gospel music has many acceptable
vowel sounds. While yes, there are some unspoken acoustic parameters
that constitute specific characteristics of a "correct" gospel vocal sound,
it would be culturally irresponsible to infer which specific vowel sounds
are correct and not correct. Instead, voice teachers and scientists may

talk in terms of "common sounds or pronunciations." Since gospel music is based on individuality, it still allows for the variation of such sounds. What is acceptable in terms of sound is defined by the culture of the music and its community. Therefore, singers need to understand the physical correlation between the production of their own sound and their pronunciation tendencies.

Learning to Control the Tongue and Limit UTT (Unnecessary Tongue Tension) Allow me to introduce the acronym **UTT**, unnecessary tongue tension.[10] As previously mentioned, tongue tension is probably the archenemy of all singers regardless of the style of music. Tongue tension can cause a singer to be off pitch, have an unstable vibrator, poor articulation, can cause fatigue, and the list goes on. However, the only way to be in a position to fix tongue issues by yourself is to understand and be able to recognize how the different areas of the tongue feel when they are contracted versus when they are relaxed. In other words, you can't fix something you can't feel or recognize exists. And how do you feel or recognize something that is not normal when the sensations are normal to you?

I want you to try something. This tongue tension/involvement test is one of the first things I do with my students. The purpose of this test is to see if you can (1) keep your tongue relaxed while your mouth is open and then (2) isolate the production of sound from engaging the tongue.

1. Sit in front of a mirror.
2. Open your mouth as if opening it for a doctor to check your tongue.
3. Rest your tongue on your bottom teeth.
4. Allow the tongue to rest in this position.
5. The tongue should look soft, with rounded edges, squishy like a pillow, and not moving.
6. In this exercise, the tongue should be so relaxed you should feel like you are about to start drooling.
7. If your tongue is moving, looks tight, flat, curled, or looks like the sides are contracted, it means your tongue is not relaxed and you have UTT. There is nothing about this position that warrants movement or contraction of the tongue, for the jaw muscles should be the only thing holding the mouth open.

8. If you open the mouth and your tongue is soft, squishy, and not moving, move on to the next step.

9. Now, keeping your mouth and tongue in this position, sustain the sound /ha/ at your speaking-pitch range and volume.

10. If your mouth remains in this position without moving and the tongue is completely relaxed, then the sound should sound like somewhat of a dormant/dead/unenergized tone and should represent what your individual sound sounds like if you didn't "do something" to make it sound like "this or that."

11. If your tongue moves once the sound starts or when sustained, you have UTT, and it is something you need to address. The tongue and the throat do not need to move nor engage to create sound.

12. Remember, the purpose of this exercise is not to create a nice sound, but to see if you can create the /a/ sound without engaging the tongue. If you have to "do something" to make the /a/ sound, you are already doing too much.

Why is this important? Once you understand what it feels like in your body when your tongue is completely relaxed, you can learn to feel and control the contraction of the tongue and actually distinguish when it's relaxed. As we start to contract and move the tongue in the pronunciation of words, and even when learning ways to use the tongue to create different vocal colors and resonances, we have to know what home base feels like in order to truly be able to track the amount of tension we are imposing during the creation of certain sounds.

COMPONENTS OF STYLE CONDITIONING

Voice production in gospel singing, like many other folk-based music styles, is closely aligned with the execution of primal sounds and vernacular speech tones. As such, style conditioning for gospel music is centered around conditioning the voice to freely execute these sounds on a variety of pitches and dynamic levels. The voice-training parameters to which style-conditioning goals and exercises should focus include vocal quality/registration, extended vocal range, **vocal timbre**, vocal agility, efficient breath management, use of vibrato, use of dynamics and emotional intensity, and ear training.[11]

Vocal Quality/Registration Style Conditioning

The most prominent vocal quality found in gospel singing is a heavy chest voice or chest-dominant, speech-like quality. This is a direct correlation to the black theological preaching styles in which the preacher would sing-speak their sermon, particularly during the climactic portion. Therefore, in gospel singing having a developed and strengthened chest register is imperative for efficient singing. If the chest register is not developed, singers default to creating a heavily pressurized sound through the use of the constrictor muscles (i.e., squeezing the throat). Upon developing the chest register as an isolated register within a small pitch range, the next level of development is to slowly coax the register in order to comfortably achieve higher pitches. An example of how this can be achieved is illustrated in the exercise below.

Style-Conditioning Exercise: Expanding Chest-Register Vocal Quality

Exercise 1: "Ah" Glides   Execute the following exercise starting within a comfortable range. Modulate up by half steps until the pitch range becomes slightly uncomfortable, then modulate back down in pitch. Only increase the pitch range of the highest note by one half step at a time and only after the highest note is performed comfortably and with ease. Never continue an exercise if it causes you pain or immense discomfort.

Exercise 2: Tell Me What You Want   Execute this exercise while maintaining a medium-loud, unpressured, chest-register speaking quality.

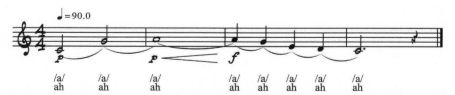

Figure 4.18.   Style-Conditioning Exercise 1: Extending Chest Register Vocal Quality

Figure 4.19. Style-Conditioning Exercise 2: Extending Chest Register Quality

Changes in vocal quality and registration are also tools or interpretation as it relates to the gospel sound; purposeful changes are often used as interpretive choice by the singer.[12] Gospel singers will sometimes employ the use of other vocal registrations. These include but are not limited to light chest mix (i.e., an unpressured, light spoken quality), pure head/falsetto voice (i.e., the sound of an owl), and brassy head/falsetto mix. The vocal quality used is often directly related to the emotional perspective of the song. Its variation closely aligns with the same variations that occur in the natural expression of animated speech. People whose voices naturally get higher in pitch when emoting with excitement will typically mirror those same sounds when expressing a song.

Below is an example of a style-conditioning exercise that focuses on change in register.

Style-Conditioning Exercise: Flipping Registration

Exercise 1: Flipping Registration Sing the following exercise starting in chest register, flip to falsetto, and then flip back into chest. This exercise can be performed at any tempo (or speed) but should be sung out of time, as interpreted by the singer.

Figure 4.20. Style-Conditioning Exercise 3: Flipping Registration

Extended Vocal Range

Having an extended vocal range that maintains this chest-dominant sound throughout the range is actually perceived by the gospel music culture as a virtuosic characteristic. In order to acquire this extended vocal range while maintaining a chest-dominant vocal quality, *both* the chest/TA register and the head/CT vocal register must first be developed in isolation and then strategically blended together in a manner that maximizes an edgier or brassier quality in a comfortable manner.

Gospel soloists are not normally categorized by voice type. Voice types only occur in the choir setting. However, the easiest way to categorize vocal ranges is to use the choral model for voice parts, although from the contemporary gospel choir perspective. The vocal range notated below for each voice part is divided into three sections. Each section represents three vocal-range goals for training the gospel soloist: **choir range**, **sustainable range**, and **solo range**. The choir range represents the vocal range consistently required of each specific voice part when singing in a gospel choir. The sustainable range represents the part of the vocal range that needs to be the most developed, as it is the pitch range used the most. Finally, the solo range represents the range of usable pitch tones that can audibly be incorporated into the interpretation of a song range. It is not uncommon for a singer to have his or her choir range fit in one voice part and his or her solo range into another. Unlike in classical or musical theater genres, soloists are not categorized by, defined by, or locked into a specific voice part or range. Gospel music is much more personal and adaptable to whatever range the soloist possesses.

The vocal texture used most consistently and objectively in a gospel choir setting is a chest-dominant, speech-quality sound. Therefore, the vocal ranges listed below are written with the understanding that the expected vocal quality used to sing the notated pitch range is a chest-dominant, belt, belt mix, or brassy head mix. The pitches notated below are not only the notes most commonly required of the different voice parts in a gospel choir, they also represent the average pitch range found in the interpretation of most gospel song melodies. Vocal models are listed for each solo voice category as voice type examples; however, many of the artists listed have vocal ranges that transcend the categories under which they are listed. This list is not exhaustive and is not intended to categorize these singers for any purpose other than to provide a listening model for students of singing.

Soprano I Voice Range (Also Called "High Soprano")

Figure 4.21. Vocal Range: Soprano I Voice Part

Gospel High Soprano Vocal Model ♪

1. Karen Clark Sheard
2. Lecresia Campbell
3. Tramaine Hawkins
4. Vanessa Bell Armstrong
5. Marion Williams
6. Tonex (Male)

Soprano II Voice Range (Also Called "Low Soprano/High Alto")

Figure 4.22.   Vocal Range: Soprano II

Gospel Low Soprano/ High Alto Vocal Models ♪

1. Yolanda Adams
2. LaShun Pace
3. Tasha Cobbs
4. Dorinda Clark Cole

Alto Voice Range

Figure 4.23.   Vocal Range: Alto

Gospel Alto Vocal Models ♪

1. Dorothy Love Coates
2. Mahalia Jackson
3. CeCe Winans

4. Juanita Bynum
5. Helen Baylor

Tenor/Tenorette Voice Range

Figure 4.24.   Vocal Range: Tenor/Tenorette

Gospel Tenor Vocal Models ♪

1. Rance Allen
2. Fred Hammond
3. Byron Cage
4. Donnie McClurkin
5. Darryl Coley

Baritone Voice Range (Also Called "Low Male Voice")

Figure 4.25.   Vocal Range: Baritone

Gospel Baritone Vocal Models ♪

1. R. H. Harris (Soul Stirrers)
2. Phil Tarver
3. Jason Nelson
4. Walter Hawkins

Bass Voice Range

Figure 4.26.   Vocal Range: Bass

Gospel Bass Vocal Mode ♪

1. Isaac "Dickie" Freedman

The bass voice part is the lowest male voice part and is not commonly represented in gospel singing, except in the gospel quartet tradition. Choir parts are generally reduced to three-part soprano-alto-tenor; however, when basses are in a choir setting, the director usually has them double the soprano or alto part an octave below or creates a bass part for them. It is also less common to find basses operating in the function of a lead soloist at a commercial level; however, having a bass voice type does not prevent one from becoming a soloist. As a soloist, your personal expression is your unique interpretation, and the anointing and Word of God does not limit itself to voice types or pitch ranges.

Vocal Texture

Vocal textures found in gospel music can range from a breathy vocal texture to a rough, gravel-sounding vocal texture. The vocal textures chosen by singers often directly correspond to the vocal textures used in normal speech during an emotional state. For example, breathy vocal textures are generally used during very intimate and/or nurturing moments during the interpretation of a song. In contrast, singers tend to use rougher or more aggressive-sounding vocal textures during an emotional climax or a portrayal of great despair or passion during interpretation. I call them *gravel* *sounds*. There are four basic types of gravel sounds: squalls, whoops, growls, and midvoice. Each type of gravel sound can be used at different points during interpretation and are often used for different reasons.

Gravel Sounds: Squall, Whoop, Growls, and Midvoice Gravel sounds are typically used in preaching and gospel singing when communicating in a heightened emotional state. Gravel vocal sounds are generally perceived as being loud and intense, but they can be produced in an unpressured manner as well. They can include the following four expressive vocal sounds: squall, whooping, growls, and midvoice.

A **squall** is a vocal texture that sounds like a quick or short yell or shout with a rough vocal quality. A squall is used as a sudden burst of excitement or energy. For example, rhythm and blues soul artist James Brown uses a squall at the beginning of his song "I Feel Good!" ♪

A **whoop**, as it is generally referred to in the context of black preaching, is an elongated squall sustained either on one pitch, a few pitches, or on a short melodic sequence. This type of gravel sound is used in climactic and/or heightened emotional states and is often known to stir up or rally the emotions of all who listen. ♪

A **growl** is a rough vocal quality that starts a word or phrase but is immediately followed by a clearer vocal quality. This gravel sound is used to bring emotional intensity or a feeling of immense conviction to a sung phrase. ♪

Midvoice is a vocal quality that sustains the gravel sound through several sung phrases. This gravel sound is also used during heightened emotional states that represent the climax and is an extended or sustained version of the whoop over several phrases. Midvoice is often considered the most passionate, convicted, and embodied state of communication in charismatic religious settings. As a result, it is also the most imitated vocal sound, as it tends to be the sound singers *try* to use to convince the listeners of their conviction to the ministry. ♪

While gravel sounds are not necessary for effective, honest worship in ministry, they are still valid and well-respected vocal sounds that are deeply ingrained within the religious experience of the black church. Thus, gravel sounds should be formally addressed in terms of production.

All four sounds are produced by slightly squeezing or contracting the back of the mouth and/or throat using the constrictor muscles. However, the specific strategies for producing this sound can be quite personal and unique (depending on the individual). Overall, the trick to producing this sound in a vocally efficient manner is to make all the contractions in the throat occur above the level of the vocal folds.[13] When creating this sound, the throat should not feel in pain or vocally strained.

As with all vocal qualities and singing styles, singers must understand the difference between true vocal production (i.e., the combination of pitch and vocal registration) and vocal effects (i.e., added manipulations to the vocal tract in order to manipulate the sound). The root of being able to create and maintain all vocal effects is to make sure the foundation of one's voice is strong and developed. For the gravel vocal effect, the necessary foundation includes a developed chest register and a chest-mix register quality. Its effective production requires the singer to have a command of his or her instrument and a keen awareness of the levels of contraction that occur in the throat.

Style-conditioning exercises for gravel sound focus more on strengthening the vocal registers and purposeful execution of the sound using a light coordination with a personalized approach.

Vocal Timbre

Vocal timbre relates to the "color" of the tone created and the many variations possible within the interpretation of music. The sung tone can have a bright, brassy timbre; it can have a nasal timbre, a warm timbre, or a dark timbre. The sound can be clear and open to create one vocal color or closed and tight to create another color. During the interpretation of a single phrase or song, a singer can choose to instantaneously change the color of a sung tone for expressive purposes, much in the manner of animated speech. Overall, a bright, full vocal texture is most common.

Style-conditioning exercises for vocal timbre include singing short musical phrases with various vocal colors.

Vowel distortion is another type of change in vocal timbre that occurs in gospel singing for stylistic purposes. Vowel distortion occurs when a singer sings a word and purposefully modifies the vowel to the point that it almost becomes unrecognizable. This is also a direct influence of the black preaching styles and animated speech.

Vocal Agility

Vocal agility is defined as the ability to change pitches and vocal qualities quickly while maintaining accuracy and clarity in the sung pitches. Many of the stylist tools used in gospel singing are largely dependent on singers having a great degree of vocal agility. This is particularly true in the execution of melodic improvisation. (Melodic improvisation will be further explained in the next chapter.)

Style-Conditioning Exercises: Vocal Agility

Figure 4.27.   Style-Conditioning Exercise 4: Vocal Agility

Efficient Breath Management

As with other styles of music that involve simultaneously singing and dancing, efficient breath management exercises for gospel singing could range anywhere from singing a series of melodic phrases while jogging on a treadmill to sustaining four- to eight-bar phrases on a set rhythmic and/or harmonic progression. The key is to learn efficient breath management by conditioning the body to stabilize the rib cage and disassociate one's breathing pattern from the tempo of the song being performed. In other words, when singing a fast song, the breath pattern of the singer should not simulate that of a person hyperventilating. It is important to understand that this type of conditioning intentionally overrides natural breathing tendencies, but it is necessary to maintain control of the breath and stabilize the sound.

Use of Vibrato

In gospel music, vibrato can be used as part of the gospel sound or used as a stylistic tool. Gospel singing is generally characteristic of heavy vibrato use through songs for both soloist and choirs, particularly on sustained tones and slow songs. However, when vibrato is not used within a phrase, it is typically omitted for stylistic purposes and added at the end of the phrase. This is referred to as ***terminal vibrato***. Terminal vibrato is a prominent stylistic device used in all styles of gospel singing. Even high-powered, belted phrases that may start with no vibrato will always add vibrato once the final tone is sustained for a number of beats.

Style-conditioning exercises for conditioning the use of vibrato focus on adding, omitting, and using terminal vibrato when singing vocal exercises.

Use of Dynamic and Emotional Intensity

Emotional intensity and dynamics are often intertwined in the execution of gospel music interpretation. Gospel music is an exciting style of music with an exciting message. It is "the good news" and the energy that stems from that belief, which directly impacts the dynamic level. Just as one wouldn't go to an exciting sporting event expecting peace and quiet, one does not go to a black church or gospel concert without expecting a celebration. As a result, the dynamic level is one that exemplifies celebration; it is often loud yet dispersed with dynamic variations as deemed appropriate by the music and the context of the song. When a singer is expressing contentment and excitement, the dynamic level tends to increase in volume the more excited the singer becomes. Even when a singer is conveying a message of sorrow, concern, or contemplation, there always remains a sense of hope and glory because the singer understands the contribution Jesus has or will make to his or her testimony or story. Thus, regardless of the subject matter, there is always a dynamic shift that occurs in the interpretation of a gospel song.

While an increase in volume is the most anticipated response to high emotional energy, singers must understand that there is more to varying dynamic levels than simply to get loud. One doesn't have to be loud to be perceived as emotionally convicted. For example, the stern yet soft voice of a parent reprimanding a child for being loud in a quiet place illustrates exactly how one can be passionate, convicted, and effective without raising his or her voice. In singing, just as when speaking, the emotional intensity and dynamic level of communication should solely depend on, and reflect, the *context* of the conversation. This includes the subject matter, to whom the conversation is directed, the inspiration that led to the conversation, and the emotional exchange that occurs during the conversation. Generally speaking, one doesn't begin a prayer shouting or crying out unless the person is already upset or in a state of unrest. These are the considerations that should be made in the interpretation of song.

Ear Training

Ear training is imperative for gospel singers, both as soloists and choir members. Modulation as a compositional device and the use of melodic improvisation are prominent expressive tools in gospel music. Both require singers to be able to hear the chord changes and chord tones in order to be executed efficiently and effectively. Also, for melodic improvisation, the most basic scales from which melodic choices are derived include a major scale, minor scale, and pentatonic scale.

Figure 4.28.   C-major Diatonic Scale

Figure 4.29.   C-major Pentatonic Scale

Figure 4.30.   C-minor Diatonic Scale

Figure 4.31.   C-minor Pentatonic Scale

Style Conditioning: Modulation and Inversions   This exercise can be executed as a choir exercise and as a soloist. The inversions outline a pentatonic scale and represent the types of inversions used in the choir arrangement during the vamp section of song. Modulate up one half step after each repetition.

Figure 4.32.   Style-Conditioning Exercise 5: Modulation and Inversions

Style Conditioning: Pentatonic Scales Exercise This exercise outlines the pentatonic scale for each chord played. Sing this exercise at a very slow tempo (around forty beats per minute) until all notes are sung clearly and comfortably. Speed this exercise up for agility training.

Figure 4.33. Style-Conditioning Exercise 6: Pentatonic Scales

NOTES

1. Trineice Robinson-Martin, "Voice Training for the Gospel Soloist" (unpublished manuscript, May 9, 2016).

2. Jeannette LoVetri, "The Necessity of Using Functional Training in the Independent Studio," *Journal of Singing* 70, no. 1 (2013): 79–86.

3. James C. McKinney, *The Diagnosis and Correction of Vocal Faults, a Manual for Teachers of Singing and for Choir Directors* (Nashville, TN: Genevox Music Group, 1994); Robinson-Martin, "Voice Training for the Gospel Soloist."

4. William Vennard, *Singing: The Mechanism and the Technic* (New York: Carl Fischer, 1967).

5. Robinson-Martin, "Voice Training for the Gospel Soloist."

6. LoVetri, "Necessity of Using Functional Training."

7. Martine E. Bestebreurtje and Harm K. Schutte, "Resonance Strategies for the Belting Style: Results of a Single Female Subject Study," *Journal of Voice* 14, no. 2 (2000): 194–204; Ronald Verle Bevan, "Belting and Chest Voice: Perceptual Differences and Spectral Correlates" (PhD diss., Teachers College Columbia University, 1989); Steven T. Kmucha, Eiji Yanagisawa, and Jo Estill, "Endolaryngeal Changes during High-Intensity Phonation Videolaryngoscopic Observations," *Journal of Voice* 4, no. 4 (1990): 346–54; Scott McCoy, "A Classical Pedagogue Explores Belting," *Journal of Singing* 63, no. 5 (2007): 545–49.

8. Jeannette LoVetri, "Somatic Voicework(™): Teacher Support Group," October 6, 2015.

9. No muscle connected to another muscle can completely be contracted in isolation. However, when I speak in terms of isolation, I refer to the use of

the specific muscle as the primary source of contraction and the contraction of the surrounding muscles being merely a byproduct of the contraction of the targeted muscle.

10. Robinson-Martin, "Voice Training for the Gospel Soloist."

11. Ibid.; Trineice Murlene Robinson-Martin, "Developing a Pedagogy for Gospel Singing: Understanding the Cultural Aesthetics and Performance Components of a Vocal Performance in Gospel Music" (PhD diss., Teachers College, Columbia University, 2010); Trineice M. Robinson-Martin, "Take My Hand: Teaching the Gospel Singer in the Applied Voice Studio," in *Teaching Singing in the 21st Century*, ed. Scott David Harrison and Jessica O'Bryan (New York: Springer, 2014), 14:335–50.

12. This is in contrast to vocal qualities chosen for functional reasons, i.e., having only one choice on a given pitch.

13. The level of the vocal folds can be experienced when clearing the throat. It should also not feel like one is consecutively clearing his or her throat.

WORKS CITED

Bestebreurtje, Martine E., and Harm K. Schutte. "Resonance Strategies for the Belting Style: Results of a Single Female Subject Study." *Journal of Voice* 14, no. 2 (2000): 194–204.

Bevan, Ronald Verle. "Belting and Chest Voice: Perceptual Differences and Spectral Correlates." PhD diss., Teachers College Columbia University, 1989.

Kmucha, Steven T., Eiji Yanagisawa, and Jo Estill. "Endolaryngeal Changes during High-Intensity Phonation Videolaryngoscopic Observations." *Journal of Voice* 4, no. 4 (1990): 346–54.

LoVetri, Jeannette. "The Necessity of Using Functional Training in the Independent Studio." *Journal of Singing* 70, no. 1 (2013): 79–86.

———. "Somatic Voicework(TM): Teacher Support Group." October 6, 2015. New York, NY.

McCoy, Scott. "A Classical Pedagogue Explores Belting." *Journal of Singing* 63, no. 5 (2007): 545–49.

McKinney, James C. *The Diagnosis and Correction of Vocal Faults, a Manual for Teachers of Singing and for Choir Directors*. Nashville, TN: Genevox Music Group, 1994.

Robinson-Martin, Trineice Murlene. "Developing a Pedagogy for Gospel Singing: Understanding the Cultural Aesthetics and Performance Components of a Vocal Performance in Gospel Music." PhD diss., Teachers College, Columbia University, 2010.

———. "Take My Hand: Teaching the Gospel Singer in the Applied Voice Studio." In *Teaching Singing in the 21st Century*, edited by Scott David Harrison and Jessica O'Bryan, 14:335–50. New York: Springer, 2014.

———. "Voice Training for the Gospel Soloist." Unpublished manuscript, May 9, 2016. Microsoft Word.

Vennard, William. *Singing: The Mechanism and the Technic*. New York: Carl Fischer, 1967.

GOSPEL STYLES, PERFORMANCE PRACTICES, AND IMPROVISATIONAL TOOLS

In chapter 4, the four components of training the gospel singer were introduced. These components include anatomical awareness, vocal fitness training, style conditioning, and style interpretation. The first three components focus on learning about and conditioning the voice to sing gospel music and were further discussed in that chapter. This chapter focuses on the fourth component: style interpretation.

Gospel singing styles are highly prized for the individuality the gospel singer can bring to the music.[1] Gospel music is not like classical art music, musical theater, or other genres in which the singer must learn to interpret his or her own emotions through the emotional intent of a given composer or character. Gospel music is a medium for the personal expression of one's own emotions, experiences, and convictions. It is a religious expression deeply rooted in the African American cultural experience. The musical and stylistic choices a singer makes when interpreting a song should thus directly reflect the emotional response to the spiritual impact that God has made in his or her own unique story.

When it comes to folk-based musical styles, there are many singers who are not necessarily great singers by the tones they produce but are considered great for their soulful and passionate expression of the text. This is especially true for gospel music. Dr. Gayle Wald describes a virtuous singer, according to African American Pentecostal audiences, as a performer who has the ability to "tap into, and give meaning to, collective emotion through the performance of a personal relation to the music."[2] Wald further explains, in describing the virtuosic style of the famous gospel and blues singer Sister Rosetta Tharpe, "the measure of a performer's value lay less in the mastery of skills associated with European art music, and more in whether the particular musical choices can induce an audience to collective joy or sorrow, awe or celebration."[3] Dr. Horace Boyer also talks of gospel singers as aiming to evoke the most emotional response from an audience.[4] As this concept of stimulating and/or capturing the emotions of the audience has the potential for misinterpretation, it should be understood that the intent to arouse emotion is not done so for entertainment purposes, as it is in secular music genres. As Dr. Glenn Hinson writes, "Any gifted singer can evoke an emotional response in a song, however it is considered the charge of the gospel singer to use the empowerment and endowment accessed in the gift of song for ministry, guiding the emotions of the listeners—by provoking thought, evoking reflection in gospel music, and eliciting praise."[5]

In order for one to execute a style of music authentically and effectively, he or she must be immersed in the culture of the music and be able to recognize and execute some of the basic style characteristics in the appropriate context. To sing gospel music, in addition to acknowledging and musically articulating the spiritual component, one must familiarize him- or herself with the various styles of African American religious music, including gospel music and its subgenres; familiarize him- or herself with the various performance mediums existing within gospel music; and ultimately recognize, analyze, internalize, and then reinterpret the improvisational tools used to musically articulate and spread the Gospel message.

TOOLS FOR INTERPRETATION: ASPECTS OF IMPROVISATION IN GOSPEL

Skilled craftsmen have tools to help them create their masterpieces. While not every tool is used on every project, each tool has a specific function and purpose. This is also true for the musical masterpieces created by the skillful performer who carefully chooses improvisation tools in order to interpret music. In gospel music, there are both sound-related and style-related improvisatory tools that can be used to effectively articulate and communicate one's emotional and spiritual conviction.

Sound-related improvisatory tools are those directly affecting the treatment of the vocal sound produced. These tools include sudden or purposeful changes in vocal quality and registration, added vocal textures, changes in vocal timbre and use of vowel distortions, use of vibrato, and use of dynamics and emotional intensity. Style-related improvisatory tools include but are not limited to melodic improvisation, textual improvisation, rhythmic improvisation, use of rhythmic "feel" and tempo, and flexibility of harmonic structure or form.[6] Sound-related improvisatory tools were introduced in the style-conditioning section. Style-related improvisatory tools will now be briefly described below as a way of introduction and preview to the types of improvisatory options possible in the interpretation of song. It is through consistent exposure to, and interactions with, the musical and social culture that represents the black church that singers can acquire a natural and genuine execution of improvisatory tools.

Melodic Improvisation

Melodic improvisation is probably the most prominent form of improvisation in gospel music. It is the generic "go to" improvisational tool for most singers who are innately musical, as it can be easier to think melody than to think intent. There are three basic types of melodic improvisation: (1) **melodic interpolations** and ornamentations (i.e., vocal runs, tails, etc.), (2) alterations to the melody, and (3) scat singing. Each type of melodic improvisation has its function and place within the song, depending on the singer's intent. This section discusses the variations that exist within each type of melodic improvisation.

Melodic Interpolations   Melodic interpolations are short, melodic insertions added to a given melody for the purpose of creating variation in the musical articulation of one's emotional expression. Melodic interpolations range from simple melodic insertions to complex melodic insertions. Simple melodic interpolations consist of simple variations to a given melody. These variations focus on the short improvisatory addition and/or special musical treatment of one or two notes in the melodic phrase. It is the simple improvisatory additions that can often have a major impact on the overall effectiveness of a song's ability to communicate the emotional intent of the singer. These improvisational tools closely align themselves with melodic tendencies often heard in animated speech; as such, their efficacy is dependent upon the skill level of the singer and knowing when and how these interpretational tools are executed.

The most common simple melodic insertions include the following:

Slides/portamentos are executed by connecting one note to the next in a continuous motion.

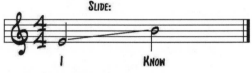

Figure 5.1.   Slides

Dramatic slides/glissandos are a slow slide from one note to the next in which all the notes in between are also emphasized as the pitch ascends.

Figure 5.2.   Glissando

Lean/appoggiatura is when a singer approaches a note by quickly sliding from the neighboring note above the intended one.

Figure 5.3.   Lean

Bends/blue note is a note sung slightly under or over pitch for expressive purposes, usually by a semitone (a half note) or less. It's usually sounded slightly above the intended pitch.

Figure 5.4.   Bends

Fall occurs when a pitch is sounded and then descends in pitch and intensity.

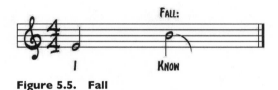

Figure 5.5.   Fall

Scoop is when the semitones are sounded as the singer slides up to the intended pitch.

Figure 5.6.   Scoop

Neighbor tone is when a note is inserted directly above or below the intended note.

Figure 5.7.   Neighbor Tone

Passing tones are when one or two notes are inserted stepwise in the same direction between two written notes.

Figure 5.8.   Passing Tone

Escape tones are when the first added note moves stepwise in one direction then skips to another note in a different direction.

Figure 5.9.   Escape Tone

Complex melodic interpolations and ornamentations are defined by the complexity of the inserted melodic motif or short phrase. These complex phrases usually consist of three or more notes inserted in between or to the end of a written or established melody. The scales from which these inserted notes stem can vary from simple scales like major, minor, or pentatonic or can stem from more complex scales like blues, chromatic, mixolydian, and half-diminished scales. Of all the various types of complex melodic interpolations and ornamentations, some have names and some do not. Complex ornamentations with names include turns or *gruppetto*, tails, runs or melismas, and fills.

Complex melodic interpolations and ornamentations are the hardest type of melodic improvisation to teach because not only do they require vocal manipulation in terms of breath pressure and vocal fold flexibility, they are melodic and rhythmic manipulations based on a feel that must be acquired through cultural exposure. Attempts to transcribe or notate a run or turn authentically using Western music notation usually results in an inaccurate or watered-down interpretation. Therefore, when learning to execute these types of ornamentations, I recommend identifying as many notes as possible in the motif, paying special attention to pivot points.

Turns are short melodic motifs that consist of five or more notes and are executed within two-beat counts in which the starting and ending note are the same. Note: Generally, turns use stepwise motions; however, more complex or exaggerated turns that integrate the use of more notes may include leaps within the melodic line. From an emotional perspective, a turn can be used as a brief emphasis of a word or note or a purposeful stutter within the flow of a musical idea.

Figure 5.10. Turns

A **tail** is approximately two to four notes added at the end of a phrase or just before a pause in the melody and descends or ascends in stepwise motion in one direction. From an emotional perspective, a tail is suggestive of the sigh or slight linger that occurs at the end of a spoken phrase.

Figure 5.11. Tails

Runs or melismas consist of the insertion of five or more notes that consist of a diatonic or pentatonic scale, chord outline, or a series of melodic sequences or turns executed in a continuous manner and are usually performed in places within the music in which a single note is sustained.

Figure 5.12. Runs

Alterations to the Melody Making alterations to the melody is a major aspect of musical interpretation. It is what one singer does to a composed melody in order to make it sound unique and distinguishable from another singer's interpretation. There are two types of melodic alterations: simple alterations to the melody and complex alterations.

Simple alterations are considered a minor change to the melody. In a simple alteration, the composed melody largely remains as written or rather close to the standard or established version of the song. The singer may make a few changes, but overall the melody remains easily recognizable and somewhat predictable in terms of its execution. It is generally advised that singers start with only simple alterations when presenting a song the first time through or through the first half of the song (depending on the length of the performance), particularly if the singer isn't experienced in the tradition of melodic improvisation. It is a way to honor the tradition from which the song stems and also allows listeners the opportunity to align themselves with the message of the song and the singer's intent without getting distracted by vocal acrobats.

To demonstrate a simple alteration, let's use the hymn "'Tis So Sweet to Trust in Jesus," written by Louisa Stead and William Kilpatrick (1882).

Figure 5.13. "'Tis So Sweet," Music by William J. Kirkpatrick (1838–1921); Lyrics by Louisa M. R. Stead (1850–1917). Original Melody

Note: The notation given above is generally performed in the gospel tradition in 12/8 or rubato (i.e., out of time). However, I have retained the use of the originally composed 4/4 time signature for simplicity.

A simple alteration of this excerpt would generally include the use of one or two simple melodic interpolations. An example of this might be something like the following:

Figure 5.14. "'Tis So Sweet" Simple Alterations

The singer may choose to use simple alterations along with rhythmic phrasing to bring a slight emphasis to certain words within the phrase. In the above example, I chose to place emphasis on the word *so* with the insertion of a neighbor tone, as if to say "'Tis soooo sweet . . ." Rhythmically, I also shortened the length of the first full phrase, "'Tis so sweet to trust in Jesus," by shortening the word *Jesus* and adding a rest or pause. Adding a rest or pause into the music allows the listener and singer time to reflect and meditate on the words previously sung.

The more skilled a singer becomes in interpretation of song, the greater his or her knack for effectively choosing the appropriate melodic interpolation to insert at any given moment. An experienced singer understands one does not have to do a lot in terms of vocal acrobatics in order to be effective.

Complex alterations are major changes integrated into an existing melody. Major changes can include the addition of complex melodic interpolations and ornaments in addition to changes in the notes of a given melody to create variation in interpretation. Complex alterations to a melody are generally executed after the first time through the song, with each repetition becoming more and more complex. Singers use complex alterations as a way to elicit excitement and to create different variations of a story that has been told repeatedly through many generations, as is the case with traditional hymns and gospel songs. Complex alterations are also a tool that allows singers to show off their vocal capabilities in terms of range, flexibility, and overall musicality. This is the number-one aspect of improvising that is consistently "overdone" by amateur singers. Amateur singers have a tendency to be more interested in executing the vocal acrobatics and eliciting the "wow factor" than in strategically and emotionally making changes to the melody that are appropriate for the emotional context of the song.

Scat Singing   When we think of scat singing, we usually think jazz, "Oop-Pop-A-Da," or merely singing an improvised melody using a collection of nonsense syllables over an established set of chord changes. Depending on the artist, his or her influence, and the context of his or her performance, a gospel singer can sound much like a jazz singer in the use of scat. Traditionally, however, it is more common to find that the scat singing in gospel music generally creates improvised melodies only using one vowel sound like /oh/ or only one or two syllables, the repetition of one or two short words, or an extension of a word. It sometimes sounds more like a slowed version of a melisma or a run than what one would consider a traditional scat due to the nature of its implementation (i.e., being executed in a fill, over a vamp, in between phrases). However, the difference between a "scat" and a "run" is found in the speed of the execution or subdivision of the notes inserted per beat, the intelligibility and importance of each note sung within the overall musical phrase, the consistency of the direction of the line being sung or lack thereof, and the use of chord tones. This is further described in table 5.1.

Textual Improvisation

> Through the text of a gospel song, a performer communicates his understanding of black survival in America and his awareness of the contribution religion has made to that survival.[7]

Another important aspect of improvisation within gospel music focuses on the text of the song. Textual improvisation can be executed in the form of textual interpolations, textual phrasing, testimony, and ad-libbing.

Table 5.1. Scat Singing versus Vocal Runs

	Scat Singing	Vocal Runs
Vowels vs. Consonants	Uses vowels and consonants	Uses only vowels
Speed of notes	Few notes per beat—usually not more than four notes per beat (a sixteenth note)	Many notes per beat—usually employs the use of four or more notes per beat
Length of phrase	Long melodic phrases lasting two or more measures in length	Short melodic phrases usually sung within one measure or at a pause in the music
Note intelligibility	Majority of the notes sung have equal importance in the overall music phrase	The first and last few notes are pivot notes and are the most important notes; others are just passing tones
Direction of line	Multi-direction, in stepwise and/or leaps	Generally stepwise or sequence
Note choices	Often emphasizes chord tones and scales	Often emphasizes chord tones and scales
Function	Self-contained melodic expression	Used as a transition tool

Textual interpolations, as described by Boyer, are the adding of extra words to the original text. For example, the phrase "Lord, I'm tired" can be executed as "Lord (*you know*) I'm (*so*) tired" when textual interpolation is used.[8] As the singer becomes comfortable with the execution of the story, inserting extra words into the lyrics should become natural.

Textual phrasing is a technique used by storytellers in which specific words are grouped together within a phrase or specific words are emphasized within a phrase in order to portray an emotion or a perspective. For example, the phrase "God has been good to me" can be sung/read as "*God* (pause) has been *good* to me" or "God has been (pause) *so good* to me." The manner in which the words are grouped, emphasized, and executed depends on the emotional perspective of the storyteller. In addition to these types of textual phrasing, lyrical and rhythmic repetition is also used. For example, "Lord, you've been good to me" could be performed "Looooord . . . Lord, Lord, Lord, you've been good to me." Textual phrasing is used in all styles of gospel singing. However, the extent of the use of repetition as a stylistic tool varies between performers and substyles within the gospel music genre.

Textual phrasing in Gospel music is very similar to the textual phrasing techniques used in African American blues and jazz and other folk-based music styles in which the grouping and execution of the lyrics are closely related to the grouping and execution of passionate, vernacular speech. The manner in which singers group text together is ultimately determined by their personal connection to the music and the established perspective from which they will tell their story. When the singer has a clear perspective from which the song stems, developing ways in which the lyrics can be grouped together becomes easier and the execution becomes more natural.

A **testimony** is a short, personal story, spoken or sung, one shares with the congregation to provide an example of how he or she believes God has worked in his or her life. Spoken testimony can be executed in the beginning of a song as a way of introducing or transitioning to the next song. Testimony may also be used in the middle of a song as a way of transitioning to a different section.

Ad-libbing is a type of textual improvisation that consists of generating short improvised phrases over a chorus or a vamp (a repeated section that extends the end of a song). The text used during an ad-libbing section can be a direct extension of the lyrics being sung by the choir or it can be a sung testimony with text that is different from that of the choir. For example, if the choir is singing "Thank You," the lead could then provide short testimonial phrases of gratitude.

While the different types of textual improvisation may be used interchangeably by some people, I reserve the use of the term *textual interpolation* for the addition of a few words within a verse; *testimony* for the addition of a short story or analogy before, during, or after a song; and *ad-libbing* for textual interpolation and testimony used during a chorus or vamp.

Rhythmic Improvisation

Melodic improvisation and textual improvisation are closely intertwined with rhythmic improvisation. Variations of rhythmic patterns, along with improvisational phrases, are typically used in combination with slurs and other vocal ornamentations in order to emphasize important words, phrases, or concepts. Rhythmic phrasing is often a key to communication and is the direct extension of one's personality and communicative tendencies. For example, if you have a naturally charismatic or animated personality, there are very distinct cadences that you will recognize in your own personal expression, especially if you are in an emotionally free environment. Even if you are not animated, there is still a tendency in communication to vary speech patterns depending on the situation and the context of that communication. The key to executing an authentic self-expression when singing is to pay attention to the manner in which you communicate and set music to your natural rhythmic expression. As you become immersed in certain cultures or are around people, you start to naturally pick up their speech patterns and phrasing tendencies. I'm sure you've heard people say, "You sounded just like [insert name here] when you said that!" Or maybe you find yourself talking like or picking up catch phrases from your friends or loved ones, without even recognizing it. Or you find yourself quoting someone and stating it just like the person you're quoting, with vocal inflections, neck roll, finger pointing, hand flapping, and/or "that look" just to make a point. "Like my daddy says, 'It's gon' *be* alright!'" This is exactly what happens with musical expression. In the context of musical interpretation, as you become immersed in the gospel style, the execution of your normal and/or animated speech pattern will subconsciously align with the cultural tendencies in gospel music.

The most significant influence on its phrasing tendencies stem from the cadences commonly heard in Southern black charismatic preaching styles. For example, the phrase "God has been so good to me" can be reinterpreted as follows:

"GOD HAS been . . . SO good to me"
"God has been, so, so, oh, oh, oh, SO good to me"
"GOD . . . HAS been . . . SO GOOD . . . he's been SO GOOD to me"
(Note: Capitalization denotes emphasis.)

The elongation and shorting of phrasing, back phrasing and front phrasing, and the use of rhythmic repetition as a communicative device all stem from these preaching styles.

Elongating Rhythmic Patterns Elongating rhythmic patterns is one way to integrate syncopation into a predefined rhythmic phrase and create a varied interpretation. When elongating a rhythmic pattern, a singer will extend the length a phrase beyond what is originally written, usually for dramatic purposes. This is done by holding a note/word a little longer than usual until it overlaps when the next note/word is supposed to come in. A form of elongation can also occur by inserting a **fermata** (a grand pause) or a retard/*retardando* (when the song slows down in an exaggerated manner) at the end of a phrase or verse.

For example, consider the phrase below as the original composed phrase.

Figure 5.15.   "Lord, We Need Your Love" Original Melody

If a singer were to hold out the word *Lord* a little longer and shorten the "we need your love" portion, it might be like the notated example below.

Figure 5.16.   "Lord, We Need Your Love" Elongated Rhythmic Phrase Example 1

Sometimes a fermata, or a hold/pause for improvisatory purposes can be inserted to elongate the rhythm for dramatic purposes. It is during this pause that singers will often insert some type of melodic or textual improvisation. An example of where a singer might place a fermata in the original melody can be seen in the example below.

Figure 5.17.   "Lord, We Need Your Love" Elongated Rhythmic Phrase Example 2

During the first fermata in the example above, the singer could use the stylistic tool of repetition by repeating the word *Lord* many times before continuing with the phrase. With each repetition, the singer would add variations to the execution of the word with the use of vocal nuances like swelling, moans, or dynamics shifts or even melodic riffs.

The second fermata could be used to recapture the whole beginning of the phrase, with some added text or testimony.

"We need . . ."
"Lord we need . . ."
"Lord . . . you're the only one who is able to love me like I need to be loved"
"Lord we need . . . your love"

Shortened/Abbreviated Rhythmic Phrases   A shortened rhythmic phrasing is usually executed in response to or is a prelude to an elongated rhythmic phrase. This rhythmic device employs more of a spoken quality or expression to its execution. Shortened rhythmic phrasing is generally used in somewhat of a reflective conversation mode of expression in which the singer may blurt something out or sing a phrase quickly and then pause as if he or she were reflective, thinking, and/or basking in that moment between the previous phrase and the next.

A shorted or abbreviated variation could be executed by speak-singing the first word *Lord* as if calling out to the Lord and in turn waiting for a response, then continued by speak-singing your request, "We need your love." An example of this is notated below.

LORD!   WE NEED YOUR LOVE!

Figure 5.18.   "Lord, We Need Your Love" Short Rhythmic Phrase

This stylistic tool is used a lot in traditional Southern gospel, as that subgenre of gospel music most closely resembles the black preaching style of expression.

Back Phrasing or Retard Phrasing   **Back phrasing** is a type of the syncopation that is executed when singing slightly behind, only to catch up to the established rhythm later but still within the phrase.

An example of back phrasing can be seen below.

Figure 5.19. "Lord, We Need Your Love" Back Phrasing

Back phrasing in often used in the interpretation to create a variation in the manner in which a song is executed. This tool should be executed with the purposeful intent of delayed speech, as when talking in a content, relaxed, or tired manner. It is during this emotional state that one may notice in his or her normal speech a bit of a lag or slur in the intent of his or her execution.

Front Phrasing or Anticipated Phrasing   **Front phrasing**, from an emotional perspective, is the type of phrase one generally uses when excited or anxious about something. Generally speaking, when in a heightened emotional state there is a tendency for a person's natural speech pattern to increase in speed. The same is true for singing. Anticipated phrasing or front phrasing is a stylistic tool used when a singer sings just before the prominent beat or originally composed melody.

An example of this type of anticipated phrasing is notated below.

Figure 5.20. "Lord, We Need Your Love" Front Phrasing

Anticipated phrasing can also be used as a musical fill-in between phrases and is most commonly used in this manner when leading a congregation or group of singers in a song. The leader will use anticipated phrasing to quickly sing the next line to be sung by the full group. This method of phrasing stems from the "lined hymn" tradition that dates back to the 1700s when the first line of the hymns was sung by the leader and the congregation followed and is currently found in all types of gospel music styles.

An example of this type of phrasing can be found in the example below.

Figure 5.21.   Anticipated Phrasing in Lead/Background Setting

Syncopation and Repetition   **Syncopation** using variations of rhythmic patterns is typically used in combination with slurs and other vocal ornamentations to emphasize important words, phrases, or melodic/harmonic concepts. Repetition specifically brings added emphasize to words by breaking up the anticipated rhythmic flow of a line and instantaneously creating variation.

Figure 5.22.   Use of Repetition

Rhythmic "Feel," Tempo, and Key

The rhythmic "feel" of gospel music or the rhythmic meter is a stylistic component that lays the musical landscape for interpretation. The gospel two-beat and triplet-based meters, such as 6/8, 9/8, 12/8, supply the rhythmic foundation of the "gospel feel" in the interpretation of traditional 2/4, 3/4, and 4/4 meters. Gospel rhythms are felt in, and expressed through, the body movement of a continuous, fluid, circular motion. Rhythm is a dance. The swaying back and forth, the waving of the hands, the hand clapping, and the foot stomping are all contributing factors to how the singer interprets the rhythm of the music. Sometimes the communication of the message in the song is so strong it far exceeds the use of a distinct tempo. The "feel" in a song with no rhythmic meter then becomes a musical reflection of a direct, emotional discussion between the singer and instrumentalists and the congregation.

Tempo marking in gospel songs is generally not set as a strict musical practice, in that most songs can be sung at any tempo (i.e., fast, med-fast, med-slow, or slow). The tempo is often derived from the tempo the singer needs in order to tell his or her story at the time of performance. It has a direct relationship with interpretation. Fast tempos usually convey excitement, and slow tempos unusually convey contentment, concern, or intimacy. Sometimes songs will start rubato (slow and out of time) and move to a consistent or even faster tempo. Sometimes gospel songs will vary in tempo throughout the song.

When singing solo, the key signature of a gospel song is usually determined by which key best fits the singer's voice. Oftentimes singers will start a song in a key that is comfortable in their voice, and the musicians, who usually can play by ear, will find the key and join the singer. Vocal range is a prominent factor of virtuosity in gospel singing. As a result, key change or modulation is expected and generally occurs for climactic purposes. Oftentimes the vamp (i.e., the repeated harmonic structure) or shout chorus (a short musical phrase in which the text and melody continuously repeat without variation) at the end of the song is where modulation takes place. Hymns and lined or metered hymns and congregational songs also employ modulation for climactic effect.

Flexibility of Harmonic Structure or Form

The composed form and harmonic structure in gospel music is intended to serve as a musical road map, the basis from which singers and musicians are expected to create an instantaneous arrangement. Not to be mistaken for lack of preparation, instantaneous arranging is a culturally accepted practice in the gospel music community. The communication between singers and musicians is to be such that musicians should be able to follow the direction of the singer as the Spirit leads him or her. The advantage of gospel musicians being able to play by ear, instead of reading a through-composed chart, is it allows for direct communication and anticipation of musical cues. During the performance, the singer will signal which sections to repeat, when to modulate, when to build in intensity, and when to break (i.e., a brief pause within the song in which all music stops simultaneously). The skill of the singer's ability to direct the music according to the ministerial needs and his or her personal interpretation is an acquired behavior.

SACRED MUSIC IN THE BLACK CHURCH

When one thinks of black sacred music, the first type of music that comes to mind is often spirituals and/or gospel. However, historically there are at least five different compositional forms used by black sacred music composers and arrangers. They include standard hymns or folk songs by European and white American composers (established in the 1600s), lined or metered hymns (established in the 1700s), spirituals (various styles established between the 1700s and 1950s), gospel hymns (established in 1900), gospel songs (established in 1940), and standard sacred classical forms in which African Americans compose (established in 1937). Each of these compositional forms has their own musical lineage, associated style, and performance practices that were established when they were created and continue to evolve and be reinterpreted with time.

European Hymns in the African American Worship Experience

Standard hymns and anthems incorporated into the African American worship experience include Greek and Latin hymns, English hymns, Lutheran chorales, European hymn anthems, and American hymns and hymn anthems.[9] These hymns can be found in the church services of many African American churches; however, the denomination of the church and its cultural practice will dictate the manner in which these hymns are interpreted. For example, the historic Methodist and Baptist church that maintained a Eurocentric perspective in terms of its worship experience and with congregants of upper-class status typically performed these songs as written, with very little musical alterations. However, with the rise of the urban Pentecostal, Holiness, and storefront churches of the city and the increased popularity of the gospel aesthetic even within traditional denominations, these hymns were commonly reinterpreted and represented using African American music aesthetics not intended in the original composition. These hymns include songs like "Amazing Grace," "What a Friend We Have in Jesus," and "Holy, Holy, Holy."

Lined or Metered Hymns (Established in the 1700s)

Sometimes referred to as "lined out" or "Dr. Watts'" hymns, metered hymns are a type of congregational song written in a short, simple form in which the lyrics consist of a few short verses. The lyrics of these hymns were taken primarily from the music of Dr. Isaac Watts and other Reformation hymn writers. However, they were combined with an African aesthetic and transmitted as an oral hymn form.[10] In this type of song, the leader will often sing or chant the lyrics of the first phrase before everyone responds. Each phrase is repeated in a line-by-line method, using a learned rhythmic and melodic form. Lots of melodic embellishments to the basic melody are expected. Rev. Dr. R. M. Simmons describes the performance of lined hymns as follows:

> Lyrics were learned, remembered and transmitted from one generation to the next. The performance tempo is slow and drawn out. The melodies are often plaintive and pensive. They are congregational in nature and carry much energy with traditional African aesthetic retentions. Two of the more popular Lined Hymns are "A Charge to Keep I Have" and "Father, I Stretch My Hand to Thee."[11]

Spirituals (Various Styles Established between the 1600s and 1950s)

Spirituals, sometimes referred to as *slave songs*, *plantation songs*, or *jubilee songs*, are a type of song established as a healing response to the trials and tribulations of African American slaves. While the lyrical content often spoke of deep despair, there was always joy and comfort in the belief that slaves would receive their promised inheritance in the life after death. Passed down through generations via the oral music tradition, the text of spirituals was largely based on stories of the Old Testament of the Bible, embraced the virtues of Christianity, and addressed a passionate longing for freedom and justice through coded meanings.

In Dr. Raymond Wise's 2002 dissertation, he describes four types of spirituals: oral, concert, congregational, and gospel.[12] The oral spiritual was created and performed by slaves with improvised vocal parts, usually without accompaniment other than rhythmic hand clapping and foot stomping. Some of the spirituals from this time are also referred to as the *moan or groan*, referring to the humming and melodic variation mixed into the interpretation of the song.[13] An example of an oral spiritual is "I've Been Buked," by an unknown composer, written during the 1700s. In the 1800s, many of the oral spirituals were reinterpreted, and others were newly composed in the concert spiritual style. The concert spiritual requires specific vocal parts and is performed with European classical vocal techniques. It gained national prominence with the Fisk Jubilee Singers touring group from Fisk University in 1871.[14]

The accompaniment for these concert spirituals can range from a choral arrangement with no accompaniment, as performed by the Fisk Jubilee Singers, to through-composed arrangements (i.e., all parts and performance cues written out by a composer/arranger instead of improvised) for piano and solo voice, as with the infamous concert spiritual by Harry T. Burleigh, "Deep River," written in 1917. The congregational spirituals of the 1900s were performed with instrumental accompaniment and performed regularly in the church during devotion. Earlier congregational spirituals appeared in *Gospel Pearls*, one of the earlier African American sacred music publications.[15] An example of the congregational spiritual is "I'm a Soldier in the Army of the Lord," composed by Charles Mason. The gospel spiritual was interpreted around the 1950s with or without accompaniment and performed in the gospel vocal style. An example of the gospel spiritual is "Plenty Good Room" as interpreted by Rev. James Cleveland.

The performance of spirituals should generally be performed as written or as learned through the oral tradition. While some improvisation is allowed, improvisation should only be executed so that it does not distort the overall effect of the song. Also, the appropriate diction (i.e., way of pronouncing the words) should be preserved and not substituted with correct English nor overexaggerated, as it would destroy both the performance and the intent of the composition. For example, words like *children* would become *chillum* in a song in order to fit the rhythm of the music.

Standard Sacred Classical Forms in Which African Americans Compose (Established in 1900)

Even before the emancipation of the slaves, black Americans were composing (i.e., writing or creating) music in the classical styles. In great prominence as early as the 1930s, black musicians composed in standard classical forms that included but were not limited to arts songs, oratorios, hymns, anthems, operas, and symphonies. The vocal requirements for this style of music correspond with those established by the bel canto singing styles of the Western European art music tradition. The oratorio "The Ordering of Moses," composed by R. Nathaniel Dett (1937), is an example of a song by an African American composer who composed using standard sacred classical form. Prominent composers of these genres include Harry T. Burleigh (1866–1949), J[ohn] Rosamond Johnson (1873–1954), James Weldon Johnson (1871–1938), R[obert] R. Nathaniel Dett (1882–1943), Shirley Graham (1896–1977), Eva Jessye (1895–1992), Francis Hall Johnson (1888–1970), and William Grant Still (1895–1978). Harry Burleigh was one of the first African American composers born after emancipation to gain broad acceptance nationally in the United States. His major contribution lies in the transformation of the Negro spiritual from the choral tradition popularized by the Fisk Jubilee Singers to the solo art song tradition of the concert stage.[16] His arrangement of "Deep River" was the first Negro spiritual to be arranged in the style of an art song for solo voice and piano. This arrangement in particular was made famous by African American classical bass baritone Paul Robeson, the first to perform an entire program of Negro spirituals in a concert setting.[17]

Gospel Hymns (Established in 1900)

Long before gospel hymns were created, black congregations were singing the hymns of the white churches when they worshiped in public. However, when blacks worshipped in secret churches and eventually in the visible black church, these hymns were adopted and converted into black songs. These "gospelized" white hymns were a result of different musical influences and often involved the improvisation of melodies and lyrics to fit the needs of the black church. While many melodies were kept intact, the rhythms and harmonies of the songs were changed to reflect the black worship experience. At the turn of the twentieth century, black composers emerged as prolific hymn writers who could not only compose in the hymn styles of the white hymn composers but also leave room within their compositions to integrate the stylistic and performance practices of African American music and worship styles. The most renowned and prolific writer of this style of music was Dr. Charles Albert Tindley (1856–1933), pastor of the Tindley Temple United Methodist Church in Philadelphia. Tindley would ultimately combine the emotion of the black spiritual with that of the emotional text of the hymns of Dr. Isaac Watts (renowned white hymn composer), coupled with the use of blues modes, jazz syncopations, and avenues of improvisation.

Gospel Songs (Established in 1940)

Gospel songs are religious songs that were actually written and performed in the black gospel style. Gospel songs exemplify the most direct connection and correspondence to their secular counterpart, the blues. This style of writing was made popular by Thomas A. Dorsey. Dorsey spent many years of his life on the blues and vaudeville circuit when he wasn't in church. He played and composed music for singers like Bessie Smith and for his own blues and jazz ensembles. When Dorsey began composing music strictly for the church—a change inspired by the great and influential music of Dr. Charles Tindley—he was greatly criticized for adapting some of this blues style into his gospel songs. Many of his songs were banished for many years in churches for being too reflective of the devil's music. However, Dorsey wrote over eight hundred songs, including his most famous, "Precious Lord, Take My Hand," "Peace in the Valley," and "The Lord Will Make a Way Somehow." From a performance standpoint, gospel songs provided unrestricted improvisation, and their written versions of the songs were intended to be a basic guide for the format of the song. Very few gospel songs are written down *exactly* how they should be performed.

GOSPEL MUSIC PERFORMANCE-STYLE CATEGORIES

Any songs composed, regardless of their genre, can be musically reinterpreted in the gospel style. According to Wise, there are eleven distinct gospel music styles. This includes the hymn style and quartet style popular from 1900 to the 1920s; the early classic gospel style popular from the 1920s to 1940; the late classic gospel style popular from 1940 to 1970; the total style, classical style, and contemporary style of the 1970s; the contemporary jazz and blues style, word style, and praise and worship style of the 1980s and 1990s; and the urban style from the 1990s to the present. While each of these styles has its own unique function and associated performance practices, I have found it helpful to categorize these eleven music styles into five broad performance-style categories for the purposes of teaching, singing, and organizing repertoire: traditional gospel style, Southern gospel style, inspirational gospel style, contemporary gospel style, and praise and worship style. Not to be confused with historic subgenres or official music industry marketing categories (although some correlations do exist), these teaching-style categories help to organize one's approach to music repertoire, particularly as it relates to musical interpretation with regard to the treatment of the melody and the musical arrangement.

Traditional Gospel Style Category ♪

The traditional gospel style category encompasses the repertoire and performance practices rooted in historic subgenres such as the hymn style of the 1900s to the late classic gospel styles of the 1950s. The modern compositions included in the category, while they may include the use of progressive harmonies in the accompaniment, still approach the musical interpretation of the song in this traditional style. The repertoire and performance practices of this style are often characteristic of long legato; continuous lines used in voices and accompaniment for slow songs; driving, bouncy continuous rhythms with vocal lines that connect one phrase to another in up-tempo songs; passionate, exaggerated melodic phrasings in which the vowel sounds of important words are typically passionately sustained within the phrase, treated with subtle melodic embellishments, or a combination; creative and dramatic use of dynamic levels; emotional intensity; simple melodic improvisation and rhythmic phrasing; and use of gospel time signatures 12/8, 6/8, and 9/8. The arrangements are generally simple and straightforward (no modulations or changes in tempo), yet the compositional form is generally extended as the Spirit leads through the use of vamps and repetitions. The vocal textures are robust, powerful, and sometimes maintain a more gravelly quality during heightened emotional states, though the rasp quality is not required. The text is most important in this style, thus the melodic and rhythmic choices rarely interrupt the intelligibility of the text. Excessive melodic embellishments are only found in modern interpretations of songs; however, even then, they are typically reserved for extending and connecting phrases. Scales used during modest interpretations include diatonic and pentatonic scales. Nonmusical elements consist of rocking, swaying, clapping, hand gestures, and hand waving.

Recommended listening examples:

Roberta Martin Singers: "God Is Still on the Throne"
Mahalia Jackson: "Precious Lord"
Dixie Hummingbirds: "When the Gates Swing Open"
Golden Gate Quartet: "Wade in the Water"
Myrna Summer: "I Found Jesus"
Jessy Dixon: "I Am Redeemed"
Kathy Taylor: "Oh How Precious"
Yolanda Adams: "Even Me"
Smokie Norful: "I Need You Now"

Southern Gospel Style Category ♪

The Southern gospel style category encompasses those repertoire and performance practices that are rooted in the historic subgenre of early classic styles and late classic gospel styles. Modern compositions are included in this style category; however, the treatment of the melody and overall approach to the arrangement is heavily influenced by historic tendencies common in the classic down-home gospel style. The repertoire and performance practices of this style are often characteristic of melodies consisting of short, speech-like phrases resembling charismatic black preaching styles and cadences; spaces between each phrase to allow for emotional and spiritual response (both audible and inaudible) by the singer, musicians, and congregation; use of colloquial speech and expression and personal testimony before, during, and at the end of the song; short yet assertive, sometimes aggressive and convicted execution of the text and melodic phrases; purposeful distortion of the text; emphasis on rhythmic improvisation through syncopation and repeated notes and rhythmic patterns; and use of gospel time signatures 12/8, 6/8, 9/8, and 2/4, with a heavy backbeat. The arrangements have simple musical forms yet employ modulations in key and tempo changes. The form is generally extended as the Spirit leads through the use of vamps and repetitions. Accompaniment is most effective when it includes a full rhythm section of piano/organ, guitar, bass, and drums. The vocal textures are robust, powerful, husky, raspy, and gravelly, particularly during heightened emotional states; this is highly characteristic of this style category.

This style category is greatly aligned with the performance practices of down-home blues and other rural black folk music. This is particularly evident in the interpretation of text and the use of textual and melodic phrasing that accentuates one's emotional response to the subject matter. It is this emotional conviction that determines the melodic and rhythmic choices used. Excessive melodic embellishments are rarely used in the style, although moans, groans, and melodic ornamentations are often used in between phrases as a way of both emotional release and emotional stimulation. As previously mentioned, singers in this style also purposefully leave space for narration and audience participation. Scales used during modest interpretations include diatonic, pentatonic, and blues scales. Nonmusical elements consist of unapologetic outward displays of emotion, high energy, rocking, swaying, hand clapping, foot stomping, hand gestures, hand waving, sudden body contortions, holy dancing, walking through the audience, or strutting across the stage/altar.

Recommended listening examples:

Albertina Walker, Shirley Caesar, and Dorothy Norwood: "I'm Going Home with Jesus"
Shirley Caesar: "I Feel Like Praising Him"
Dorothy Norwood: "A Denied Mother"
Dottie People: "He's an On-Time God"
Rev. James Cleveland: "Jesus Is the Best Thing"
Neal Roberson: "Don't Let the Devil Ride"
Bishop Paul Morton: "Your Tears"

Rev. Timothy Wright: "Jesus, Jesus, Jesus"
LaShun Pace Rhodes: "I know I've Been Changed"

Inspirational Gospel Style Category ♪

The inspirational gospel style category combines the core musical elements of traditional and contemporary gospel music with the musical characteristics and performance practices of Western European classical art songs, white folk songs, white Southern gospel, contemporary Christian music, and jazz. The historic subgenres associated with this style category are rooted in historical styles such as total style, classical style, word style, and contemporary style. The repertoire and performance practices of this style are often characteristic of through-composed melodies with strings or full orchestral arrangements; moderate to complex forms; and arrangements that include key modulations, tempo changes, retards, tags, and orchestral interludes. A signifying characteristic of the lyrical content associated with this style category can be divided into two types. One type consists of inspirational songs about love and encouragement that don't specifically use the names Jesus, Lord, God, or Christ in the lyrics; rather, the source of love and encouragement is implied. The other type of lyrics tells stories of Christ and Christian life through elaborate through-composed melodies. During the performance of the inspirational style, the flow and evenness of the melodic line and the exemplified technical command of one's instrument is valued more than improvisational skills. Melodic embellishments are lyrically executed in slow and even fashion and are usually reserved for sustained notes within and at the end of a melodic phrase. While a variety of vocal textures and timbres can be found in inspirational styles, the smooth, aesthetically pleasing, formally trained singers with a wide vocal range typically dominate this style. Some of the nonmusical core elements represented include rocking, swaying, walking, clapping, hand gestures, and hand waving.

Recommended listening examples:

Andraé Crouch: "My Tribute"
Nicole C. Mullen: "My Redeemer Lives"
James Cleveland and the Southern Community Choir: "God Is"

CeCe Winans: "Alabaster Box"
Wintley Phipps: "Ordinary People"
Jessy Dixon: "Gone"
Yolanda Adams and Donnie McClurkin: "My Prayer"
Tramaine Hawkins: "What Shall I Do?"

Contemporary Gospel Style Category ♪

The contemporary gospel style category combines the core musical elements of the traditional and Southern gospel style categories with the musical characteristics and performance practices of blues, jazz, rhythm and blues, soul, hip-hop, rap, and rock. The historic subgenres associated with this style category include word style, contemporary style, contemporary jazz and blues style, and urban style. The music and the approach to musical interpretations so closely resemble its secular counterparts that the only distinguishing factor of the secular and sacred styles is the lyrical content. The repertoire and performance practices of this style are often characteristic of moderate to complex newly composed music or traditional songs with new modern arrangements; elaborate introductions, musical transitional passages, and bridges; horn riffs, licks, riffs, and countermelodies; solo instrumental and scat singing; virtuoso-melismatic singing; major vocal and emotional dynamic changes; and extended use of vocal range. Accompaniment not only includes a full rhythm section with horns but can also include drum machines, synthesizers, and studio-produced vocal effects. Vocal textures associated with this style can vary from one singer to the next; however, vocal flexibility, accurate intonation, conviction, vocal power, and vocal stamina are consistent throughout. Nonmusical core elements include sway, bounce, hand clapping, hand genres strut, and often highly choreographed dance routines.

Recommended listening examples:

Walter Hawkins: "What Is This"
Commissioned: "Running Back to You"
Clark Sisters: "You Brought the Sunshine"
BeBe and CeCe Winans: "Addicted Love"
Fred Hammond: "This Is the Day"

Kirk Franklin: "Stomp"
Kim Burrell: "Try Me Again"
Mary Mary: "Shackles"

Praise and Worship Style Category ♪

Because praise and worship music is such a broad category, it deserves a separate style category. Praise and worship have direct lineages in slave songs and spirituals, the lined and metered hymns of the 1700s, and the devotional and congregational songs of the 1900s. This musical influence combines core musical and emotional elements of black gospel music with the core musical elements of Christian contemporary music to form an emotional and energetic style of worship designed to give praise and worship to God. Welcomed in most contemporary Christian churches around the world, this type of Christian music lends itself to be freely reinterpreted as a spiritual and cultural collaboration for all who participate. The majority of contemporary praise and worship music compositions stem from white megachurches and is often reinterpreted in the black church using core musical and nonmusical elements of gospel music. In terms of the approach to musical interpretation, praise and worship music can fit into all four gospel style categories (traditional, Southern, inspirational, and contemporary), depending on the church and the context of the performance.

The repertoire and performance practices of this style are often characteristic of simple and repetitive melodies, song texts that range from those easily learned to more involved scripture-based texts, vocal parts predominately in unison, leader-directed songs, call-and-response compositional structures, war cry (a simple melodic motif sustained on the vowel sound "oh" or [o]), modulation in key, elaborate musical interludes and bridges, and emotional dynamic changes starting low in the beginning and becoming loud and energetic in the end. In addition, each song typically lasts between seven and twelve minutes (with a musical set lasting between twenty to ninety minutes). Accompaniment can range from a full rhythm section with synthesizers and horns to studio-produced tracks. Vocal textures associated with this style can vary between each singer; however, vocal flexibility, conviction, vocal power, and vocal stamina are consistent throughout. Nonmusical core elements include sway, bounce, jumping, hand clapping, and choreographed dance routines.

Recommended listening examples:

Judith McAllister: "To Our God"
Byron Cage: "The Presence of the Lord Is Here"
Israel Houghton: "Lord You Are Good"
Micah Stampley: "Our God Is Greater"
Carlton Pearson: "Catch on Fire"
Andraé Crouch, featuring Marvin Winans: "Let the Church Say Amen"
Tasha Cobbs: "Break Every Chain"
Helen Baylor: "Awesome God"

PERFORMANCE MEDIUMS

A performance medium can be defined as the combination of voices and/or instruments used in the performance of music. There are many performance mediums found in gospel music. These mediums can include anything from a solo vocal or instrumental performance with or without instrumental accompaniment to a choir performance with members totaling more than three hundred accompanied by an orchestra. The five most prominent performance mediums in gospel music are gospel ensembles, gospel quartets and groups, gospel choirs, gospel duos and trios, and gospel soloists. See chapter 1 for more information about the history of gospel performances.

Gospel Ensembles ♪

When the performance of sacred music made its first transition from congregational singing to a traveling feature performer(s), the a cappella singing groups took the lead. These groups were called *jubilee singers* and consisted of between nine and twenty singers performing the concert spiritual repertoire, most groups stemming from historically black colleges. As gospel music evolved, this medium-size ensemble was replaced as the most prominent performance medium—first with the gospel quartet, then eventually with the choir—only to return to its now-prominent status. This performance medium has evolved to include instrumental accompaniment and is represented in all subgenres and style categories of the gospel genre, particularly in the praise and worship style. Examples of gospel ensembles include but are not limited to Fisk Jubilee Singers, Kurt Carr Singers, Donald Lawrence and the Tri-City Singers, Tye Tribbett and GA (Greater Anointing), and James Fortune and FIYA.

Gospel Quartets and Groups ♪

Out of the early jubilee singer tradition came the gospel quartets. The gospel quartet performance medium, first with all-male quartets, then with all-female quartets, remained the dominant performance medium for performing gospel music for the first half of the twentieth century. Since its creation, the gospel quartet has expanded from the traditional four singers to as many as six members, as represented in the contemporary styles. It would ultimately be the five-membered group, which featured two lead singers (one who would start the song and another who would finish the song), that became the standard for this performance medium. As with the evolution of gospel music, the gospel quartet style has expanded in instrumentation and has groups represented in all gospel music style categories. This was and still is the most popular performance medium for family-based gospel groups. Examples of gospel quartets and groups include but are not limited to the Caravans, Dixie Hummingbirds, Mighty Clouds of Joy, Commissioned, the Clark Sisters, and Soul Stirrers.

Gospel Choirs ♪

Consisting of twenty or more singers with instrumental accompaniment, the gospel choir is the most beloved performance medium within the local church, outside of congregational singing. From the inception of Thomas Dorsey's National Convention of Gospel Choirs and Choruses in 1932 to the later-established Rev. James Cleveland's Gospel Music Workshop of America National Convention in 1967, the popularity of gospel choirs began to spread greatly throughout the country.

While the choir has always remained a popular performance medium in the church, it was during the 1970s and 1980s when gospel choirs became the most prominent touring and featured performance medium in gospel music. While touring choirs often featured a number of soloists in a given concert, the "featured performer" was typically the choir director, as he or she remained the most significant member of the group. In the gospel choir, it is the choir director who composes, arranges, and/ or selects the repertoire for the choir. The spiritual effectiveness of the choir is often directly related to the director's ability to align the energy and output of each choir member in order to create one dynamic, ministerial music force. Directing styles can vary from person to person, although it is typically the regional style characteristics (in terms of vocal outputs, musical characteristics, and performance arrangements) that best distinguish one gospel choir sound from another. Examples of gospel choirs include but are not limited to James Cleveland and the Angelic Choir, Chicago Mass Choir, Colorado Mass Choir, New Life Community Choir, Mississippi Mass Choir, Hezekiah Walker and the Love Fellowship Choir, Ricky Dillard and Nu G (New Generation), and Thompson Community Singers (Rev. Milton Brunson).

Gospel Duos and Trios ♪

Throughout the history of gospel music, there have been gospel duos and trios. As with the gospel quartets and groups, this performance medium is often composed of relatives. Gospel duos and trios are a derivative of the gospel quartet tradition, particularly in their approach to the split lead when interpreting song. While this performance medium has never maintained a prominent status in comparison to others, it is certainly an established force in the performance of gospel music. Examples of gospel duos and trios include but are not limited to the O'Neal Twins, BeBe and CeCe Winans, the Boyer Brothers, and the Barrett Sisters.

Gospel Soloists

The gospel soloist has been a performance medium in every church from the beginning of gospel to the present day. While it was the lead singer of gospel quartets and ensembles who established the early vocal sound, style characteristics, and performance practices, it would be in the late 1940s and 1950s that the solo voice would become a dominant performance medium.

CONCLUSION

As singers immerse themselves in the religious culture of gospel music and become more familiar with the gospel genre and its substyles and performance mediums, they will start to recognize and acquire the tools used to interpret the music. There are many components influencing how the sound and style tools are executed in the context of performance. This includes the singer's own style of emotional communication as influenced by the musical vocabulary and performance practices specific to the substyle of gospel music; the geographical region from which the composers and performers stem (i.e., North, South, West, Midwest); the influence of the musical culture within the Christian denomination (i.e., Pentecostal, Holiness, Baptist, African American Methodist Episcopal); and even the influence of other musical styles outside of gospel music upon the singer. Listening is the key to recognizing how these tools are executed in a culturally viable manner.

NOTES

1. Pearl Williams-Jones, "Afro-American Gospel Music: A Crystallization of the Black Aesthetic," *Ethnomusicology* 19, no. 3 (1975): 373–85.

2. Gayle Wald, "From Spirituals to Swing: Sister Rosetta Tharpe and Gospel Crossover," *American Quarterly* 55, no. 3 (2003): 398.

3. Ibid.

4. Horace Clarence Boyer, "Gospel Music," *Music Educators Journal* 64, no. 9 (1978): 34–43.

5. Glenn Douglas Hinson, "When the Words Roll and the Fire Flows: Spirit, Style and Experience in African-American Gospel Performance" (PhD diss., University of Pennsylvania, 1989), 316–17.

6. Trineice Murlene Robinson-Martin, "Developing a Pedagogy for Gospel Singing: Understanding the Cultural Aesthetics and Performance Components

of a Vocal Performance in Gospel Music" (PhD diss., Teachers College, Columbia University, 2010); Robinson-Martin, "Take My Hand: Teaching the Gospel Singer in the Applied Voice Studio," in *Teaching Singing in the 21st Century*, ed. Scott David Harrison and Jessica O'Bryan (New York: Springer, 2014), 14:335–50.

7. Mellonee Burnim, "The Black Gospel Music Tradition: A Complex of Ideology, Aesthetic, and Behavior," in *More than Dancing: Essays on Afro-American Music and Musicians*, ed. Irene Jackson (Westport, CT: Greenwood, 1985),164.

8. Horace Clarence Boyer, "Contemporary Gospel Music," *The Black Perspective in Music* 7, no. 1 (1979): 27.

9. R. M. Simmons, *Good Religion: Expressions of Energy in Traditional African-American Worship* (Columbus, OH: Layman Christian Leadership, 1998).

10. Ibid.

11. Ibid., 119.

12. Raymond Wise, "Defining African American Gospel Music by Tracing Its Historical and Musical Development from 1900 to 2000" (PhD diss., Ohio State University, 2002).

13. See www.negrospirituals.com, accessed February 2, 2015.

14. Wise, "Defining African American Gospel Music."

15. Simmons, *Good Religion*.

16. Josephine R. B. Wright, "Art/Classical Music: Chronological Overview," in *African American Music: An Introduction*, ed. Mellonee Burnim and Portia K. Maultsby (New York: Taylor and Francis, 2006).

17. Mellonee Burnim, "Religious Music," in *African American Music: An Introduction*, ed. Mellonee Burnim and Portia K. Maultsby (New York: Taylor and Francis, 2006).

WORKS CITED

Boyer, Horace Clarence. "Contemporary Gospel Music." *The Black Perspective in Music* 7, no. 1 (1979): 5–58.

———. "Gospel Music." *Music Educators Journal* 64, no. 9 (1978): 34–43.

Burnim, Mellonee. "The Black Gospel Music Tradition: A Complex of Ideology, Aesthetic, and Behavior." In *More than Dancing: Essays on Afro-American Music and Musicians*, edited by Irene Jackson, 147–67. Westport, CT: Greenwood, 1985.

————. "Religious Music." In *African American Music: An Introduction*, edited by Mellonee Burnim and Portia K. Maultsby. New York: Taylor and Francis, 2006.

Hinson, Glenn Douglas. "When the Words Roll and the Fire Flows: Spirit, Style and Experience in African-American Gospel Performance." PhD diss., University of Pennsylvania, 1989.

Robinson-Martin, Trineice Murlene. "Developing a Pedagogy for Gospel Singing: Understanding the Cultural Aesthetics and Performance Components of a Vocal Performance in Gospel Music." PhD diss., Teachers College, Columbia University, 2010.

————. "Take My Hand: Teaching the Gospel Singer in the Applied Voice Studio." In *Teaching Singing in the 21st Century*, edited by Scott David Harrison and Jessica O'Bryan, 14:335–50. New York: Springer, 2014.

Simmons, R. M. *Good Religion: Expressions of Energy in Traditional African-American Worship*. Columbus, OH: Layman Christian Leadership, 1998.

Wald, Gayle. "From Spirituals to Swing: Sister Rosetta Tharpe and Gospel Crossover." *American Quarterly* 55, no. 3 (2003): 387–416.

Williams-Jones, Pearl. "Afro-American Gospel Music: A Crystallization of the Black Aesthetic." *Ethnomusicology* 19, no. 3 (1975): 373–85.

Wise, Raymond. "Defining African American Gospel Music by Tracing Its Historical and Musical Development from 1900 to 2000." PhD diss., Ohio State University, 2002.

Wright, Josephine R. B. "Art/Classical Music: Chronological Overview." In *African American Music: An Introduction*, edited by Mellonee Burnim and Portia K. Maultsby. New York: Taylor and Francis, 2006.

6

GOSPEL IN CONTEXT

As mentioned in previous chapters, gospel music serves as a platform to musically testify about who God is, what he has already done, and what the Word says about what he is going to do. The effectiveness of a singer's ability to communicate the gospel message lies more in his or her own conviction and personal testimony, rather than simply in his or her ability to sing the melody and the words of a song in a stylistically appropriate manner. Therefore, repertoire selection in the gospel genre is a very personal and conscious selection process. Many amateur or preprofessional singers often overlook this process, particularly those not well versed in the ministerial aspect of gospel singing or the gospel music repertoire as a whole. The tendency for these singers is to perform popular gospel songs that they like, particularly ones that might also show off their vocal skills, rather than picking songs to best articulate their story. While this is a good place to start in terms of learning repertoire in order to become familiar with the gospel style, ultimately this is not how professional gospel singers select their music.

When selecting music for the intended ministerial function, singers first have to recognize where they are in their Christian walk and then match their experience with theological subject matters that can be articulated in a genuine manner. There is no spiritual prequalification level necessary to sing gospel songs, for God uses whomever he chooses to do his work. There is no hierarchy in repertoire; one song is not holier than the next. Singers can write their own songs or collaborate with others to create new music. But the most important aspect about a gospel singer before he or she ministers is authenticity and awareness. In other words, the singer must be aware of where he or she is spiritually and minister from that awareness. Singers must sing from an honest and humble place and allow themselves to be used by God so that they, and those to whom they are ministering, can have a genuine religious experience. There are many other aspects of God's word, power, and glory to which singers can attest, whether the singer is a seasoned Christian, a new Christian, or simply an admirer of Christ. One does not need to feel obligated to minister about topics or subjects in which he or she cannot relate. For example, a person does not have to minister about God being a healer if he or she has never been in a position in which God's healing power was needed and/or verified. There are many other topics from which one can testify that will align with his or her personal testimony. As people grow in their spiritual walk and relationship with Christ, so will their abilities to minister, and thus, the content of their repertoire will expand.

DEVELOPING INTERPRETATION OF SELF-EXPRESSION

True and honest self-expression lies in the vulnerability of outwardly acknowledging and expressing one's genuine emotions. This ability is often directly related to one's cultural upbringing and emotive environment. Meaning if a singer was raised in an environment in which the outward display of extreme emotion, good or bad, was discouraged, then the singer will tend to have difficulty outwardly displaying passion and conviction while singing. Conversely, people who are comfortable outwardly displaying an array of emotions in everyday life tend to emote more easily in the context of music. The charismatic culture of Pentecostal and Holiness churches standardizes this outward display of emotion as normal behavior in their worship experience when communicating with God and singing his praises. It is with the continual immersion in this setting that one acquires the release of both expressive and spiritual bondage.

The individuality of musical expression comes from the ability to musically articulate an authentic representation of self. To do so, one must first recognize how he or she naturally emotes and then learn to musically articulate those emotions using the musical vocabulary of gospel music. In other words, the singer must recognize how he or she displays and communicates emotions during everyday speech and everyday interaction. This includes recognizing natural mannerisms such as tone of voice, inflections in pitch, hand gestures, body movements, facial expression, and so on, that all comprise emotional expression. With this recognition of self-expression, singers can apply and articulate those mannerisms in the interpretation of the song using established stylistic tools in gospel music.

The ministry aspect of gospel music suggests that in gospel music, the musical interpretation is not simply the personal expression of emotion. It is musically articulating the emotional response to the reality of Christ's influence on the singer's life story. It is a reflection of one's personal relationship with God and the recognition and acknowledgment of the impact God has made on his or her life. "Who is God to me?" "How has what I know about him and his word impacted my life?" "What is my situation and how do I feel about it?" "What does God say about my situation according to his word?" "How do I feel about what God says about my situation?" The answer to these very personal questions, combined with the internal desire to share one's revelation with others, is the epitome of testimony and a major component as it pertains to honest worship and ministry.

FINDING THE WORDS: MATTERS OF THE HEART

There are reoccurring themes from which most gospel lyrics are based. More often than not, gospel singers are in the position to give testimony or further ad lib on these topics and need to feel prepared when doing so. To achieve this, it may be helpful to journal on the following seven topics and ask yourself questions regarding how you feel about these topics.

Scripture: Musical Setting of Specific Scripture. Choose some scriptures that resonate well with your spirit. Journal about what these scriptures mean and how your faith in the written words impacts your daily life.

Love: Love of Christ, Loving Christ, Loving One Another. Think about the many ways Christ shows his love to you. Perhaps there are scriptures specifically about love that you want to share with others. What are some personal situations in which you undeniably experienced God's love or shared God's love with others? How are you a better person knowing that God loves you?

Faith/Trust: Believing That the Word Is True and That God Keeps His Promises. List some scriptures illustrating God's faithfulness. Why do you trust God? What do you want to tell someone regarding trusting God?

Encouragement: Encouraging Oneself or Someone Else in the Lord. What are some scriptures that show that even in biblical days, people of God still needed to be encouraged? Were there times when you needed to be encouraged? How did you overcome your situation? How do you deal with doubt? What do you want to tell someone who needs to be encouraged about what God can do in his or her situation?

Submission: Jesus Is the Messiah, He Is Lord, the Way, the Truth, and the Light. How does the Lord direct your path? Why should you surrender to him? Talk about your struggles without him. What is the significance of this submission, and how has it affected your life?

Gratitude: Being Grateful for What God Has Done, His Mercy, His Grace, His Sacrifice. What are all the things you are grateful for? What are some situations in which God has made a move on your behalf that you want to celebrate him for? What does the Bible say about his grace, mercy, and sacrifice? How would you tell others about the goodness of the Lord? What do you want to say?

Role of Christ: Identifying and Acknowledging Christ for Who He Is (e.g., Savior, Provider, and/or Redeemer). How and why do you show reverence to God? What role does Jesus play in your life? How would you describe the role of Christ to those who do not know him or to those who want to know him better? What personal experience have you had that illustrates God's work in your life?

Journaling and devotion is key. Regardless of where you are on your Christian journey, there is always at least one theme or one aspect of a theme that directly resonates with you. Ministry is a process. The more you understand Christ and your relationship with Christ, the better you will become at expounding on various subject matters related to him. The process that occurs in preparation for ministry also nourishes the process of spiritual growth for the minister him- or herself. It is as a result of this process that the conviction of your testimony is given fuel, substance, and validity.

When picking songs, it is important to acknowledge and sing your own story. You should start with the topics you can best articulate so that when singing a song, you can sing your own words from a personal place rather than the words of someone else. Stop and take time to understand the message of the song. Some singers will default to simply imitating verbatim what the singer on a recording does with the song, hoping to evoke the same response from the listener. As a result, his or her performance is merely an imitation of stylistic expression and serves primarily as entertainment rather than true ministry. Everyone has a story, and each person's story is unique and worthy of telling.

ANOINTING VERSUS ENTERTAINMENT

Knowledge of gospel aesthetics can be quite beneficial to singers of all genres as it promotes personal interpretation and emotional communication through music. One does not have to believe in God, sing gospel songs, or even totally sing in the gospel style to incorporate gospel aesthetics. For example, many singers incorporate the gospel style into secular music styles such as soul, rhythm and blues, jazz, and musical theater. Even within the gospel genre, some vocalists sing gospel music not for the purpose of ministry but for personal or artistic enjoyment. In the mid-1950s and 1960s, gospel music became so popular that gospel nightclubs were established for entertainment purposes.[1] Headliners in these clubs would openly admit they were in the clubs to perform music rather than to minster to the people.

I would be remiss not to admit that within the church and gospel music industry, not all singers are concerned with singing in the Spirit, nor do they take praise as their purpose or accept ministry as their mandate. These types of gospel performers are seen by gospel tradition bearers as entertainers who sing gospel music just to be seen or for the ego satisfaction of audience acclaim or even for the private and monetary perk of musical prestige. Their goal is to entertain and minister to a person's emotions through songs of empathetic subjects and through the purposeful execution of the emotion-stirring practices found within the gospel aesthetics. While these performances result in what appears to be a Spirit-driven performance, Dr. Glenn Hinson explains that the source is self rather than the Spirit, and the shouts are outbursts of emotion and devotional excitement rather than spiritual receipt and holy joy. Hinson writes, "Like shouts of the spirit, these experiences draw believers into fleeting epiphanies of passion; unlike holy shouts, however, they meet needs only on the emotional plane, leaving believers' souls and spirits unfulfilled."[2]

There are also people who sing gospel music outside the church simply because they like the style. For example, there are many gospel choirs and ensembles, though mainly outside of the United States, whose members are composed of nonbelievers singing gospel music solely for entertainment purposes. There are choirs in schools and universities within the United States that include a gospel song or two as part of a diverse repertoire. In this context, the gospel performance will have more of an entertainment and educational function, much like an academic performance of George Frideric Handel's *Messiah*. One can argue that any music performed outside its intended context, whether church music or music for cultural rituals or ceremonies, will lack authenticity in its performance.

It is important to recognize that it *is* the Spirit-driven aspect of the gospel music performance that separates the concepts of gospel music as ministry from that of being merely entertainment. Gospel performers who sing gospel music as part of their ministry do so with the purposeful intent of ministry—to minister the Word of God to all who listen, including themselves. Thus, gospel performers who maintain ministry to be their purpose consider themselves to be spiritual leaders, musical evangelists, or simply vessels through which the Word of God is spread.[3] Dr. Pearl Williams-Jones, one of gospel music's most revered scholars, is often quoted as saying "that in seeking to communicate the gospel message, there is little difference between the gospel singer and the gospel preacher in the approach to his subject."[4] When these artists perform, there is a commitment to stretch beyond entertainment and emotions and minister to the listener's spirit. Dr. Mellonee Burnim quotes gospel legend Clara Ward as saying, "I have always felt it is not enough to merely sing a song well—without having communicated God's message in the audience that listens."[5] For when a gospel performer ministers to a person's spirit, the message of the song continues to dwell in the heart of the listener long after the performance is over.[6] A gospel music performance that does not contain this spiritual element is often viewed as superficial by gospel tradition bearers and is often seen as "squandering the true potential of worship."[7]

VOCAL TECHNIQUE AND THE ANOINTING

When it comes to gospel music, nurturing the spiritual aspect of vocal students as part of their overall musical development is not the obligation of a vocal instructor unless he or she is qualified to do so. However, it is vital that vocal instructors understand and respect that singing with the anointing is an integral part of a gospel performance. Most important, teachers must recognize that when singing in the Spirit, the singer assumes a semiconscious state (or as gospel tradition bearers would suggest, the body transcends the mortal state as the Spirit takes over[8]), at which time the execution of proper vocal technique is no longer a priority. This concept makes it imperative for vocal instructors to encourage their singers to understand the voice, its function, and its limitations in order to make educated choices about the types of vocal productions to use and the frequency of use during performance.

During more controlled settings, such as when singing in the choir or along with the congregation; during most, if not all, rehearsals (Note: Some rehearsal settings are conducted like a church service.); when singing just for fun; and even when conversing in social settings, vocal instructors should encourage singers to use a healthy vocal technique. This does not mean that if singers know what types of vocal productions can damage the voice and what types do not, they will always choose the healthier vocal production. However, it allows singers to make choices on how to pace themselves during a single concert, busy performance weekend, or a lengthy tour.

ESTABLISHING AND ORGANIZING REPERTOIRE

Professional gospel singers should have a diverse repertoire of songs they are prepared to sing on command for church services and special events, weddings, and funerals. Depending on a person's church, associated responsibilities, and/or the singer's primary function as a soloist, there are two primary ways repertoire can be categorized. Songs can be categorized by Christian theological topics or the liturgical calendar.

Three Christian Theological Categories

All Christian theological content can be organized into three broad categories: defining/describing the Holy Trinity, Word of God/works of Christ, and reverence, prayer, and faith. As a result, music that supports this teaching can also be categorized into these three broad categories. As singers become familiar with these theological concepts and their associated functions, singers can better align their song choice with the theological topic of the day/event.

Defining/Describing the Holy Trinity   When Christians speak of the Holy Trinity, most use this language to describe the nature of God. As Father, Son, and Holy Spirit, gospel singers use melody to do theology; that is to say, much of their contribution in the worship event is not just musical but theological. They sing lyrics that biblically assist the congregation in understanding the triune nature of God and the relationship God the Father has with God the Son and the Holy Spirit. During Pentecost, for example, singers will introduce songs that speak to the power of the Holy Spirit as an advocate, comforter, and guide. During Easter, songs that speak to the blood and power of Jesus Christ, the atoning work done at the cross, and his resurrection help inform the congregation of their belief. This does not always happen in a sermon—more often than not, it happens in and through songs.

Purpose   To introduce and reintroduce the Holy Trinity (the Father, Son, and Holy Spirit) and their respective role/function to the people of God, as defined in the scriptures.

Theological Themes   Position and power of God; birth, role, and function of Jesus Christ; function and power of the Holy Spirit; acknowledging Christ for who he is (i.e., savior, provider, redeemer).

Repertoire Examples

"Jesus, Oh What a Wonderful Child" (Traditional spiritual)
"Wonderful Counselor" (Traditional spiritual)
"Hark! The Herald Angels Sing" (Charles Wesley)
"Joy to the World" (Isaac Watts)
"The Blood Will Never Lose Its Power" (Andraé Crouch)
"Changed" (Walter Hawkins)
"You Are God Alone" (Rodney Hubb Hubbard)
"You Are" (Kierra "Kiki" Sheard, J. Drew Sheard II, Angel Chisholm)
"God So Loved the World" (Lanny Wolfe)
"I Am God" (Donald Lawrence)
"Because He Lives" (Gloria Gaither and William Gaither)

Word of God/Works of Christ   Most Christians prize the scriptures as the highest authority in institutionalized Christianity. That is to say, the Bible communicates truth to the believer. Thus, in order to transmit that truth, gospel singers will often use lyrics from their song to recite scripture. These words of the song are literally taken from the Word of God for reinforcement, edification, and to assist with memorization. Psalm 119:11 says, "Thy word have I hid in my heart that I might not sin against thee." When gospel singers include scriptures in their songs, they heighten the congregations' ability to memorize scripture through the medium of music. The Word of God also invokes several redemptive themes of grace, love, mercy, and forgiveness—all subjects that many gospel singers and writers share in ministry with others who need empowerment and encouragement.

Purpose   To illustrate the Word of God and work of Christ through the acknowledgment of scripture.

Theological Themes   God's covenant/promises, teaching parables, love, miracles, grace, redemption, and mercy.

Repertoire Examples

"Great Is Thy Faithfulness" (Thomas O. Chisholm and William M. Runyan)

"I'm So Glad (Jesus Lifted Me)" (Traditional spiritual)

"Watch God Work a Miracle" (Chester D. T. Baldwin)

"He Looked beyond My Faults" (Londonderry Irish traditional melody and Dottie Rambo)

"His Eye Is on the Sparrow" (Civilla D. Martin and Charles H. Gabriel)

"God Has Smiled on Me" (Isaiah Jones Jr.)

"God Never Fails" (George Jordan)

"Jesus Is Love" (Lionel Richie)

"He's So Real" (Charles H. Nicks)

"I Am Redeemed" (Jesse Dixon)

Reverence, Prayer, and Faith   Because prayer and fasting, worship, and praise are not just songs but spiritual disciplines, many gospel singers compose lyrics that assist the Christian in prayer time with God. These songs of reverence, worship, and prayer are written and sung in such a way that the lyrics take the center focus, over and above the skillfulness of the singer.

Purpose   To describe man's relationship with and disposition toward Christ, as defined in the scriptures.

Theological Themes   Submission and acknowledgment of God's strength; significance and importance of prayer and devotion; having a relationship with God; significance and importance of worship, honor, praise, glory, adoration, and gratitude; believing and trusting in the Word of God, covenant, faith, trust, inspiration, and encouragement.

Repertoire Examples

"Christ Is All" (Kenneth Morris)

"Great Is Thy Faithfulness" (Thomas O. Chisholm and William M. Runyan)

"Jesus, I Love Calling Your Name" (Shirley Caesar)

"Precious Lord, Take My Hand" (Thomas A. Dorsey)
"It Is Well in My Soul" (Horatio G. Spafford)
"Order My Steps" (Glenn Burleigh)
"Psalm 8: O Lord, How Excellent" (Richard Smallwood)
"My Tribute" (Andraé Crouch)
"Good News" (Chester D. T. Baldwin)
"This Too Shall Pass" (Connie Harrington and Ty Lacy)

Liturgical Calendar

The liturgical calendar depicts the church calendar year according to specific events or time periods commemorating the history of salvation. Developed and implemented by the Catholic Church, other liturgical churches such as the Presbyterian, Episcopal, Methodist, and African Methodist Episcopal (AME) use this calendar on which to base their theological themes, colors, and approaches to worship. The church calendar or liturgical year is generally divided into six seasons: Advent, Christmas, Epiphany, Lent, Easter, and Pentecost. Depending on the church, Ordinary days can consist of days between Epiphany and Lent (for those churches that only recognize Epiphany as a day and not a season[9]) and Pentecost and Advent.

While each denomination may incorporate other holy days and feast days into their calendar year, developing a repertoire organized into seven liturgical categories (including Ordinary) may be an efficient way to build one's repertoire. This is particularly true as more Protestant and nondenominational churches are trending toward incorporating liturgical seasons other than Christmas and Easter into their calendar year.[10]

Advent Season: Coming of Christ

Time Period   Four Sundays before Christmas. The first day generally falls on the last Sunday of November or the first Sunday in December, and it lasts until Christmas Eve.

Purpose   The beginning of the Christian year is marked by the first day of the Advent season. Advent marks a season that commemorates the preparation for the coming of Christ and the preparation for Christmas. It is a season of hope and longing, of joyful expectation and peaceful preparation.[11]

Theological Themes   Waiting, expecting, hoping, yearning, needing a savior, the coming of the Messiah, and hoping for the second advent of the Messiah.[12]

Repertoire Examples

"I Want to Be Ready" (Traditional spiritual)

"O Come, O Come, Emmanuel" (Thomas Helmore, John Mason Neale, and Henry Sloane Coffin)

"Soon and Very Soon Music" (Andraé Crouch)

"We Shall Behold Him" (Dottie Rambo)

"Sign Me Up" (Kevin Yancy and Jerome Metcalfe)

"Already Here" (Brian Courtney Wilson)

"I'm Going Away" (Walter Hawkins)

"O Come" (Israel Houghton)

"For Your Glory" (Mia Booker)

Christmas Season: Birth of Christ

Time Period   Twelve days of Christmas, December 25–January 5.

Purpose   The Christmas season commemorates a twelve-day season celebrating the birth of Jesus Christ through many different symbols and traditions, special music, and activities.[13]

Theological Themes   Celebration of the incarnation of the Word of God, salvation, joy, kingdom, peace, and giving.[14]

Repertoire Examples

"Go Tell It on the Mountain" (Negro spiritual, adapted by John W. Work)

"O Holy Night" (by Adolphe Adam; John S. Dwight)

"Heaven's Christmas Tree" (Charles Tindley)

"Messiah Now Has Come" (Nolan Williams Jr.)

"Messiah Has Come" (Donnie McClurkin)

"All Because a Child Was Born" (BeBe Winans)

"Now Behold a Lamb" (Kirk Franklin)

"Born to Die" (Hezekiah Walker)

Epiphany: Jesus Is Lord

Time Period   Day of Epiphany, January 6, through Transfiguration Sunday (or Last Epiphany), according to most liturgical denominations.[15]

Purpose   In the Christian tradition, Epiphany marks the miraculous manifestation or shining forth of God in human form, that is, in the person of Jesus. The day of Epiphany represents the day the wise men or three kings came to give Jesus gifts and the universal import of salvation in Christ.[16] This season recognizes the other momentous events that include Jesus being baptized by John the Baptist, Jesus's first miracle of turning water into wine, and his transfiguration, where he metamorphosed into a divine state, becoming radiant with the light of God as he communed with the Father on a mountaintop (Mark 9:2–8).

Theological Themes   Miracles of Jesus, three kings, giving and receiving, hospitality, baptism, and living as "children of light."[17]

Repertoire Examples

"Behold the Star" (Traditional spiritual)
"Jesus, What a Wonderful Child" (Traditional spiritual)
"Jesus, the Light of the World" (George D. Elderin; Charles Wesley)
"Christmas Star" (Kevin Savigar and Kimmie Rhodes)
"Because This Child Was Born" (Shelton Becton)
"Follow That Star" (Edwin Hawkins)
"What Shall I Render" (Margaret Pleasant Douroux)
"Watch God Work a Miracle" (Chester D. T. Baldwin)
"Lamb of God" (David Mullen and Nicole C. Mullen)

Lent: Dying of Self

Time Period   Forty days prior to Easter (not including Sundays), starting with Ash Wednesday. Holy Week is the last week of Lent.

Purpose   As a period of preparation, Lent has historically included the instruction of persons for baptism and profession of faith on Easter Sunday; the calling back of those who have become estranged from the church; and efforts by all Christians to deepen their piety, devotion, and readiness to mark the death and resurrection of their Savior.[18]

Theological Themes   Baptismal spirituality, importance of heart-felt repentance, morality, human limitations, need for a savior, self-denial, the death of Jesus and its meaning, love for one another (Maundy Thursday), preparation for Good Friday and Easter.[19]

Repertoire Examples

"I Surrender All" (Judson W. Van De Venter; Winfield S. Weeden)
"He Looked beyond My Fault" (Traditional; Dottie Rambo)
"I Need Thee Every Hour" (Robert Lowry and Annie Hawkes)
"I Need You Now" (Smokey Norful)
"I'm Available to You" (Carlis Moody Jr.)
"I Give Myself Away" (Sam Hinn and William McDowell)
"Open My Heart" (James Quentin Wright, James Samuel Harris III, Terry Lewis, and Yolanda Adams)
"I Need Your Glory" (James Fortune)
"Take Me to the King" (Kirk Franklin)

Easter: Season of Resurrection

Time Period   Easter Sunday through Pentecost Sunday, fifty days.

Purpose   The resurrection of Christ is the basis of the Christian faith. The Apostle Paul wrote, "If Christ is not risen, our faith is in vain" (1 Cor. 15:12–20). The resurrection of Christ culminates in his ascension into heaven and the descent of the Holy Spirit on Pentecost, which inaugurates the mission of the church to spread the good news of salvation to all the world.[20]

Theological Themes   Salvation, victory, new life, joy, Christ reigns.[21]

Repertoire examples

"He Lives" (Alfred H. Ackley)
"He Decided to Die" (Margaret Douroux)
"Because He Lives" (Gloria Gaither and William J. Gaither)
"When Sunday Comes" (Donald Lawrence)
"Celebrate (He Lives)" (Noel Hall and Fred Hammond)
"Oh! What Man" (Tyrone J. Hemphill)
"That Name" (Richard Smallwood)
"I Will Serve Him" (Chester D. T. Baldwin)
"Don't Cry" (Kirk Franklin)

Pentecost Season

Time Period Starts on the day of Pentecost, ending date varies. Some denominations only celebrate the day of Pentecost and treat the other dates during the season as Ordinary Time. Other single-day celebrations that occur during this season are Trinity Sunday (the Sunday after Pentecost), Christ the King Sunday (the last Sunday before Advent), Reformation Sunday, and All Saints' Day.

Purpose The name *Pentecost* from the Greek word for "fifty." According to the book of Acts, on the fiftieth day after Easter, the day of Pentecost, believers of Christ were gathered in the upper room and the Holy Spirit descended upon them. They became filled with the Spirit, and they began to speak in other tongues as the Spirit enabled them (Acts 2:1–6).

Theological Themes The outpouring of the Holy Spirit; the birth of the church; power for service in the church and the world; the inclusion of all of God's people in ministry; recognizing the presence, power, and majesty of the King.[22]

Repertoire Examples

"Sweet, Sweet, Spirit" (Doris Akers)
"In the Presence of Jehovah" (Geron Davis and Becky Davis)
"What Is This?" (Joseph May)
"Awesome God" (Rich Mullins)
"Let Us Worship Him" (Armirris Palmore)
"Spirit Fall Down" (Melvin Barnes)
"Holy Ghost Power" (Percy Gray Jr.)
"The Presence of the Lord in Here" (Kurt Carr)
"Rain on Us" (Daniel Moore)
"Fill Me Up" (William Reagan)

Ordinary: Christian Life

Time Period Ordinary Time comprises two periods in the church year. The first period of Ordinary Time can last as long as December 26 to the day before Easter Sunday (for some denominations). The second and longest period can last as long as the day after Pentecost up to the first day of Advent.

Purpose   Ordinary Time takes its name from the fact that the weeks are numbered (ordinal numbers are numbers indicating positions in a series, such as fifth, sixth, and seventh).[23] This time period is dedicated to the teaching of other topics of Christian life and one's walk with Christ.

Theological Themes   Various.

Suggested Repertoire   See the three theological categories.

SONGS FOR FUNERALS

As a professional singer, singing for funerals is inevitable, and depending on one's position on the music ministry staff at church, it is required. While it is typical for the family to specifically request songs for the services, it is just as typical for the family to ask the singer for recommendations. Below are a few suggestions to get singers started with repertoire for this occasion.

"Precious Lord, Take My Hand" (Thomas Dorsey)
"How Great Thou Art" (Stuart K. Hine)
"It Is Well in My Soul" (Horatio G. Spafford)
"I Know Who Holds Tomorrow" (Ira F. Stamphill)
"'Tis So Sweet to Trust in Jesus" (Louisa M. R. Stead)
"What a Friend We Have in Jesus" (Joseph M. Scriven)
"His Eye Is on the Sparrow" (Civilla D. Martin)
"Going Up Yonder" (Walter Hawkins)
"I Can Only Imagine" (Bart Millard)
"'Till We Meet Again" (Kirk Franklin)

SONGS FOR WEDDINGS

As with funerals, singing at weddings is also inevitable, and depending on one's position on the music ministry staff at church, it is also required. While it is typical for the family to specifically request songs for the services, professional singers should be prepared to provide recommendations. Below are a few suggestions to get singers started with repertoire for this occasion.

"The Prayer" (Carole Bayer Sager and David Foster)
"The Lord's Prayer" (Albert Hay Malotte)
"Ave Maria" (Johann Sebastian Bach, Charles Gounod)
"Amazing Grace" (John Newton)
"I Found You (Cindy's Song)" (BeBe Winans)
"I Promise (Wedding Song)" (K. O. Thomas)
"Once in a Lifetime" (Smokie Norful and Derrick D. O. A. Allen)
"Dance with Me" (Chris Payne Dupre)
"My Heart Says Yes" (Troy Sneed)
"Love" (Kirk Franklin)

CONCLUSION

Regardless of the song, gospel singers should always strive to minister from an honest and genuine place. Song selections should be chosen carefully to ensure that they have both personal and spiritual meaning and relevance. Even in situations in which singers are not performing gospel for ministerial purposes, passionate execution of the text will help to bring the music alive. Take the time to analyze the lyrics of the song so that at the very least, the story can be told with conviction and emotional variation.

NOTES

1. Raymond Wise, "Defining African American Gospel Music by Tracing Its Historical and Musical Development from 1900 to 2000" (PhD diss., Ohio State University, 2002).

2. Glenn Douglas Hinson, "When the Words Roll and the Fire Flows: Spirit, Style and Experience in African-American Gospel Performance" (PhD diss., University of Pennsylvania, 1989), 326.

3. Horace Clarence Boyer, "A Comparative Analysis of Traditional and Contemporary Gospel Music," in *More than Dancing: Essays on Afro-American Music and Musicians*, ed. Irene V. Jackson (Westport, CT: Greenwood,

1985), 127–45; Mellonee Burnim, "The Black Gospel Music Tradition: A Complex of Ideology, Aesthetic, and Behavior," in *More than Dancing: Essays on Afro-American Music and Musicians*, ed. Irene V. Jackson (Westport, CT: Greenwood, 1985), 147–67; Burnim, "Functional Dimensions of Gospel Music Performance," *Western Journal of Black Studies* 12, no. 2 (1988): 112–21; Lloyd Benjamin Mallory Jr., "The Choral Singing of the Negro Spiritual versus the Singing of Contemporary Gospel without Harming the Vocal Apparatus: A Choral Concept" (DMA diss., University of California, Los Angeles, 2006; ProQuest Order No. 3240942); Wise, "Defining African American Gospel Music."

4. Pearl Williams-Jones, "Afro-American Gospel Music: A Crystallization of the Black Aesthetic," *Ethnomusicology* 19, no. 3 (1975): 381.

5. Burnim, "Functional Dimensions of Gospel Music Performance," 117.

6. Hinson, "When the Words Roll and the Fire Flows."

7. Ibid., 327.

8. Ibid.

9. Presbyterian Church (U.S.A.), *Liturgical Year (Supplemental Liturgical Resources)* (Louisville, KY: Westminster/John Knox Press, 1992); Calvin Institute of Christian Worship Library Resource, "Calvin Institute of Christian Worship: Songs for Ordinary Time," Calvin Institute of Christian Worship website August 8, 2014, http://worship.calvin.edu/resources/resource-library/songs-for-ordinary-time/.

10. Kate Shellnutt, "Evangelicals Making Liturgical Traditions Their Own," *Houston Chronicle*, April 23, 2011, www.chron.com/life/houston-belief/article/Evangelicals-making-liturgical-traditions-their-1597378.php.

11. Felix Just, J.S., "Resources for Liturgy and Prayer for the Seasons of Advent and Christmas," Catholic Lectionary website, December 7, 2015, http://catholic-resources.org/Lectionary/Seasons-Advent-Christmas.htm.

12. Mark D. Roberts, "Introduction to the Christian Year: How Can It Make a Difference in Your Relationship with God?" *Reflections on Christ, Church, and Culture* (blog), 2011, www.patheos.com/blogs/markdroberts/series/introduction-to-the-christian-year/.

13. Just, "Resources for Liturgy and Prayer."

14. Roberts, "Introduction to the Christian Year."

15. Calvin Institute of Christian Worship Library Resource, "Songs for Ordinary Time"; Presbyterian Church (U.S.A.), *Liturgical Year*.

16. Roberts, "Introduction to the Christian Year."

17. Joan Huyser-Honig, "Epiphany in Missional Churches," Calvin Institute of Christian Worship website, December 22, 2006, http://worship.calvin.edu/resources/resource-library/epiphany-in-missional-churches/.

18. Calvin Institute of Christian Worship, "Lent Planning Guide," Calvin Institute of Christian Worship website, February 1, 2005, http://worship.calvin.edu/resources/resource-library/lent-planning-guide.

19. Ibid.; Roberts, "Introduction to the Christian Year."

20. Scott Richert, "When Is Easter This Year?" About Religion & Spirituality, About.com, 2016, http://catholicism.about.com/od/easter/f/When-Is-Easter.htm.

21. Roberts, "Introduction to the Christian Year."

22. Ibid.

23. Richert, "When Is Easter This Year?"

WORKS CITED

Boyer, Horace Clarence. "A Comparative Analysis of Traditional and Contemporary Gospel Music." In *More than Dancing: Essays on Afro-American Music and Musicians*, edited by Irene V. Jackson, 127–45. Westport, CT: Greenwood, 1985.

Burnim, Mellonee. "The Black Gospel Music Tradition: A Complex of Ideology, Aesthetic, and Behavior." In *More than Dancing: Essays on Afro-American Music and Musicians*, edited by Irene V. Jackson, 147–67. Westport, CT: Greenwood, 1985.

———. "Functional Dimensions of Gospel Music Performance." *Western Journal of Black Studies* 12, no. 2 (1988): 112–21.

Calvin Institute of Christian Worship. "Lent Planning Guide." Calvin Institute of Christian Worship website, February 1, 2005. http://worship.calvin.edu/resources/resource-library/lent-planning-guide.

Calvin Institute of Christian Worship Library Resource. "Calvin Institute of Christian Worship: Songs for Ordinary Time." Calvin Institute of Christian Worship website, August 8, 2014. http://worship.calvin.edu/resources/resource-library/songs-for-ordinary-time/.

Hinson, Glenn Douglas. "When the Words Roll and the Fire Flows: Spirit, Style and Experience in African-American Gospel Performance." Doctoral Dissertation, University of Pennsylvania, 1989.

Huyser-Honig, Joan. "Epiphany in Missional Churches." Calvin Institute of Christian Worship website, December 22, 2006. http://worship.calvin.edu/resources/resource-library/epiphany-in-missional-churches/.

Just, Felix, J. S. "Resources for Liturgy and Prayer for the Seasons of Advent and Christmas." The Catholic Lectionary website, December 7, 2015. http://catholic-resources.org/Lectionary/Seasons-Advent-Christmas.htm.

Mallory, Lloyd Benjamin, Jr. "The Choral Singing of the Negro Spiritual versus the Singing of Contemporary Gospel without Harming the Vocal Apparatus: A Choral Concept." DMA diss., University of California, Los Angeles, 2006. ProQuest Order No. 3240942.

Presbyterian Church (U.S.A.). *Liturgical Year (Supplemental Liturgical Resources)*. Louisville, KY: Westminster/John Knox Press, 1992.

Richert, Scott. "When Is Easter This Year?" About Religion & Spirituality, About.com, 2016. http://catholicism.about.com/od/easter/f/When-Is-Easter.htm.

Roberts, Mark D. "Introduction to the Christian Year: How Can It Make a Difference in Your Relationship with God?" *Reflections on Christ, Church, and Culture* (blog), 2011. www.patheos.com/blogs/markdroberts/series/introduction-to-the-christian-year/.

Shellnutt, Kate. "Evangelicals Making Liturgical Traditions Their Own." *Houston Chronicle*, April 23, 2011. www.chron.com/life/houston-belief/article/Evangelicals-making-liturgical-traditions-their-1597378.php.

Williams-Jones, Pearl. "Afro-American Gospel Music: A Crystallization of the Black Aesthetic." *Ethnomusicology* 19, no. 3 (1975): 373–85.

Wise, Raymond. "Defining African American Gospel Music by Tracing Its Historical and Musical Development from 1900 to 2000." PhD diss., Ohio State University, 2002.

NOTES FOR THE PROFESSIONAL

There are many aspects to being a professional singer that cannot be taught and must be acquired through experience. This chapter is intended to be a starting point and provide the guidelines necessary to develop one's own strategies for being efficient as a soloist, director, and/or teacher. When reading this chapter, use the suggestions as a launching point from which each component can be further refined according to one's own needs, circumstances, and schedule. The considerations listed will not work for every singer in every circumstance. However, understanding the reasoning or explanation behind the consideration will allow singers to personalize each aspect as necessary.

CONSIDERATIONS FOR ALL SINGERS

No matter the medium through which one chooses to sing gospel music, professional singers need strategies to keep them mentally and physically prepared for the tasks. There are many aspects to preparing and maintaining the body for singing in a performance or rehearsal setting. The most prominent consideration for the gospel singer includes the following: proper sleep, proper hydration, warming up/cooling down the

voice, monitoring vocal output, use of amplification, and being mindful
of one's vocal limitations.

Proper Sleep

Sleep is possibly the most undervalued healing remedy by students
and amateur performers. It is during sleep that the body is able to reju-
venate cells and produce hormones to help keep the body healthy and
functioning at an optimal level. The National Institute of Health states
that people who get the recommended amount of sleep at night tend
to perform better at mentally challenging tasks and creative problem
solving than those without the recommended amount of sleep.[1] Worship and ministry should not be done while sleep walking/singing. The
purposeful and improvisatory nature of gospel music requires its participants to be actively engaged, body, mind, and spirit; otherwise the
energized delivery of the message will be compromised.

When singing, if a person is tired the whole body is affected, including the voice. With lack of sleep, the energy necessary to properly support the body is compromised, it takes longer to warm the voice, and
depending on the level of fatigue, vocal stamina can be greatly compromised and vocal fatigue can ensue.[2] Vocal fatigue is defined by the feeling of laryngeal discomfort along with an increase in vocal or respiratory
effort needed to produce a normal tone.[3] Without ample time to recover
and with continued heavy vocal use—as when having to sing in more
than one service in a day—it becomes progressively more difficult to recover.[4] Singers may use caffeine, energy drinks, and other supplements
to help "wake the body up," but these products are often dehydrating
and still ineffective when used in excess. There are no shortcuts to getting proper sleep. While lack of sleep isn't the only contributor to vocal
fatigue, it can certainly be an avoidable factor.

Proper Hydration

Professional singers need to be strategic about their water intake.
Literature in voice science readily recognizes that the hydration level of
the vocal folds significantly impacts vocal function and states that proper
hydration significantly contributes to the maintenance and recovery of

the vocal folds.[5] There is actually a thin layer of mucus that sits on the outermost layer of the vocal folds (the epithelium) and functions as a protective coating. Studies show that the hydration level of this layer of liquid is directly related to how easily the vocal folds vibrate and achieve regular vibratory patterns.[6] When the vocal folds become dehydrated and the mucus becomes thick and sticky, the vocal folds become stiff, and the vibratory pattern that results is inconsistent (sometime audibly noticeable in the form of the voice breaking/cracking when trying to sustain a tone).[7] Under these conditions it takes more lung pressure and overall physical effort to start and sustain a sung tone, in addition to the vocal folds themselves generating more heat as a result of increased friction during vocal fold vibration.[8] Vocal fatigue, in addition to other vocal problems, will commonly result.

Proper maintenance of hydration is the typical treatment for the prevention of vocal fold dehydration; therefore, professional singers need to be mindful of their hydration levels at all times. Generally speaking, a good measurement for calculating how much water a person should consume in one day is to take a person's weight and divide that number by two to get the number of ounces of water.[9] For example, a person weighing 150 pounds should consume 75 ounces of water ($150 \div 2 = 75$), a little over 2 liters per day. Singers may find it helpful to drink twenty to thirty ounces of water forty-five minutes to an hour before singing in rehearsals or services. This gives the body ample time to absorb water intake and gives the singer enough time to use the restroom before it is time to perform. The temperature of the water can be based on the singer's preference. Singers performing in multiple services should strive to drink sixteen to twenty ounces of water per service, ideally before and during the service if possible (understanding that most praise and worship teams and choirs do not or cannot drink water during their fifteen- to forty-five-minute performance set).

Aiming to drink at least one and a half liters of water by noon may be a great way to jump-start the daily requirements without having to worry about having too much water too late in the evening. For those who have a hard time drinking their total required water intake, certain foods such as cucumbers, applesauce, watermelon, lettuce, pineapple, and carrots can help meet the hydration requirement.[10] In addition to drinking water to hydrate the vocal folds, singers can incorporate environmental hydration into their routine by applying moisture directly to the vocal folds. Steamers and humidifiers are commonly used to add moisture to the air quality, so when a person inhales the moisture can reach the vocal folds more quickly. This is particularly important when traveling or spending long periods of time in spaces with dry air.

Singers should also be aware of dehydrating substances and activities, such as certain foods and medications, poor air quality, and even perspiration. Dehydrating foods and beverages include alcohol, certain prescription and over-the-counter medications, certain herbs, protein, asparagus, cured meats, fried foods, sugary drinks, and caffeine (when consumed in excess). Environmentally dehydrating effects singers need to be aware of and prepared for include dry air or certain air-conditioning and environmental pollutions and/or allergens. Finally, when a person sweats his or her body loses water, whether due to physical activity or simply hot, humid weather.[11] If the person does not replenish the water lost, he or she will become dehydrated. Singers ultimately need to be prepared for all circumstances by increasing their water intake as needed, as determined by how much water they are taking in and how much water they are losing in a given day.

Warming Up and Cooling Down

While unfortunately not the most common practice within the church community, it is imperative for singers to warm up their voices before worship service or rehearsal in order to physically prepare their instruments for the tasks to be performed. The typical strategy of using the first song as a warm-up piece only works when the first song is strategically selected for that purpose. Most songs do not fit in this category. The time required to warm up the voice varies from person to person, as well as depending on the time of the day and on the vocal health of the singers. In other words, a well-rested, well-hydrated singer may only require a fifteen- to thirty-minute warm-up first thing in the morning. A tired, dehydrated singer may need thirty- to forty-five minutes to warm the voice. It is very personal and requires singers to be in tune with their bodies and be able to recognize what their voice feels like when warm. With a warm voice, the physical effort required to produce sound is greatly decreased, it is easier to sustain breath flow and maintain breath support, and it becomes easier to sing throughout one's vocal range.[12] Much like any other physical or mental exercise, the better conditioned the body is to perform a specific task, the easier it will be to execute that task.

Singers need to be strategic about how to vary their warm-up routine depending on the different times of the day. In other words, the vocal warm-up one uses first thing in the morning or after a long nap has a very different focus from the warm-up singers use for a midday or evening performance or rehearsal. For example, warm-up exercises performed first thing in the morning or after the body has been resting for an extended period of time must incorporate warming up the entire body as part of the warm-up routine. This might include but is not limited to deep breathing, stretching, neck rolls, jumping, squatting, panting like a dog, humming, and singing easy slides from the bottom to the top of the vocal range. A warm-up routine for someone who has already been physically and/or vocally active might be centered on recalibrating vocal effort, stabilizing the breath flow for singing, and focusing the sound. This might include deep breathing, stretching, singing long tones, and easy slides but might not add aggressive physical warm-ups like jumping or squatting.

Vocal cool-down exercises are just as important as vocal warm-ups. The rigor of rehearsal and performance can tax the voice, even if the singer does not perceive it. While the concept of implementing cool-down exercises is a relatively new standard in voice training, studies are showing that singers who cool down after a performance recover faster and experience a decreased effort the following day.[13] Physiologically, the function of specific cool-down exercises for the voice is synonymous to the cool-down exercises recommended after extensive physical exercises like running or lifting weights. Its purpose is to gently coax the voice back from the extreme vocal range and dynamic levels achieved during a performance or rehearsal through specific exercises that strategically induce a comfortable, unpressured speaking range.[14] These exercises include but are not limited to Ingo Titze's straw-phonation exercises (i.e., singing slides from the bottom to the top of the range through a straw), humming, and lightly vocalizing in the vocal registration that was less dominant during the performance (i.e., head voice for the gospel singer).[15]

Monitoring Vocal Effort

Previously discussed in this book was the importance of anatomical and kinesthetic awareness for the sake of understanding how the voice functions. Professional singers should also use this awareness to monitor their vocal effort. There are two aspects of vocal effort that singers need to be able to self-monitor: vocal strain and vocal fatigue. Vocal strain occurs when the voice is pushed past its comfortable limits in terms of singing or speaking too high or too loud or through other vocal behavior yielding excessive pressure at the level of the vocal folds for extended periods of time. Vocal fatigue, as previously mentioned, occurs when there is a feeling of laryngeal discomfort along with an increase in vocal or respiratory effort needed to produce a normal tone. While proper hydration, vocal fitness training, and style conditioning can help prevent vocal fatigue and vocal strain, there will always be instances in which a performance or rehearsal may push the performer past his or her vocal limits.

The vigilance in recognizing that one's vocal limit has been reached or even surpassed is imperative for singers so that they can make educated decisions regarding how to proceed for the rest of the performance or rehearsal. For example, a singer might feel an increased sense of vocal fatigue after giving an emotionally intense performance of a song or might feel his or her throat close in response to being emotionally overwhelmed in the middle of a song. In these cases, getting through the rest of the song or performance may include strategic decisions like ending the song in a lighter sound, getting the congregation or audience to sing a repeated vamp section or refrain, or extending a segment of a song during which the music gets quiet and the singer allows for and encourages corporate worship (i.e., the collective praise, gratitude, love, and honor of God through congregational songs, prayers, scripture reading, and other collective actions). Singers may also, depending on the vocal effort extended, recognize that they should do less talking in the days that follow, systematically hydrate the body and voice, and get some rest so that the body can fully recover before the next performance or rehearsal. When singers carefully monitor their vocal effect, they will also be able to recognize if their voice takes longer than normal to recover or if the voice doesn't fully recover at all and can thus get the necessary help from voice-care professionals in a timely manner.

Consider developing a personalized vocal intensity chart as found in the appendix section.

Amplification Is a Must

Gospel singers must use amplification in rehearsals and performances. There is a common misconception that just because a person can sing loud or can project their voice it means he or she does not need amplification. This is synonymous to a body builder who regularly lifts five hundred pounds during weight training deciding to carry one hundred pounds for ninety minutes straight because she or he can. It may not feel like much weight at first, but that same one hundred pounds will feel heavier and heavier as time progresses. This is also true for singers. Rehearsing or performing without amplification may feel all right at the time, but it is usually accompanied by vocal fatigue by the end of the session or even the next day.

Always request a microphone for rehearsals and ensure that there is appropriate amplification for the performance, particularly if you are singing for more than five minutes. Most churches/venues in which gospel music is performed or rehearsed are not acoustically designed to carry the voice. When electronic instruments are added, the voice cannot compete. Therefore, singers should consider purchasing a small amp or monitor that can be taken to rehearsals, as well as owning their own sound system to use for performances if such a system is not readily available. It's better to have something than nothing at all.

When amplification is provided, singers have to pay close attention to where monitors or speakers are placed in comparison to where they will stand when performing. Not all churches have great sound systems and in-ear monitors run by experienced sound persons. In fact, the majority of churches do not, particularly older and smaller churches. Oftentimes there may not be any monitors at all for singers, and singers will have to depend on the speakers that feed into the congregation to hear themselves. When singing under these circumstances, singers need to locate where the sound is coming from and then try to position themselves as best they can so that they can hear themselves well. This might mean standing farther away from the drums and electronic instruments, standing closer to the congregation, or even standing in the middle aisle (if the cords reach that far). Singers need not be concerned with being too close to the congregation, as it can be considered an opportunity to become more intimate. Singers only need to focus on finding the best place to hear themselves so that they do not feel the need to push their voice to be heard.

Recognize the Limitations of the Human Voice

Singers cannot reproduce sounds acoustically that are produced electronically. Often soloists and choirs will burn out trying to sing a song exactly like it was heard on a recording, vocal effects and all. Singers and directors must recognize that not only are electronic enhancements added to every aspect of a well-produced recording, but there may be a certain level of precision or vocal effects that just cannot be reproduced without electronic manipulations and thus should not be attempted.

Singers also need to be true to their own expression and instrument. It is not beneficial for the singer to imitate a sound that his or her body was not designed to create. Trying to imitate the vocal expressions of another recording artist when the body types and vocal capacities are not similar only results in fatigue and can potentially damage the voice. Singers should always strive to achieve their version of a particular style or emotional expression. Everyone can't sing every sound the same way with the same level of ease and expertise. But every person can sing to his or her true potential.

NOTES FOR THE WORSHIP LEADER

A worship leader has the important function of leading the congregation in corporate worship. Corporate worship emphasizes the offering of words, songs, and actions, which enables a collective praise, gratitude, love, and honor of God. Through the use of song, scripture, and testimony, worship leaders are responsible for engaging the congregation and leading them in the recognition and reverence of God's power and works. As a result, there are a few considerations that worship leaders should be aware of. They include selecting music, stage presence, engaging the audience, communing with God, and keeping the worship experience God centered.

Selecting Music for Worship

Do not let trends in music determine the worship music for praise and worship; focus on those songs that speak to the congregation.[16] Worship leaders should always be mindful of their congregation and pick songs to inspire the congregants to collective worship. Sometimes the latest worship songs do not resonate with the majority of the congregation, and the last thing a worship leader should want is for an intended time period of corporate worship to become a self-service concert in which the congregants are focused on the singer and not the worship of God.

Stage Presence

Do the worship leaders appear to believe what they are singing about? Do they seem disengaged? Do they seem inauthentic in their presentation? These are all important questions that every worship leader and team member should consider and address. As it is the worship leader's goal to encourage congregants to collectively worship the Lord, his or her own stage presence, and the presence of everyone else on stage, can be a prominent factor in his or her effectiveness as a worship leader. There is a thin line between performance and authentic worship. Singers are perceived as being more effective in their delivery when they look and sound convincing. This is not to say that worship leaders should be good actors, as discerning congregants will be able to tell when a heart is not pure for ministry. However, one's stage presence has a direct correlation to believability. The use of body language, expressive gestures, and maintaining eye contact with the congregation are a few things that help leaders to engage their audience.[17]

Perfecting the art of worship leading is a skill leaders have to continuously nourish throughout their careers. Singers should watch videos of themselves to assess if there might be anything they do during worship that comes across as awkward, disengaging, or distracting to congregants. This includes their physical presentation (i.e., their outer appearance and body language), their musical presentation (i.e., whether they are singing too loud, too complex, or singing so much that they overpower the congregation), and their dynamic with the congregation (i.e., engaging the audience through words and scriptures).

Engaging the Audience

A worship leader is not effective if the congregation is not involved in the worship process. Worship leaders should actively look into the congregation to see if people are actively participating in worship, whether in terms of singing along, rocking, or waving their hands. If they are not participating, the worship leader needs to make purposeful moves to encourage the congregation to get involved. Sometime congregants need to be instructed and/or reminded that their participation is required and expected. If the congregants are not participating because the song is unfamiliar, it may mean taking the time to teach it to the congregation as a worship tool by explaining and reinforcing the message of each phrase. This can be accomplished by repeating a particular section of the song or refrain and then calling out encouraging demands like, "Now let me hear you sing it" or "If you know God is worthy, sing it like you mean it!" Worship leaders have to be prepared to interject scripture, personal testimony, or encouraging words that aim to nourish the worship process and to help the congregation focus on giving their all when expressing God's worthiness.

Communing with God

Worship leaders should be diligent about spending time with God throughout the week in private devotion and worship. An experienced worship leader recognizes that in order to lead others in worship efficiently, he or she has to be intentional when it comes to the continual commitment to spiritual formation (i.e., the process of Christian formation: being formed into the image of Christ)[18] and spiritual disciplines (e.g., prayer, devotions, and the reading of scriptures) of his or her own self.[19] Preparation for worship is not something that begins the morning of the service or even the night before. However, the night before and morning of can be the time period during which prayer requests might shift from personal spiritual development and communication to humbly ask God to use the worship leader's body, mind, and spirit as he pleases during worship to ensure that it is not for oneself but that God be glorified.

Keeping Worship God Centered

One of the worst things a worship leader can do is make the worship experience about the glorification of him- or herself, his or her talents, or his or her abilities to lead the congregation in having an emotional experience. A God-centered worship experience is defined as directing or formulating the worship experience toward honoring or focusing on God.[20] According to John 4:23–24, genuine worship is worship executed in Spirit (meaning one cannot worship fully without the Holy Spirit) and in truth (meaning the truth of God as depicted in the scriptures).[21] This includes maintaining a philosophy that worship is for God, acknowledging that worship is performed with the help of the Holy Spirit, selecting songs based on biblical principles, directing all praise efforts to God, and consistently reinforcing all these concepts to the congregation.

NOTES FOR THE CHOIR MEMBER/CHOIR DIRECTOR

The choir is the most prominent performance medium in the church setting. Since choirs generally contain singers of varying abilities and performance experiences, there are some things choir directors and choir members need to consider when worshiping and rehearsing in this medium. The most prominent considerations for gospel choir directors and choir members are the following: incorporating warming up and cooling down, running a structured rehearsal, preserving the voice when in rehearsal mode, recording rehearsals, and rehearsing in a U shape or circle.

Warming Up and Cooling Down

Church choir rehearsals are generally held on weekday evenings. In most cases, everyone involved, including the director, is coming off a long day of work or school and may feel tired and out of focus. Directors should carve out time in the beginning of a rehearsal to warm up the singers before they start rehearsing songs. Choir warm-up should consist of deep breathing and stretching, light aerobic exercises (e.g., rocking from side to side or marching/walking around the sanctuary while singing), and strategically chosen songs or vocalises focusing on sustaining vowels sounds and using staccato. This could be accomplished by taking the chorus or vamp of a song already in the choir's repertoire, starting the song in a lower key than usual, and then modulating the chorus up by half steps.

For example, I would use eight bars or the full sixteen-bar chorus of the song "Lord, Help Me to Hold Out" by Harrison E. Johnson as performed by Rev. James Cleveland or as performed by John P. Kee because it is up tempo (which means the choir can rock to the beat), it uses sustained notes in each phrase (to help strengthen and stabilize the tone), it includes a melodic pattern that can be performed as staccato (to engage the support muscles), and it has a range of a perfect fifth. Instead of singing the song in the original key of G with the original lyrics, choirs can start the song a major third lower in the key of E♭, and sing a vowel sound [u] in place of the words. After one chorus or excerpt is complete, modulate the excerpt by one half step to the key of E and change the vowel sound to [o], then F and change the vowel sound, then F♯ and change the vowel sound, and so on. Because of the simplicity of the song, as the modulations continue, I could add style-conditioning components like swells and crescendos as desired in order to increase the attentiveness and synchronization of the choir.

Depending on the demands of the songs the choir will be performing, each vocal section should warm up to, at minimum, one whole step higher than their highest note as notated in their vocal part. In other words, comparing all the songs in terms of pitch range for each part for all the songs to be rehearsed or performed that day, determine the highest note in each part (e.g., the soprano part might be an F5), and then make sure to warm up each vocal section one whole step higher than their highest note (e.g., the soprano section would warm up to a G5).

Choirs should also consider reserving time for a vocal cooldown at the end of the rehearsal. The function of cool-down exercises is to bring the voice back to an unpressured speaking range after having being extensively used.[22] Cool-down exercises don't have to be long; five to ten minutes can do wonders for the voice. An example of a choir cool-down regimen is one that begins with taking slow, deep breaths and then singing an unpressured descending sigh starting on a pitch near the top of one's range and descending to the bottom of one's range with every exhale. Then using the chorus of a song like Walter Hawkins's "Be Grateful"—which I would use because of its small range of a major third, use of stepwise motion, and long, sustained melodic phrases—the choir can sing the chorus on the [u] vowel sound softly and unpressured, meditating on God, while someone gives the dismissal prayer. This regimen at the end of rehearsal functions both as vocal cooldown and as a spiritual and mental reinforcement that the rehearsal and performance intend to glorify God. Gospel choir songs generally sit in a high tessitura (i.e., the upper part of the vocal range). Therefore, singers may tire sooner or take longer to recover from vocal fatigue if the voice is not properly warmed up and cooled down after rehearsals.

Running a Structured Rehearsal

Good preparation typically yields good results. Prepare goals for rehearsal ahead of time. Structure the rehearsal, depending on the time allotted, so that the choir has time to: (1) pray and warm up; (2) run through or learn the new song(s); (3) take a short break for announcements; (4) rehearse the songs to be performed for the upcoming service; and (5) pray and cool down. If the songs being performed for the month or season are preselected, consider giving the choir the song list or a CD of the recordings so they can make themselves familiar with the material before it is taught. Recording artist and minister of music Lonnie Hunter says he maximizes rehearsal time by teaching the hardest vocal part first, which is usually the alto part, and asking other sections to join in with their part one section at a time without teaching it. This way he only has to correct the wrong notes instead of teach the whole part note by note.[23] Experienced gospel choir members can generally pick out their part, so it is perfectly fine to give them the authority to take that initiative. When choir members are involved in the learning process, it helps strengthen their skills as musicians, it builds their confidence as individual singers, and it also helps with the overall retention and accuracy of their part. Overall, when preparing for and running rehearsals, establish goals and expectations and be consistent about seeing them through, with little down time in between. Choir members tend to be more attentive when structure is in place.

Preserving the Voice When in Learning/Teacher Mode

Choir directors should reserve singing at performance volumes and intensity for the final run-through of a song, not while learning it. During the learning process, neither the choir director nor choir members should sing the parts at the same intensity level used to perform the music. Consider using a light, unpressured registration such as falsetto/head voice or a light chest mixed registration when teaching and learning parts. Both choir directors and designated section leaders should use amplification. Directors often want to multitask by telling the choir what notes to sing and how to sing them, often while the choir is singing. In these situations, the director runs the risk of oversinging in the effort to being heard. This is not only vocally taxing on the director but also on the choir, as they continuously sing sections over and over for the thirty minutes or so it takes to learn a new song. Take the time to teach the pitches separately from the stylistic execution, and everyone will benefit in the long run.

Recording Rehearsals

If possible, arrange for media services to make a recording of the rehearsal so singers can take it home with them. This will allow the singers to practice their parts during the week. Individuals can make recordings using their own portable recording devices or with free recording apps available on smartphones. This reduces the amount of rehearsal time needed to work on a particular song.

Rehearsing in a U Shape or a Circle

When choir members can clearly hear their part and how it relates to the whole group, they tend to be more accurate in their parts and better at blending their sound together. Depending on the size of the choir, as well as on the point in the learning process the choir has achieved, each vocal section can create their own U shape or circle or the whole ensemble can create one big U shape or circle. This also prevents choir members from having to oversing, particularly when members are oversinging to compensate for others who don't sing as loud or don't readily know their part.

NOTES FOR THE SINGING TEACHER

It important for voice teachers to understand their function in the development of the gospel singer. Unlike in the Western European classical approach to teaching voice in which the voice studio is the primary source for the development and nurturing of a singer, the voice studio for gospel singers is a secondary source. The primary source for learning gospel music, as mentioned at the beginning of this book, is in the church and particularly through the anointing, as declared by the culture bearers of the gospel music tradition.[24]

Role of the Instructor

The role of the voice teacher is that of a vocal fitness trainer and style coach. The voice teacher is responsible for training the voice as an instrument, conditioning the voice so the singer can easily execute stylistic vocal expressions, and if the voice teacher is also a style coach, teaching the singer how to stylistically articulate his or her own emotional expression in song. When determining technical goals for the gospel singer, the parameters should be particularly sensitive to the value system as defined by the cultural aesthetics of gospel music. Because the sound of gospel music is heavily influenced by the charismatic emotional expression heard in the natural speaking voice, voice teachers should train singers on how to use their voice in this manner, freely. Finding the singer's natural voice—the way the voice sounds without the intentional manipulation of trying to make it "sound good"—voice teachers should focus on developing and freeing this sound so its most prominent characteristics and tone colors are accentuated. In other words, don't change the voice; make it free.

In terms of style, the instructor should not try to teach the cultural and musical aesthetic components of gospel music to a singer who does not have experience in singing gospel music or who has never listened to gospel music. That is, unless the teacher is merely introducing the style for educational purposes. Singers who genuinely want to learn gospel music to minister or perform the style in an authentic manner do so through immersion, because there are many nuances found in the style vocabulary and performance practice that cannot be articulated in words and cannot be demonstrated but must be experienced in order to be understood and embodied. Once the cultural and musical aspects are obtained by the singer and become familiar, the instructor can then guide the execution of those components. The instructor can also assist the singer in determining which components will be most appropriate for his or her instrument and in determining which components will be most effective in portraying the singer's emotional intent.

While the spiritual aspect is the most prominent component of a gospel music performance, voice teachers should not feel obligated to develop the spiritual aspect of the gospel singer unless the teacher is qualified to do so. The singer's spiritual development is the singer's responsibility and the responsibility of the singer's spiritual leader or mentor. The voice instructor should guide the singer in recognizing and determining the most appropriate manner in which to musically express the emotional component that arises as a result of the singer's spiritual conviction.

Repertoire Selection

In terms of selecting repertoire for voice students, the easiest songs to learn are congregational praise songs, spirituals, and praise and worship songs. These songs are great songs for beginning students because they are repetitive, easy to learn, have small vocal ranges, and intentionally have a simple text that is easy to comprehend. In terms of repertoire, the next level of technical difficulty are hymns and traditional gospel songs. These songs generally have wider ranges than praise songs, yet for the most part, they still remain within an octave or so, making them accessible to all levels of singers. However, the lyrical content of hymns tends to be more involved and complex than average praise and worship songs. The text typically requires a deeper level of understanding in order to translate the poetry into everyday language and expression and may need some scaffolding by the voice teacher for the student to comprehend its meaning.

Repertoire from the Southern gospel style category, as defined in the previous chapter, is easy in terms of range and lyrical context but is very difficult in terms of the emotional expression and vocal nuances required. Since music in the Southern gospel style category is closely related to performance practices found in down-home blues, it is the effective portrayal of the emotional perspective of the songs that makes its interpretation effective. This style of music can be challenging for singers who do not possess the skill of emotion-driven musical interpretation. Where hymns will use the melody and words to tell a story, songs from the Southern gospel repertoire accentuate the emotional response when telling the story.

The most difficult gospel music repertoire is found in the categories of inspirational and contemporary styles. These songs tend to have wide vocal ranges, sitting in a high tessitura for longer than the refrain of the hymn, and are often standardized by an elite artist, which often makes it challenging for beginners and new artists to reinterpret. While these songs, aside from praise and worship songs, are most popular in terms of what is considered mainstream gospel according to the current generation, there are many other styles to be considered.

Students should have a wide variety of songs in their repertoire. They should be encouraged to write new songs, create new arrangements of old songs, and even consider adding songs to their repertoire from every decade so they can experience the growth and development of gospel music for themselves.

SUPPLEMENTAL RESOURCES FOR LEARNING TO SING AND TEACH GOSPEL MUSIC

Most chapters of this book contain a list of resources to gain a further understanding of the history, spirituality, vocal technique, and performance practices associated with singing gospel music. Outside of learning gospel music from participating in church, listening to gospel music, and watching videos on YouTube, the following section lists the most prominent books and conferences specifically focusing on furthering the teaching and learning of gospel singing.

Books

Gospel Music: Vocal Cords and Related Issues, by Eustace A. Dixon
Gospel Vocalises: Engaging Mind, Body, and Spirit, by Charsie Randolph Sawyer
Vocal Improvisation: Techniques in Jazz, R&B, and Gospel Improvisation, by Gabrielle Goodman
Voice Training for the Gospel Soloist, by Trineice Robinson-Martin

Course Packets

Vocal Training for the Gospel Singer, by Raymond Wise
Tips on Teaching Vocal Parts, by Raymond Wise
Music Ministry for the Gospel Singer, by Raymond Wise
Interpreting the Gospel, by Raymond Wise

Conferences

Gospel Music Workshop of America Inc. National Convention—www.gmwanational.net/ (held annually in the last week of July, location varies each year)

National Convention of Gospel Choirs and Choristers (Dorsey Convention)—www.ncgccinc.com/wp/ (held annually in August, location varies each year)

Calvin Symposium on Worship—http://worship.calvin.edu/symposium/ (held annually in January, at Calvin College, Grand Rapids, Michigan)

Hampton University Choir Directors' and Organists' Guild Workshop—http://minconf.hamptonu.edu/ (held annually in June at Hampton University, Hampton, Virginia)

CONCLUSION

Learning to be a professional singer is an ongoing learning process in any genre that one chooses to perform. In the ministry of gospel music, singers should strive to be their best in body, mind, spirit, and effort so God will be glorified. This means taking care of the body in terms of diet and exercise, it means getting the proper musical training so the voice is appropriately conditioned to do God's work, and it means establishing and maintaining a personal relationship with Christ so the divine inspirations and communication can become clear and apparent. The professional gospel singer actively chooses to be an open vessel through which the anointing will provide the mental, spiritual, and physical strength necessary to minister. Therefore, the professional singer must learn to nurture and protect his or her temple.

NOTES

1. U.S. Department of Health and Human Services, *Your Guide to Healthy Sleep*, NIH Publication No. 11-5271 (Washington, DC: U.S. Department of Health and Human Services, National Institutes of Health, National Heart, Lung, and Blood Institute, 2005; revised August 2011, www.nhlbi.nih.gov/files/docs/public/sleep/healthy_sleep.pdf.

2. Leslie Ferreira et al., "Influence of Abusive Vocal Habits, Hydration, Mastication, and Sleep in the Occurrence of Vocal Symptoms in Teachers," *Journal of Voice* 24, no. 1 (2008): 86–92.

3. Thomas Carroll et al., "Objective Measurement of Vocal Fatigue in Classical Singers: A Vocal Dosimetry Pilot Study," *Otolaryngology—Head and Neck Surgery* 135, no. 4 (2006): 509–602.

4. Eric Hunter and Ingo Titze, "Quantifying Vocal Fatigue Recovery: Dynamic Vocal Recovery Trajectories after a Vocal Loading Exercise," *Annals of Otology, Rhinology, and Laryngology* 118, no. 6 (2009): 449–60.

5. Shuai Yang, Randal D. Mills, and Jack J. Jiang, "Quantitative Study of the Effects of Dehydration on the Viscoelastic Parameters in the Vocal Fold Mucosa," *Journal of Voice* (in press), doi:http://dx.doi.org/10.1016/j.jvoice.2016.05.002; Ferreira et al., "Influence of Abusive Vocal Habits"; Ingo Titze and Katherine Verdolini Abbott, *Vocology: The Science and Practice of Voice Habilitation* (Salt Lake City, UT: National Center for Voice and Speech, 2012); Ingo Titze, *Principles of Voice Production*, 2nd printing (Iowa City, IA: National Center for Voice and Speech, 2000); Wendy DeLeo LeBorgne and Marci Daniels Rosenberg, *The Vocal Athlete* (San Diego, CA: Plural Publishing, 2014).

6. Yang, Mills, and Jiang, "Quantitative Study of the Effects of Dehydration"; Ferreira et al., "Influence of Abusive Vocal Habits"; Ciara Leydon et al., "Vocal Fold Surface Hydration: A Review," *Journal of Voice* 23, no. 6 (2009): 658–65.

7. Yang, Mills, and Jiang, "Quantitative Study of the Effects of Dehydration"; Leydon et al., "Vocal Fold Surface Hydration"; Ferreira et al., "Influence of Abusive Vocal Habits"; LeBorgne and Rosenberg, *Vocal Athlete*.

8. LeBorgne and Rosenberg, *Vocal Athlete*, 253.

9. Joanna Cazden, *Everyday Voice Care* (Milwaukee, WI: Hal Leonard, 2012).

10. Ibid.; LeBorgne and Rosenberg, *Vocal Athlete*; Ashley E., "Four Foods and Drinks That Make You Dehydrated," The Joint . . . the Chiropractic Place, June 3, 2013, http://chiropractorsandiego-thejoint.com/mission-valley/four-foods-and-drinks-that-make-you-dehydrated/; "Eating When You're Dehydrated," BreastCancer.org, accessed June 24, 2016, www.breastcancer.org/tips/nutrition/during_treat/side_effects/dehydrated:EF.

11. "Dehydration Causes—Mayo Clinic," MayoClinic.org, accessed June 30, 2016, www.mayoclinic.org/diseases-conditions/dehydration/basics/causes/CON-20030056.

12. LeBorgne and Rosenberg, *Vocal Athlete*.

13. Renee Gottliebson, "The Efficacy of Cool-Down Exercises in the Practice Regimen of Elite Singers" (PhD diss., University of Cincinnati, 2011); Kari Ragan, "The Impact of Vocal Cool-Down Exercises: A Subjective Study of Singers' and Listeners' Perceptions," *Journal of Voice* (in press), www.jvoice.org/article/S0892-1997(15)00227-1/abstract.

14. Brenda J. Smith and Robert Thayer Sataloff, "Choral Pedagogy and Vocal Health," in *Vocal Health and Pedagogy: Science and Assessment 1*, 2nd ed. (San Diego, CA: Plural Publishing, 2006), 215; LeBorgne and Rosenberg, *Vocal Athlete*.

15. Ragan, "Impact of Vocal Cool-Down Exercises"; Smith and Sataloff, "Choral Pedagogy and Vocal Health."

16. "Top 10 Worship Leading Tips," ChurchLeaders.com, June 1, 2016, www.churchleaders.com/worship/worship-how-tos/145412-10-very-best-worship-leading-tips.html/2.

17. Alexis Abernethy et al., "Corporate Worship and Spiritual Formation: Insights from Worship Leaders," *Journal of Psychology and Christianity* 34, no. 3 (2015): 266–79; "10 Tips for Worship Leaders: How to Enhance On-Stage Presence," TheWorshipCommunity.com, accessed June 28, 2016, www.theworshipcommunity.com/10-tips-for-worship-leaders-how-to-enhance-on-stage-presence/.

18. Abernethy et al., "Corporate Worship and Spiritual Formation," 267.

19. Ibid.

20. Ibid.

21. Mark D. Roberts, "What Is a Successful Worship Leader?" *Reflections on Christ, Church, and Culture* (blog), accessed June 28, 2016, www.patheos .com/blogs/markdroberts/series/what-is-success-for-a-worship-leader/.

22. Smith and Sataloff, "Choral Pedagogy and Vocal Health."

23. Lonnie Hunter, "Effective Choir Rehearsal Strategies," Pastors' and Laymen's Power of God Convocation, June 8, 2016, Bethany Baptist Church, Gibbsboro, NJ.

24. Eustace A. Dixon, *Gospel Music: Vocal Cords and Related Issues* (Mantua, NJ: Eureka Publications, 1992).

WORKS CITED

"10 Tips for Worship Leaders: How to Enhance On-Stage Presence." TheWorshipCommunity.com. Accessed June 28, 2016. www.theworshipcommunity .com/10-tips-for-worship-leaders-how-to-enhance-on-stage-presence/.

Abernethy, Alexis, Brittany E. Rice, Laura Rold, Kevin R. Kurian, Gillian D. Grannum, and Heather Jones. "Corporate Worship and Spiritual Formation: Insights from Worship Leaders." *Journal of Psychology and Christianity* 34, no. 3 (2015): 266–79.

Ashley E. "Four Foods and Drinks That Make You Dehydrated." The Joint . . . the Chiropractic Place, June 3, 2013. http://chiropractorsandiego-thejoint .com/mission-valley/four-foods-and-drinks-that-make-you-dehydrated/.

Carroll, Thomas, John Nix, Eric Hunter, Kate Emerich, Ingo Titze, and Mona Abaza. "Objective Measurement of Vocal Fatigue in Classical Singers: A Vocal Dosimetry Pilot Study." *Otolaryngology—Head and Neck Surgery* 135, no. 4 (2006): 509–602.

Cazden, Joanna. *Everyday Voice Care*. Milwaukee, WI: Hal Leonard, 2012.

"Dehydration Causes—Mayo Clinic." MayoClinic.org. Accessed June 30, 2016. www.mayoclinic.org/diseases-conditions/dehydration/basics/causes/ CON-20030056.

Dixon, Eustace A. *Gospel Music: Vocal Cords and Related Issues*. Mantua, NJ: Eureka Publications, 1992.

"Eating When You're Dehydrated." Breastcancer.org. Accessed June 24, 2016. www.breastcancer.org/tips/nutrition/during_treat/side_effects/dehyd rated:EF.

Ferreira, Leslie, Maria do Rosario Dias de Oliveira Latorre, Susana Pimentel Pinto Giannini, Ana Carolina de Assis Moura Ghirardi, Delmira de Fraga e Karmann, Eliana Egerland Silva, and Silmara Figueira. "Influence of Abusive Vocal Habits, Hydration, Mastication, and Sleep in the Occurrence of Vocal Symptoms in Teachers." *Journal of Voice* 24, no. 1 (2008): 86–92.

Gottliebson, Renee. "The Efficacy of Cool-down Exercises in the Practice Regimen of Elite Singers." Doctoral Dissertation, University of Cincinnati, 2011.

Hunter, Eric, and Titze, Ingo. "Quantifying Vocal Fatigue Recovery: Dynamic Vocal Recovery Trajectories after a Vocal Loading Exercise." *The Annals of Otology, Rhinology, and Laryngology* 118, no. 6 (2009): 449–60.

Hunter, Lonnie. "Effective Choir Rehearsal Strategies." Presented at the Pastors' and Laymen's Power of God Convocation, Bethany Baptist Church, Gibbsboro, NJ, June 8, 2016.

LeBorgne, Wendy DeLeo, and Marci Daniels Rosenberg. *The Vocal Athlete*. San Diego: Plural Publishing, 2014.

Leydon, Ciara, Mahalakshmi Sivasankar, Danielle Falciglia, Christopher Atkins, and Kimberly Fisher. "Vocal Fold Surface Hydration: A Review." *Journal of Voice* 23, no. 6 (2009): 658–65.

Ragan, Kari. "The Impact of Vocal Cool-down Exercises: A Subjective Study of Singers' and Listeners' Perceptions." *Journal of Voice* (in press). www.jvoice.org/article/S0892-1997(15)00227-1/abstract.

Roberts, Mark D. "What Is a Successful Worship Leader?" *Reflections on Christ, Church, and Culture* (blog). Accessed June 28, 2016. www.patheos.com/blogs/markdroberts/series/what-is-success-for-a-worship-leader/.

Smith, Brenda J., and Robert Thayer Sataloff. "Choral Pedagogy and Vocal Health." In *Vocal Health and Pedagogy: Science and Assessment 1*, 2nd ed., 215. San Diego, CA: Plural Publishing, 2006.

Titze, Ingo. *Principles of Voice Production*. 2nd printing. Iowa City, IA: National Center for Voice and Speech, 2000.

Titze, Ingo, and Katherine Verdolini Abbott. *Vocology: The Science and Practice of Voice Habilitation*. Salt Lake City, UT: National Center for Voice and Speech, 2012.

"Top 10 Worship Leading Tips." ChurchLeaders.com, June 1, 2016. www.churchleaders.com/worship/worship-how-tos/145412-10-very-best-worship-leading-tips.html/2.

U.S. Department of Health and Human Services. *Your Guide to Healthy Sleep*. NIH Publication No. 11-5271. Washington, DC: U.S. Department of Health and Human Services, National Institutes of Health, National Heart, Lung, and Blood Institute, 2005; revised August 2011. www.nhlbi.nih.gov/files/docs/public/sleep/healthy_sleep.pdf.

Yang, Shuai, Randal D. Mills, and Jack J. Jiang. "Quantitative Study of the Effects of Dehydration on the Viscoelastic Parameters in the Vocal Fold Mucosa." *Journal of Voice* (in press). doi:http://dx.doi.org/10.1016/j.jvoice.2016.05.002.

8

USING AUDIO ENHANCEMENT TECHNOLOGY

Matthew Edwards

In the early days of popular music, musicians performed without electronic amplification. Singers learned to project their voices in the tradition of vaudeville performers with a technique similar to operatic and operetta performers, who had been singing unamplified for centuries. When microphones began appearing on stage in the 1930s, vocal performance changed forever since the loudness of a voice was no longer a factor in the success of a performer. In order to be successful, all a singer needed was an interesting vocal quality and an emotional connection to what he or she was singing; the microphone would take care of projection.[1]

Vocal qualities that may sound weak without a microphone can sound strong and projected when sung with one. At the same time, a singer with a voice that is acoustically beautiful and powerful can sound harsh and pushed if he or she lacks microphone technique. Understanding how to use audio equipment to get the sounds a singer desires without harming the voice is crucial. The information in this chapter will help the reader gain a basic knowledge of terminology and equipment commonly used when amplifying or recording a vocalist as well as providing tips for singing with a microphone.

THE FUNDAMENTALS OF SOUND

In order to understand how to manipulate an audio signal, you must first understand a few basics of sound, including frequency, amplitude, and resonance.

Frequency

Sound travels in waves of compression and rarefaction within a medium, which for our purposes is air (see figure 8.1). These waves travel through the air and into our inner ears via the ear canal. There they are converted, via the eardrums, into nerve impulses that are transmitted to the brain and interpreted as sound. The number of waves per second is measured in hertz (Hz), which gives us the frequency of the sound that we have learned to perceive as pitch. For example, we hear 440 Hz (440 cycles of compression and rarefaction per second) as the pitch A above middle C.

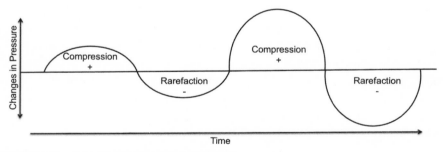

Figure 8.1. Compression and rarefaction.
Creative Commons

Amplitude

The magnitude of the waves of compression and rarefaction determines the amplitude of the sound that we call its "volume." The larger the waves of compression and rarefaction, the louder we perceive the sound to be. Measured in decibels (dB), amplitude represents changes in air pressure from the baseline. Decibel measurements range from zero decibels (0 dB), the threshold of human hearing, to 130 dB, the upper edge of the threshold of pain.

Harmonics

The vibrating mechanism of an instrument produces the vibrations necessary to establish pitch (the fundamental frequency). The vibrating mechanism for a singer is the vocal folds. If an acoustic instrument, such as the voice, were to produce a note with the fundamental frequency alone, the sound would be strident and mechanical like the emergency alert signal used on television. Pitches played on acoustic instruments consist of multiple frequencies, called *overtones*, which are emitted from the vibrator along with the fundamental frequency. For the purposes of this chapter, the overtones that we are interested in are called *harmonics*. Harmonics are whole-number multiples of the fundamental frequency. For example, if the fundamental is 220 Hz, the harmonic overtone series would be 220 Hz, 440 Hz (fundamental frequency times two), 660 Hz (fundamental frequency times three), 880 Hz (fundamental frequency times four), and so on. Every musical note contains both the fundamental frequency and a predictable series of harmonics, each of which can be measured and identified as a specific frequency. This series of frequencies then travels through a hollow cavity (the vocal tract) where they are attenuated or amplified by the resonating frequencies of the cavity, which is how resonance occurs.

Resonance

The complex waveform created by the vocal folds travels through the vocal tract, where it is enhanced by the tract's unique resonance characteristics. Depending on the resonator's shape, some harmonics are amplified and some are attenuated. Each singer has a unique vocal tract shape with unique resonance characteristics. This is why two singers of the same voice type can sing the same pitch and yet sound very different. We can analyze these changes with a tool called a *spectral analyzer*, as seen in figure 8.2. The slope from left to right is called the *spectral slope*. The peaks and valleys along the slope indicate amplitude variations of the corresponding overtones. The difference in spectral slope

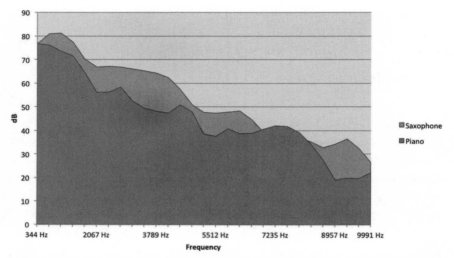

Figure 8.2. The figure above shows two instruments playing the same pitch. The peak at the far left is the fundamental frequency and the peaks to the right are harmonics that have been amplified and attenuated by the instrument's resonator resulting in a specific timbre.
Matthew Edwards

between instruments (or voices) is what enables a listener to aurally distinguish the difference between two instruments playing or singing the same note.

Because the throat and mouth act as the resonating tube in acoustic singing, changing their size and shape is the only option for making adjustments to timbre for those who perform without microphones. In electronically amplified singing, the sound engineer can make adjustments to boost or attenuate specific frequency ranges, thus changing the singer's timbre. For this and many other reasons discussed in this chapter, it is vitally important for singers to know how audio technology can affect the quality of their voice.

SIGNAL CHAIN

The signal chain is the path an audio signal travels from the input to the output of a sound system. A voice enters the signal chain through a microphone, which transforms acoustic energy into electrical impulses.

The electrical pulses generated by the microphone are transmitted through a series of components that modify the signal before the speakers transform it back into acoustic energy. Audio engineers and producers understand the intricacies of these systems and are able to make an infinite variety of alterations to the vocal signal. While some engineers strive to replicate the original sound source as accurately as possible, others use the capabilities of the system to alter the sound for artistic effect. Since more components and variations exist than can be discussed in just a few pages, this chapter will discuss only basic components and variations found in most systems.

Microphones

Microphones transform the acoustic sound waves of the voice into electrical impulses. The component of the microphone that is responsible for receiving the acoustic information is the diaphragm. The two most common diaphragm types that singers will encounter are dynamic and condenser. Each offers advantages and disadvantages depending on how the microphone is to be used.

Dynamic Dynamic microphones consist of a dome-shaped Mylar diaphragm attached to a free-moving copper wire coil that is positioned between the two poles of a magnet. The Mylar diaphragm moves in response to air pressure changes caused by sound waves. When the diaphragm moves, the magnetic coil that is attached to it also moves. As the magnetic coil moves up and down between the magnetic poles, it produces an electrical current that corresponds to the sound waves produced by the singer's voice. That signal is then sent to the soundboard via the microphone cable.

The Shure SM-58 dynamic microphone is the industry standard for live performance because it is affordable, nearly indestructible, and easy to use. Dynamic microphones such as the Shure SM-58 have a lower sensitivity than condenser microphones, which makes them more successful at avoiding feedback. Because of their reduced tendency to feedback, dynamic microphones are the best choice for artists that use handheld microphones when performing.

Condenser Condenser microphones are constructed with two parallel plates: a rigid posterior plate and a thin, flexible anterior plate. The

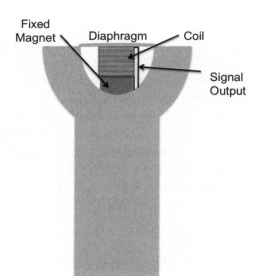

Figure 8.3. This is the basic design of a dynamic microphone.
Matthew Edwards

anterior plate is constructed of either a thin sheet of metal or a piece of Mylar that is coated with a conductive metal. The plates are separated by air, which acts as a layer of insulation. In order to use a condenser microphone, it must be connected to a soundboard that supplies "phantom power." A component of the soundboard, phantom power sends a 48-volt power supply through the microphone cable to the microphone's plates. When the plates are charged by phantom power, they form a capacitor. As acoustic vibrations send the anterior plate into motion, the distance between the two plates varies, which causes the capacitor to release a small electric current. This current, which corresponds with the acoustic signal of the voice, travels through the microphone cable to the soundboard, where it can be enhanced and amplified.

Electret condenser microphones are similar to condenser microphones, but they are designed to work without phantom power. The anterior plate of an electret microphone is made of a plastic film coated with a conductive metal that is electrically charged before being set into place opposite the posterior plate. The charge applied to the anterior plate will last for ten or more years and therefore eliminates the need for an exterior power source. Electret condenser microphones are often used in head-mounted and lapel microphones, laptop computers, and smartphones.

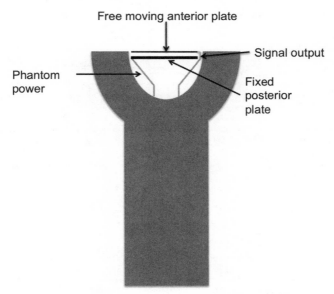

Figure 8.4. This is the basic design of a condenser microphone.
Matthew Edwards

Recording engineers prefer condenser microphones for recording applications due to their high level of sensitivity. Using a condenser microphone, performers can sing at nearly inaudible acoustic levels and obtain a final recording that is intimate and earthy. While the same vocal effects can be recorded with a dynamic microphone, they will not have the same clarity as those produced with a condenser microphone.

Frequency Response   *Frequency response* is a term used to define how accurately a microphone captures the tone quality of the signal. A "flat response" microphone captures the original signal with little to no signal alteration. Microphones that are not designated as "flat" have some type of amplification or attenuation of specific frequencies, also known as *cut* or *boost*, within the audio spectrum. For instance, the Shure SM-58 microphone drastically attenuates the signal below 300 Hz and amplifies the signal in the 3 kHz range by 6 dB, the 5 kHz range by nearly 8 dB, and the 10 kHz range by approximately 6 dB. The Oktava 319 microphone cuts the frequencies below 200 Hz while boosting everything above 300 Hz with nearly 5 dB between 7 kHz and 10 kHz (see figure 8.5). In practical terms, recording a bass singer with the Shure

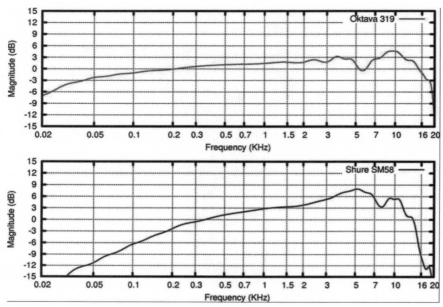

Figure 8.5. Example frequency response graphs for the Oktava 319 and the Shure SM-58.
Wikimedia Commons

SM-58 would drastically reduce the amplitude of the fundamental frequency, while the Oktava 319 would produce a slightly more consistent boost in the range of the singer's formant. Either of these options could be acceptable depending on the situation, but the frequency response must be considered before making a recording or performing live.

Amplitude Response The amplitude response of a microphone varies depending on the angle at which the singer is positioned in relation to the axis of the microphone. In order to visualize the amplitude response of a microphone at various angles, microphone manufacturers publish polar pattern diagrams (also sometimes called a *directional pattern* or a *pickup pattern*). Polar pattern diagrams usually consist of six concentric circles divided into twelve equal sections. The center point of the microphone's diaphragm is labeled "0°" and is referred to as "on-axis," while the opposite side of the diagram is labeled "180°" and is described as "off-axis."

Although polar pattern diagrams appear in two dimensions, they actually represent a three-dimensional response to acoustic energy. You can use a round balloon as a physical example to help you visualize a three-dimensional polar pattern diagram. Position the tied end of the balloon away from your mouth and the inflated end directly in front of your lips. In this position, you are singing on-axis at 0 degrees with the tied end of the balloon being 180 degrees, or off-axis. If you were to split the balloon in half vertically and horizontally (in relationship to your lips), the point at which those lines intersect would be the center point of the balloon. That imaginary center represents the diaphragm of the microphone. If you were to extend a 45-degree angle in any direction from the imaginary center and then drew a circle around the inside of the balloon following that angle, you would have a visualization of the three-dimensional application of the two-dimensional polar pattern drawing.

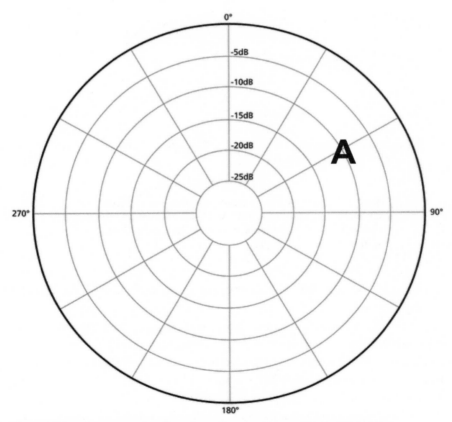

Figure 8.6. An example of a microphone polar pattern diagram.
Wikimedia Commons

The outermost circle of the diagram indicates that the sound pressure level (SPL) of the signal is transferred without any amplitude reduction, indicated in decibels (dB). Each of the inner circles represents a -5 dB reduction in the amplitude of the signal up to -25 dB. For example, look at figure 8.7.

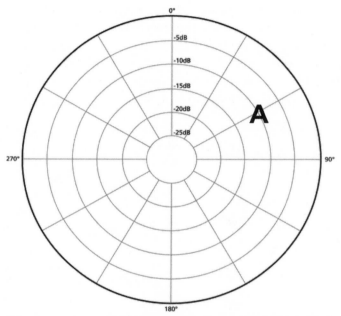

Figure 8.7. If the amplitude response curve intersected with point A, there would be a -10 dB reduction in the amplitude of frequencies received by the microphone's diaphragm at that angle.
Wikimedia Commons

Figures 8.8, 8.9, and 8.10 show the most commonly encountered polar patterns.

When you are using a microphone with a polar pattern other than omnidirectional (a pattern that responds to sound equally from all directions), you may encounter frequency-response fluctuations in addition to amplitude fluctuations. Cardioid microphones in particular are known for their tendency to boost lower frequencies at close proximity to the sound source while attenuating those same frequencies as the distance between the sound source and the microphone increases. This

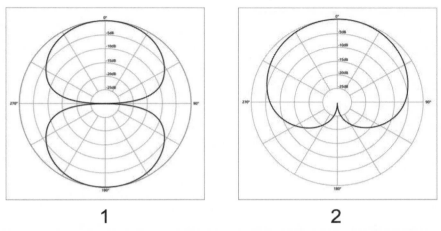

1   2

Figure 8.8.   Diagram one represents a bi-directional pattern, diagram two represents a cardioid pattern.
Creative Commons

is known as the *proximity effect*. Some manufacturers will notate these frequency-response changes on their polar pattern diagrams by using a combination of various lines and dashes alongside the amplitude-response curve.

Sensitivity   While sensitivity can be difficult to explain in technical terms without going into an in-depth discussion of electricity and elec-

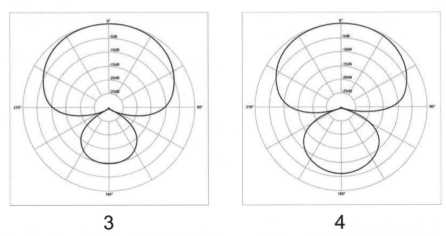

3   4

Figure 8.9.   Diagram three represents a super-cardioid pattern, and diagram four represents a hyper-cardioid pattern.
Creative Commons

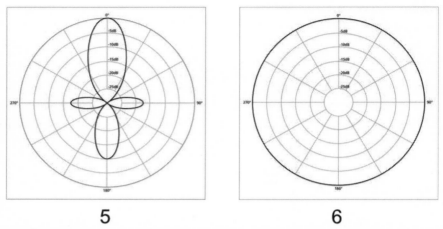

5 6

Figure 8.10. Diagram five represents a shotgun pattern, and diagram six represents an omnidirectional pattern.
Creative Commons

trical terminology, a simplified explanation should suffice for most readers. Manufacturers test microphones with a standardized 1 kHz tone at 94 dB in order to determine how sensitive the microphone's diaphragm will be to acoustic energy. Microphones with greater sensitivity can be placed farther from the sound source without adding excessive noise to the signal. Microphones with lower sensitivity will need to be placed closer to the sound source in order to keep excess noise at a minimum. When shopping for a microphone, the performer should audition several next to each other, plugged into the same soundboard, with the same volume level for each. When singing on each microphone at the same distance, the performer will notice that some models replicate the voice louder than others. This change in output level is due to differences in each microphone's sensitivity. If a performer has a loud voice, they may prefer a microphone with lower sensitivity (one that requires more acoustic energy to respond). If a performer has a lighter voice, they may prefer a microphone with higher sensitivity (one that responds well to softer signals).

Equalization (EQ)

Equalizers enable the audio engineer to alter the audio spectrum of the sound source and make tone adjustments with a simple electronic interface. Equalizers come in three main types: shelf, parametric, and graphic.

Shelf   Shelf equalizers cut or boost the uppermost and lowermost frequencies of an audio signal in a straight line (see figure 8.11). While this style of equalization is not very useful for fine-tuning a singer's tone quality, it can be very effective in removing room noise. For example, if an air-conditioner creates a 60 Hz hum in the recording studio, the shelf can be set at 65 Hz, with a steep slope. This setting eliminates frequencies below 65 Hz and effectively removes the hum from the microphone signal.

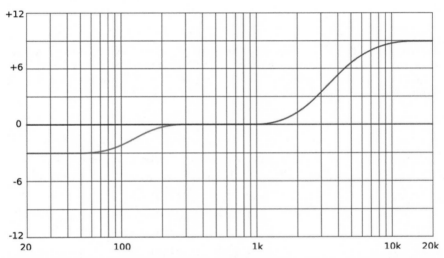

Figure 8.11.   The frequency amplitude curves above show the effect of applying a shelf EQ to an audio signal.
Wikimedia Commons

Parametric   Parametric units simultaneously adjust multiple frequencies of the audio spectrum that fall within a defined parameter. The engineer selects a center frequency and adjusts the width of the bell curve surrounding that frequency by adjusting the "Q" (see figure 8.12). They then boost or cut the frequencies within the bell curve to alter the audio spectrum. Parametric controls take up minimal space on a soundboard and offer sufficient control for most situations. Therefore, most live-performance soundboards have parametric EQs on each individual channel. With the advent of digital workstations, engineers

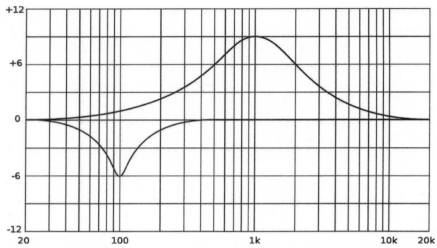

Figure 8.12. The frequency amplitude curves above display two parametric EQ settings. The top curve represents a boost of +8 dB set at 1 kHz with a relatively large bell curve—a low Q. The lower curve represents a high Q set at 100 Hz with a cut of -6 dB.
Wikimedia Commons

can now use computer software to fine-tune the audio quality of each individual channel using a more complex graphic equalizer in both live and recording studio settings without taking up any additional physical space on the board. However, many engineers still prefer to use parametric controls during a live performance since they are usually sufficient and are easier to adjust mid-performance.

Parametric adjustments on a soundboard are made by rotary knobs similar to those in figure 8.13 below. In some cases, you will find a button labeled "low cut" or "high pass" that will automatically apply a shelf filter to the bottom of the audio spectrum at a specified frequency. On higher-end boards, you may also find a knob that enables you to select the high-pass frequency.

Graphic   Graphic equalizers enable engineers to identify a specific frequency for boost or cut with a fixed-frequency bandwidth. For example, a ten-band equalizer enables the audio engineer to adjust ten specific frequencies (in Hz): 31, 63, 125, 250, 500, 1k, 2k, 4k, 8k, and 16k. Graphic equalizers are often one of the final elements of the signal chain, preceding only the amplifier and speakers. In this position, they can be used to adjust the overall tonal quality of the entire mix.

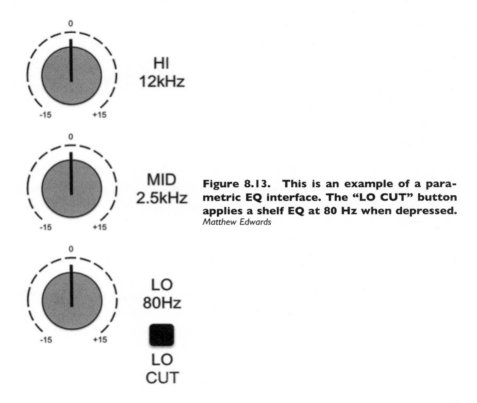

Figure 8.13. This is an example of a parametric EQ interface. The "LO CUT" button applies a shelf EQ at 80 Hz when depressed.
Matthew Edwards

Utilizing Equalization   Opinions on the usage of equalization vary among engineers. Some prefer to only use equalization to remove or reduce frequencies that were not a part of the original sound signal. Others will use EQ if adjusting microphone placement fails to yield

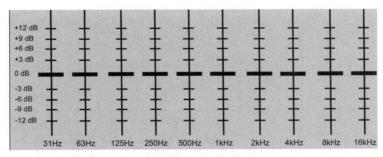

Figure 8.14.   This is an example of a graphic equalizer interface.
Matthew Edwards

acceptable results. Some engineers prefer a more processed sound and may use equalization liberally to intentionally change the vocal quality of the singer. For instance, if the singer's voice sounds dull, the engineer could add "ring" or "presence" to the voice by boosting the equalizer in the 2 k to 10 kHz range.

Compression

Many singers are capable of producing vocal extremes in both frequency and amplitude levels that can prove problematic for the sound team. To help solve this problem, engineers often use compression. Compressors limit the output of a sound source by a specified ratio. The user sets the maximum acceptable amplitude level for the output, called the *threshold*, and then sets a ratio to reduce the output once it surpasses the threshold. The typical ratio for a singer is usually between 3:1 and 5:1. A 4:1 ratio indicates that for every 4 dB beyond the threshold level, the output will only increase by 1 dB. For example, if the singer went 24 dB beyond the threshold with a 4:1 ratio, the output would only be 6 dB beyond the threshold level (see figure 8.15 below).

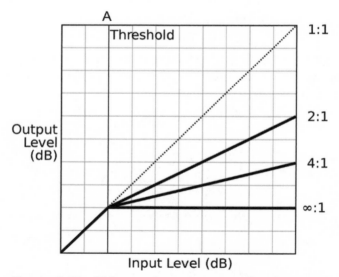

Figure 8.15. This graph represents the effects of various compression ratios applied to a signal. The 1:1 angle represents no compression. The other ratios represent the effect of compression on an input signal with the threshold set at line A.
Wikimedia Commons

Adjusting the sound via microphone technique can provide some of the same results as compression and is preferable for the experienced artist. However, compression tends to be more consistent and also gives the singer freedom to focus on performing and telling a story. The additional artistic freedom provided by compression is especially beneficial to singers who use head-mounted microphones, performers who switch between vocal extremes such as falsetto and chest voice, and those who are new to performing with a microphone. Compression can also be helpful for classical singers whose dynamic abilities, while impressive live, are often difficult to record in a manner that allows for consistent listening levels through a stereo system.

Multiband Compression   If a standard compressor causes unacceptable alterations to the tone quality, engineers can turn to a multiband compressor. Rather than affecting the entire spectrum of sound, multiband compressors allow the engineer to isolate a specific frequency range within the audio signal and then set an individual compression setting for that frequency range. For example, if a singer creates a dramatic boost in the 4 kHz range every time they sing above an A4, a multiband compressor can be used to limit the amplitude of the signal in only that part of the voice. By setting a 3:1 ratio in the 4 kHz range at a threshold that corresponds to the amplitude peaks that appear when the performer sings above A4, the engineer can eliminate vocal "ring" from the sound on only the offending notes while leaving the rest of the signal untouched. These units are available for both live and studio use and can be a great alternative to compressing the entire signal.

Reverb

Reverb is one of the easier effects for singers to identify; it is the effect you experience when singing in a cathedral. An audience experiences natural reverberation when they hear the direct signal from the singer, and then milliseconds later they hear multiple reflections as the acoustical waves of the voice bounce off the sidewalls, floor, and ceiling of the performance hall.

Many performance venues and recording studios are designed to inhibit natural reverb. Without at least a little reverb added to the sound, even the best singer can sound harsh and even amateurish. Early reverb

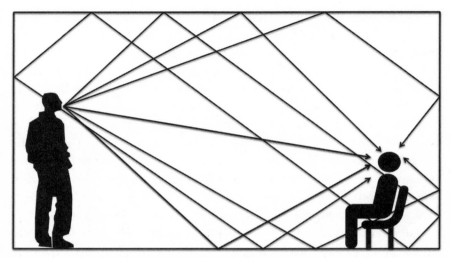

Figure 8.16. This diagram illustrates the multiple lines of reflection that create reverb.
Matthew Edwards

units transmitted the audio signal through a metal spring, which added supplementary vibrations to the signal. While some engineers still use spring reverb to obtain a specific effect, most now use digital units. Common settings on digital reverb units include wet/dry, bright/dark, and options for delay time. The wet/dry control adjusts the amount of direct signal (dry) and the amount of reverberated signal (wet). The bright/dark control helps simulate the effects of various surfaces within a natural space. For instance, harder surfaces such as stone reflect high frequencies and create a brighter tone quality, while softer surfaces such as wood reflect lower frequencies and create a darker tone quality. The delay time, which is usually adjustable from milliseconds to seconds, adjusts the amount of time between when the dry signal and wet signals reach the ear. Engineers can transform almost any room into a chamber music hall or concert stadium simply by adjusting these settings.

Delay

Whereas reverb blends multiple wet signals with the dry signal to replicate a natural space, delay purposefully separates a single wet signal from the dry signal to create repetitions of the voice. With delay, you

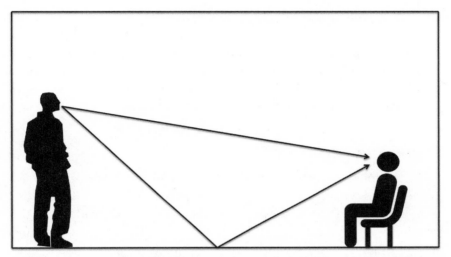

Figure 8.17.   This diagram illustrates how a direct line of sound followed by a reflected line of sound creates delay.
Matthew Edwards

will hear the original note first and then a digitally produced repeat of the note several milliseconds to seconds later. The delayed note may be heard one time or multiple times, and the timing of those repeats can be adjusted to match the tempo of the song.

Auto-tune

Auto-tune was first used in studios as a useful way to clean up minor imperfections in otherwise perfect performances. Auto-tune is now an industry standard that many artists use, even if they are not willing to admit it. Auto-tune has gained a bad reputation in the last few years, and whether or not you agree with its use, it is a reality in today's market. If you do not understand how to use it properly, you could end up sounding like T-Pain.[2]

Both Antares and Melodyne have developed auto-tune technology in both "auto" and "graphical" formats. "Auto" auto-tune allows the engineer to set specific parameters for pitch correction that are then computer controlled. "Graphical" auto-tune tracks the pitch in the selected area of a recording and plots the fundamental frequency on a linear graph. The engineer can then select specific notes for pitch correction. The engineer can also drag selected pitches to a different frequency, add or reduce vibrato, and change formant frequencies above the fundamental. To simplify, the "auto" function makes general corrections while the "graphic" function makes specific corrections. The "auto" setting is usually used to achieve a specific effect (for instance "I Believe" by Cher), while the "graphic" setting is used to correct small imperfections in a recorded performance.

Digital Voice Processors

Digital voice processors are still relatively new to the market and have yet to gain widespread usage among singers. While there are several brands of vocal effects processors available, the industry leader as of this printing is a company called TC-Helicon. TC-Helicon manufactures several different units that span from consumer to professional grade. TC-Helicon's premiere performer-controlled unit is called the Voice-Live 3. The VoiceLive 3 incorporates over twelve vocal effects, eleven guitar effects, and a multitrack looper with 250 factory presets and 250 memory slots for user presets. The VoiceLive 3 puts the effects at the singer's feet in a programmable stomp box that also includes phantom power, MIDI in/out, a USB connection, guitar input, and monitor out. Onboard vocal effects include equalization, compression, reverb, and "auto" auto-tune. The unit also offers μMod (an adjustable voice modulator), a doubler (for thickening the lead vocal), echo, delay, reverb, and several other specialized effects.[3]

One of the most impressive features of digital voice processors is the ability to add computer-generated harmonies to the lead vocal. After the user sets the musical key, the processor identifies the fundamental frequency of each sung note. The computer then adds digitized voices at designated intervals above and below the lead singer. The unit also offers the option to program each individual song, with multiple settings for every verse, chorus, and bridge.

THE BASICS OF LIVE SOUND SYSTEMS

Live sound systems come in a variety of sizes from small practice units to state-of-the-art stadium rigs. Most singers only need a basic knowledge of the components commonly found in systems that have one to eight inputs. Units beyond that size usually require an independent sound engineer and are beyond the scope of this chapter.

Following the microphone, the first element in the live signal chain is usually the mixer. Basic portable mixers provide controls for equalization, volume level, auxiliary (usually used for effects such as reverb and compression), and on some units, controls for built-in digital effects processors. Powered mixers combine an amplifier with a basic mixer, providing a compact solution for those who do not need a complex system. Since unpowered mixers do not provide amplification, you will need to add a separate amplifier to power this system.

The powered mixer or amplifier connects to speaker cabinets, which contain a "woofer" and a "tweeter." The "woofer" is a large, round speaker that handles the bass frequencies, while the "tweeter" is a horn-shaped speaker that handles the treble frequencies. The crossover, a component built into the speaker cabinet, separates high and low frequencies and sends them to the appropriate speaker (woofer or tweeter). Speaker cabinets can be either active or passive. Passive cabinets require a powered mixer or an amplifier in order to operate. Active cabinets have an amplifier built in and do not require an external amplifier.

If you do not already own a microphone and amplification system, you can purchase a simple setup at relatively low cost through online vendors such as Sweetwater.com and MusiciansFriend.com. A dynamic microphone and a powered monitor are enough to get started. If you would like to add a digital voice processor, Digitech and TC-Helicon both sell entry-level models that will significantly improve the tonal quality of a sound system.

Monitors

Monitors are arguably the most important element in a live sound system. The monitor is a speaker that faces a performer and allows them to hear him- or herself and/or the other instruments on stage. On-stage volume levels can vary considerably, with drummers often producing sound levels as high as 120 dB. Those volume levels make it nearly impossible for singers to receive natural acoustic feedback while performing. Monitors can improve aural feedback and help reduce the temptation to oversing. Powered monitors offer the same advantages as powered speaker cabinets and can be a great option for amplification when practicing. They are also good to have around as a backup plan in case you arrive at a venue and discover they do not supply monitors. In-ear monitors offer another option for performers and are especially useful for those who frequently move around the stage.

MICROPHONE TECHNIQUE

The microphone is an inseparable part of the contemporary commercial music singer's instrument. Just as there are techniques that improve singing, there are also techniques that will improve microphone use. Understanding what a microphone does is only the first step to using it successfully. Once you understand how a microphone works, you need hands-on experience.

Practicing with a Microphone

The best way to learn microphone technique is to experiment. Try the following exercises to gain a better understanding of how to use a microphone when singing.

- Hold a dynamic microphone with a cardioid pattern directly in front of your mouth, no further than one centimeter away. Sustain a comfortable pitch and slowly move the microphone away from your lips. Listen to how the vocal quality changes. When the microphone is close to the lips, you should notice that the sound is louder and has more bass response. As you move the microphone away from your mouth, there will be a noticeable loss in volume and the tone will become brighter.
- Next, sustain a pitch while rotating the handle down. The sound quality will change in a similar fashion as when you moved the microphone away from your lips.
- Now try singing breathy with the microphone close to your lips. How little effort can you get away with while producing a marketable sound?

- Try singing bright vowels and dark vowels, and notice how the microphone affects the tone quality.
- Also experiment with adapting your diction to the microphone. Because the microphone amplifies everything, you may need to underpronounce certain consonants when singing. You will especially want to reduce the power of the consonants t, s, p, and b.

CONCLUSION

Since this is primarily an overview, you can greatly improve your comprehension of the material by seeking other resources to deepen your knowledge. There are many great resources available online, in addition to those found in the works cited, that may help clarify some of these difficult concepts. Most importantly, you must experiment. The more you play around with sound equipment on your own, the better you will understand it and the more comfortable you will feel when performing or recording with audio technology.

NOTES

1. Paula Lockheart, "A History of Early Microphone Singing, 1925–1939: American Mainstream Popular Singing at the Advent of Electronic Amplification," *Popular Music and Society* 26, no. 3 (2003): 367–85.
2. For example, listen to T-Pain's track "Buy You a Drank (Shawty Snappin')."
3. "VoiceLive3," TC-Helicon website, accessed May 2, 2016. www.tc-helicon.com/products/voicelive-3/.

WORKS CITED

Lockheart, Paula. "A History of Early Microphone Singing, 1925–1939: American Mainstream Popular Singing at the Advent of Electronic Amplification." *Popular Music and Society* 26, no. 3 (2003): 367–85.
"VoiceLive3." TC-Helicon website. Accessed May 2, 2016. www.tc-helicon.com/products/voicelive-3/.

APPENDIX
EXAMPLE VOCAL INTENSITY CHART

A vocal intensity chart is a personalized document singers can use to measure and articulate the physical effort used when producing various dynamic levels. The intensity levels are ranked on a scale of 1–10. One (1) represents the most sound with the least amount of effort (i.e., the quietest tone possible before whispering), and ten (10) represents the most sound with most effort (i.e., pushing as hard as one can in attempts to sing as loud as one can). When establishing a personalized version of this chart, singers will be able to comfortably articulate what their body feels like when they are singing or speaking very softly, medium soft, loud, and when screaming or shouting. This awareness is crucial to understanding the body's capabilities and limitations when producing sound. The purpose is to increase one's kinesthetic awareness so that a singer can self-monitor his or her vocal output and make educated choices as to how to use his or her body.

When creating a personalized chart, a singer will record this demonstration (audio or video) so he or she can analyze what is happening in the body when the various sounds are produced. While one would never sing at an intensity level of ten on purpose, it is important for singers to recognize and be able to articulate what an intensity level of ten sounds like and feels like in his or her body to help determine a point of limitation.

Intensity	1	2	3	4	5	6	7	8	9	10
Description	Most sound; least effort									Most sound; Most effort
Sounds like:	The softest sound you can make without whispering		Talking softly in small group discussion in the library		Normal talking volume, not loud, not soft		Talking loudly, projecting, but not shouting, as if when addressing a large crowd		Shouting and yelling	Screaming at the top of your lungs
Possible physical sensations	Small breath, very little physical effort if any, completely no pressure in body		Less breath pressure than when talking at a normal volume, but more than just above a whisper. Body is physically engaged, but little physical effort		Breath pressure no greater than used for normal speech, comfortable amount of effort and energy, body is engaged		Medium to large amount of breath pressure, no pressure in the neck and shoulders, pressure in the torso, takes more energy and effort than normal speech, but not as much as shouting, can be tiring if body is not conditioned		Large amounts of breath pressure, lots of effort, pressure felt through-out torso, some pressure felt in neck muscles, will feel tired with prolonged use if the body is not conditioned for this type of vocal intensity	Maximum breath intake, pressure felt in every part of the body, head to toe, most physical effort possible, lots of energy, typically results in face is turning colors or a headache when sustained longer than 10-15 seconds, throat squeezes and it hurts
Contraction level of support muscles	Support muscles are barely contracted		Support muscles are slightly contracted		Support muscles are distinctly contracted		Support muscles are firmly contracted		Support muscles are contracted to maximum, possibly recruits help from other muscles	Support muscles are contracted to maximum level, other muscles are also at maximum

Singers who regularly belt or sing loudly can sometimes be so accustomed to the way they produce their sound that they don't realize how much effort their body is actually using to create that sound. Conversely, singers who do not project their voice often also recognize how much more their body has to be engaged to project a sound.

Note: This is an exploratory assignment by design. After doing the initial documentation on what these various intensity levels feel like on levels 1–10, try to perform levels 1–9 on a specific pitch. Try singing levels 1–9 toward the bottom of your range, then in the middle, then on a high note. Try it in chest voice and in falsetto. You may notice that while the intensity level will physically feel the same or very similar on these notes, the volume level may greatly decrease or increase depending on the pitch and how well that part of the voice is developed.

GLOSSARY

ad-libbing: a type of textual improvisation consisting of generating short improvised phrases over a chorus or over a vamp (a repeated section that extends the end of a song)

articulators: parts of the mouth used to create vowel and consonant sounds during speech

back phrasing: a type of the syncopation that is executed when singing slightly behind only to catch up to the established rhythm later but within the same phrase

balanced onset: when the start of the breath and the start of the tone are coordinated to start smoothly

bends/blue note: a note sung slightly under- or over-pitch for expressive purposes, usually by a semitone (a half note) or less

black theology: the theological explication of the blackness of black people

breathy onset: when an audible breathy sound starts before the vocal folds close/vibrate to make a sound

call-response: musical structures and musical expectations for expression that constitute gospel music

choir range: the vocal range consistently required of each specific voice part when singing in a gospel choir

constriction: when a muscle is stuck in the contracted position and is not easily pliable; when this occurs, limitation in stamina also occurs, which eventually results in fatigue and may cause damage

constrictor muscles: the three sets of muscles that can contract and close the throat (like when swallowing or gargling)

contraction: the tightening and shortening of a muscle; necessary to produce and/or sustain vocal sounds

cricothyroid (CT) muscle: one of the two primary sets of muscles that control the thickness and length of the vocal folds; when contracted, the vocal folds are lengthened and thinned

dramatic slides/glissandos: a slow slide from one note to the next in which all the notes in between are also emphasized as the pitch ascends

energized worship: the relationship between spirituality and spiritual perception, affectivity, and cognition

escape tones: when the first added note to a melody moves stepwise in one direction, then skips to another note in a different direction

fall: when a pitch is sounded and then descends in pitch and intensity

fermata: a hold/pause for improvisatory purposes can be inserted to elongate the rhythm for dramatic purposes

front phrasing: a stylistic tool used when a singer sings just before the prominent beat or originally composed melody

gravel: rough or aggressive-sounding vocal textures during an emotional climax or a portrayal of great despair or passion during interpretation (four basic types of gravel sounds: **squalls**, **whoops**, **growls**, and **midvoice**)

gravel onset: when the tone starts as a vocal fry (i.e., a toneless popping sound) and then slides into a pitched tone

growl: a rough vocal quality that starts a word or phrase but is immediately followed by a clearer vocal quality; used to bring emotional intensity or a feeling of immense conviction to a sung phrase

hard onset: when the vocal folds are firmly pressed together and air pressure builds up underneath the vocal folds creating a harsh, pressurized sound when the tone starts

inferior constrictors: constricts the pharynx and lifts the larynx; attached to both sides of the thyroid cartilage (the cartilage that primarily houses the vocal folds), wraps around the base of the vocal tract, which includes connection to the cricoid cartilage (a cartilage to which a portion of the vocal folds are also attached), and attaches at the top of the esophagus

intercostal muscles: several groups of muscles that help move the chest wall and are involved in the mechanical aspect of breathing

interpolation: insertion of flatted or blues thirds and sevenths

larynx: the hollow muscular organ forming a passage of air to the lungs and holding the vocal cords

lean/appoggiatura: when a singer approaches a note by quickly sliding from the neighboring note above the intended note

melismas: a group of notes sung to one syllable of text

melodic interpolations: short melodic insertions added to a given melody for the purpose of creating variation in the musical articulation of one's emotional expression

middle constrictor muscles: set of muscles connected to the hyoid bone (note: the base of the tongue connects to the front of the hyoid bone) and connects around the vocal tract about the level of the bottom jaw; functions to narrow the back of the throat and assist in pushing food to the esophagus

midvoice: a vocal quality sustaining the gravel sound through several sung phrases; used during heightened emotional states that represent the climax

neighbor tone: when a note is inserted directly above or below the intended note

onset: the start of a tone

passaggio: specific transition areas of the voice (around E♭, E, F and B♭, B, and C above middle C) where "breaks" in the voice are most obvious for both men and women

passing tones: when one or two notes are inserted to a melody stepwise in the same direction between two written notes

pentatonic scales: a specific five-note scale from which many cultures base their melodies

performance medium: the combinations of voices and/or instruments used in the performance of music

pharyngeal shape: positions created by changing the position of the pharyngeal wall (the walls of the throat), the position of the tongue, the position of the soft palate, the position of the jaw, and the height position of the larynx, giving specific acoustic properties and characteristics to result in a distinct sound

pharyngeal wall: the throat; a part of the vocal tract

pharynx or vocal tract: all the open space in the head and neck above the vocal folds, including the oral cavity (mouth), nasal cavity (nose), and pharynx (throat)

resonating chamber: the area of the instrument allowing its sound to carry or project; the chamber from which vocal sounds resonate is called the *pharynx or vocal tract*

runs or melismas: the insertion of five or more notes that consist of a diatonic or pentatonic scale, chord outline, or a series of melodic sequences or turns executed in a continuous manner; usually performed in places within the music in which a single note is sustained

scoop: when the semitones are sounded as the singer slides up to the intended pitch

signifyin(g): a **call-response** consisting of improvisatory and performance characteristics found in the performance of black folk music, such as moans, slurs, shouts, and call-and-response

slides/portamentos: connecting one note to the next in a continuous motion

soft palate: soft part of the top back of the mouth from which the uvula hangs

solo range: the range of usable pitch tones that can audibly be incorporated into the interpretation of a song

speak in tongues: a signifying capturing of the spirit through a fluent kind of utterance filled with Hebraic-sounding syllables

squall: a vocal texture that sounds like a quick or short yell or shout with a rough vocal quality; used as a sudden burst of excitement or energy

superior muscles: upper set of constrictor muscles located at the top of the vocal tract, behind the nose and throat; functions to narrow the back of the throat and assist in pushing food to the esophagus

sustainable range: the vocal range that is used the most

syncopation: rhythms that accentuate the weak beats of a meter

tail: approximately two to four notes added at the end of a phrase or just before a pause in the melody; descends or ascends in stepwise motion in one direction

terminal vibrato: vocal vibration once a final tone is sustained for a number of beats

testimony: a short, personal story, spoken or sung, in which one shares with the congregation in order to provide an example of how he or she believes God has worked in his or her life

textual interpolations: the adding of extra words to the original text

textual phrasing: a technique used by storytellers in which specific words are grouped together within a phrase or specific words are emphasized within a phrase in order to portray an emotion or a perspective

thyroarytenoid (TA) muscle: one of the two primary sets of muscles that control the thickness and length of the vocal folds; when contracted, these muscles shorten and thicken the vocal cords

turns: a short melodic motif that consists of five or more notes and is executed within two-beat counts in which the starting and ending note are the same

UTT: unnecessary tongue tension; could cause singers to go off pitch, have an unstable vibrator, poor articulation, and fatigue

vocal agility: one's ability to change pitches and vocal qualities quickly while maintaining accuracy and clarity in the sung pitches

vocal registration or vocal register: a particular series of tones (or ranges) produced in the same manner (or same muscular coordination) and that has the same basic vocal quality

vocal timbre: the "color" of the tone created

vowel distortion: when a singer sings a word and purposefully modifies the vowel to the point that it almost becomes unrecognizable

whoop: an elongated squall sustained either on one pitch, a few pitches, or on a short melodic sequence; used in climactic and/or heightened emotional states; often known to stir up or rally emotions

INDEX

hymns: Dr. Watts, 142; European, 141–42; lined or metered, 141, 142; Methodist hymnal, 10; white, 144, 145. *See also* gospel hymns
hyoid bone, 53

"If I Don't Get There," 16
"I'll Overcome Someday," 14
inferior constrictors, 100, 230–31
inhalation phase, of breath cycle, 82–83
inharmonic overtones, 48
inspirational contemporary artists, 26
inspirational gospel style category, 149–50, 195
intercostal muscles, 40, 41, 231
internal intercostal muscles, 40, 41
internal obliques, 41
interpolation, 231; textual, 134, 233. *See also* melodic interpolations
"It's Tight Like That," 16

Jackson, Mahalia, 15, 16, 20–21
jaw positions, vowels and, 97
jazz: gospel singing and, xx–xxi, 20, 21; musicians and black church music, 3, 13; scat singing, 132; voice study, xx
Johnson, Harrison E., 190
jubilee quartets, 13–14; gospel quartets and, 17, 21; gospel style and, 15
jubilee singers, 13–14, 152; Fisk Jubilee Singers, 9, 143, 144
jubilee songs, 142
jubilee spiritual, 11

key, 140
Kilpatrick, William, 130
King, Martin Luther, Jr., 21

lamina propria, 44
laryngeal dryness, 57, 59, 61
laryngopharyngeal reflux (LPR), 62–63
larynx, 58, 59, 231; as voice vibrator, 43–48
Lawrence, Van, 57
lean/appoggiatura, 126, 231
Lent, 171–72
lined or metered hymns, 141, 142
lips, as articulator, 52–54, 104
liturgical calendar: Advent season, 169–70; Christmas season, 170; Easter, 172; Epiphany, 171; Lent, 171–72; Ordinary Time, 173–74; overview, 169; Pentecost season, 173
loft voice, 89
"Lord, Help Me to Hold Out," 190
LoVetri, Jeanette, xxii, 78
LPR. *See* laryngopharyngeal reflux
lungs, 38–39

male quartets, 15, 16
Martin, Roberta, 15, 17–18, 22, 24
Martin, Sallie, 16
Martin and Frye Singers, 18
Mason, Charles, 143
McAllister, Judith Ëhristie, 26
Meade, Donald, xx
medications: reflux, 63; voice and, 61–62
melismas, or runs, 129–30, 231, 232
melodic improvisation: alterations to melody, 125, 130–32; overview, 125; scat singing, 125, 132
melodic interpolations: bends/blue note, 127, 229; dramatic slides/ glissandos, 126, 230; escape tones, 128, 230; fall, 127, 230; lean/

ABOUT THE AUTHOR

Creator of Soul Ingredients, **Dr. Trineice Robinson-Martin** holds doctoral and master's degrees from Teachers College, Columbia University, in music education with an emphasis in contemporary commercial music vocal pedagogy. In addition, Dr. Robinson-Martin holds master's and bachelor's degrees in jazz studies from Indiana University–Bloomington and San Jose State University, respectively, and is certified in Somatic Voicework: The LoVetri Method. Her published works are in the *Journal of Singing*; *Teaching in the 21st Century* (Scott D. Harrison and Jessica O'Bryan, eds.); and in the recently authored and upcoming publications of *Voice Training for the Gospel Soloist* and *So You Want to Sing Gospel* sponsored by the National Association of Teachers of Singing.

As an accomplished performer, teacher, and scholar, Dr. Robinson-Martin has traveled and taught students from all over the world and lectures nationally and internationally on a variety of Soul Ingredients topics. Her performance experience spans a variety of musical styles, venues, and settings: the intimacy of private parties and local clubs, the grand stages of musical arts centers and large music festivals, and international stages. She has performed with concert choirs and chorales, large and small jazz ensembles, Latin music ensembles, corporate bands, a pop orchestra, and rhythm and blues (R&B) groups, including tours with international R&B recording group CHANGE and Standing in the Shadows of Motown Live.

Dr. Robinson-Martin currently teaches private voice lessons and directs the Jazz Vocal Collective Ensemble at Princeton University; serves on the national faculty of the Gospel Music Workshop of America, Inc.; and is the executive director of the African American Jazz Caucus, Inc. For more information, visit www.DrTrineice.com.